CR ConsumerReports™

Buying Guide™ 2017

FROM
THE
EDITORS OF
CONSUMER
REPORTS

Contents

Shop Smart in 2017

Quick Guides & Product Ratings

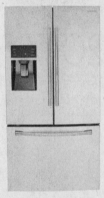

Autos

Buying Advice at Your Fingertips

The Consumer Reports Buying Guide for 2017 is your handy one-stop source for making informed, money-saving purchases. Consult it before you shop, then bring it to the store or keep it beside your computer to help you compare brands. Here's how to make the best use of this guide:

Packed with highlights from our exclusive buying advice and ratings for more than 2,000 specific product models, this little book will be an invaluable shopping tool for squeezing the most value from every dollar you spend.

Preceding each ratings chart, you'll find a Quick Guide to our buying advice. You can access our full buying advice by using the website address provided with each category.

But before you delve into the best stuff to buy, be sure to read about the best places to buy it–whether online or at a walk-in store–in the Comparing Retailers section, starting on page 5. Based on valuable information provided to us by thousands of CONSUMER REPORTS readers, we discuss buying trends and provide information on the service, selection, and prices of dozens of retailers of appliances, electronics products. After you've brushed up on your shopping savvy, turn to the Product Ratings section, starting on page 11, for guidance from the experts at CONSUMER REPORTS on 33 product categories, presented in alphabetical order. Along with the ratings, you'll find brand reliability estimates for some products that reflect survey results from thousands of readers about breakages and problems they've had with various brands.

Are you in the market for a car? The Autos section, starting on page 145, has the latest ratings and data on new models. In addition to highs and lows of the 2017 vehicles, there's a section on the best and worst used cars, and reliability ratings for more than 200 models currently in the marketplace. The tires section includes more than 150 models.

So grab this handy little book whenever you shop. Whether you are shopping online or in a store, we're certain it will save you money and help you get the best value every time you pick it up.

CR ConsumerReports™

About the Consumer Reports Family of Products

Founded as a magazine in 1936, Consumer Reports now brings you its unbiased, trusted information in many formats. Products and publications include Consumer Reports magazine; buying guides, books, and special issues from Consumer Reports Publications Development; a newsletter, Consumer Reports on Health; and Consumer Reports TV News, a nationally syndicated consumer news service.

> **ConsumerReports.org** offers site subscribers a searchable version of our test findings and advice, as well as access to **Consumer Reports Mobile.**

> **Consumer Reports' Build & Buy Car Buying Service** helps you know what you should pay for a vehicle before visiting a dealership. You can find prices, subscription rates, and more information on all of those products and services at ConsumerReports.org. Go to "Consumer Reports Bookstore" at the bottom of the home page. For more reporting on consumer news and issues, go to Consumerist.com.

> **Consumer Reports** magazine specializes in head-to-head, brand-name comparisons of autos and household products. It also provides informed, impartial advice on a broad range of topics, from health and nutrition to personal finance and travel.

> **Consumer Reports** buys all of the products it rates and accepts no free samples. We accept no advertising from outside entities, nor do we let any company use our information or ratings for commercial purposes.

> **Consumer Reports** is an independent, nonprofit testing and information organization—the largest such organization in the world. Since 1936 our mission has been to test products, inform the public, and protect consumers. Our income is derived solely from the sale of our publications and online information and services, and from nonrestrictive, noncommercial contributions, grants, and fees.

Comparing Retailers

Our product testers can tell you which refrigerator or computer delivers the most value. But then you have to find the lowest price and good service. To help you find the best places to shop, we survey tens of thousands of Consumer Reports subscribers annually about their experiences buying appliances, and electronics in-store and online.

APPLIANCES

Most appliance purchases are still made in brick-and-mortar stores, but more than two-thirds of subscribers use the Internet to check prices, read reviews, and research features and performance. More than half of large appliance shoppers visit a retailer's website before making a purchase at its store or website as do 48 percent of small appliance shoppers.

The Appliance Shopper Satisfaction survey, conducted by the Consumer Reports National Research Center, uses subscribers' experiences in making over 80,000 appliance purchases from Fall 2014 to Fall 2015 to help evaluate the best places to shop. It provides insight into details such as checkout ease and shipping in the purchase of major appliances, such as refrigerators, washers and dryers, as well as smaller appliances, such as coffeemakers, blenders and vacuum cleaners.

Small Appliances Thrive Online

Online buying is growing fastest for small appliances, with around one out of four items purchased that way in recent years. Abt Electronics and Appliances followed by Amazon.com topped the list of 23 small-appliance chains and independent retailers in our survey and outdid all the others for selection. Favorable prices and checkout ratings for online retailers are likely part of their strong showing. But other retailers scored near the top of the ratings, too. Costco, QVC, and Williams-Sonoma please their customers overall.

Research Can Yield a Good Price

Doing online research is useful, according to more than 90 percent of our readers who tried that approach. Comparing prices on the websites of various retailers topped their list of strategies.

Who Provides the Best Support?

Once you've purchased your appliance, you need to figure out where to turn if it suddenly breaks down. In another survey, subscribers were much more satisfied when they called an independent repair shop for service than when they called the manufacturer or major retailer. Most outlets got only average scores for solving the problem.

WHERE TO BUY ELECTRONICS

Overall, consumers are quite happy with their shopping experience at electronic retailers and online shoppers tend to be significantly more satisfied in all aspects of the transaction experience compared to their in-store shopping counterparts. However, more than half of consumers in our ratings sample are still making their electronic purchases at walk-in retailers.

Even so, you're likely to hit the mall for many electronics purchases if you're anything like the consumers we surveyed.

Online Retailers

Overall, shoppers are quite satisfied with these online retailers. BHPhotovideo.com and Crutchfield.com with reader scores of 96 are among the highest rated online electronic retailers. Both of these retailers received top marks for all rated categories. Although Abt.com cannot be called out as among the highest online retailers for overall satisfaction, it still received an overall reader score of 95 and received the highest marks for all rated categories. In addition, Adorama.com and Amazon.com with reader scores of 94 also received high marks for all rated categories.

Walk-In Stores

Abt Electronics and Appliances, B & H Photo, Navy Exchange, and Nebraska Furniture Mart are among the highest rated walk-in electronic retailers for overall customer satisfaction. All four of these retailers received top marks for product quality, customer service, price, selection, and checkout ease.

You can skip the warranty

Retailers make a lot of profit on extended warranties, so brace yourself for a sales pitch. Almost two out of three in-store shoppers were asked to buy an extended warranty. Fifteen percent of walk-in buyers bought one, as did 10 percent of online buyers.

Don't be tempted to buy a service plan. Many consumer products are reliable and don't break during the period covered. Plans can cost as much as you'd pay for a repair that may never be required.

One exception: It's worth considering Apple's extended warranty/service plan if you want phone or online support for more than the standard 90 days. Apple consistently stands out in our surveys for offering the best computer tech support in the business.

Appliance Retailers

In order of highest reader score, within appliance type.

Legend (WORSE → BETTER): ▼ = worst, ▽ = worse, ● = middle, ▲ = better, ▲▲ = best

Retailer	Reader Score	Price Paid	Selection	In-Store Service	Checkout Ease	Website Usability	Shipping	Installation	Haul-Away
MAJOR APPLIANCES									
Abt Electronics and Appliances	93	▲	▲▲	▲▲	▲▲	▲	▲▲	▲▲	▲▲
Amazon.com	90	▲	▲	–	▲▲	▲▲	▲	–	–
Nebraska Furniture Mart	90	▲	▲▲	▲	▲▲	●	▲	▲▲	▲▲
Costco	89	▲	▽	–	▲▲	▲	▲	▲	▲▲
Independents	89	●	●	▲	▲▲	▽	▲▲	▲▲	▲▲
Warner's Stellian Appliance	89	▽	●	▲	▲	–	▲	▲	▲▲
R.C. Willey Home Furnishings	87	●	▲	▲	●	–	▲	–	–
Menards	86	●	▽	●	▲	●	–	–	–
Pacific Sales	85	●	▲	▲	▲	●	▲	▲	▲▲
Lowe's	85	●	●	●	▲	●	▲	▲	▲▲
Best Buy	84	●	●	●	▲	●	▲	▲	▲▲
P.C. Richard & Son	84	●	▲	●	▲	●	▲	▲	▲
Home Depot	84	●	●	●	▲	●	▲	▲	▲
HHGregg	83	●	●	●	●	●	●	▲	▲
Sears	83	●	●	●	●	▽	●	▲	▲
SMALL APPLIANCES									
Abt Electronics and Appliances	94	▲▲	▲▲	▲▲	▲▲	▲	–	–	–
Amazon.com	93	▲▲	▲▲	–	▲▲	▲▲	–	–	–
Costco	91	▲▲	▽	▽	▲	●	–	–	–
QVC	91	▲	▲	–	▲▲	▲	–	–	–
Williams-Sonoma	90	●	▲	▲▲	▲	▲	–	–	–
Meijer	88	▲	●	–	▲	–	–	–	–
Independents	88	●	●	▲▲	▲	●	–	–	–
ACE Hardware	88	●	▽	▲	▲	–	–	–	–
Bed Bath & Beyond	88	●	●	●	▲	●	–	–	–
HSN	88	▲	●	–	▲	▲	–	–	–
Kohl's	87	▲	●	▽	●	●	–	–	–
Macy's	85	●	●	●	●	●	–	–	–
P.C. Richard & Son	85	●	●	▲	●	–	–	–	–
BJ's Wholesale Club	85	▲	▽	▽	●	–	–	–	–
Lowe's	84	●	▽	●	●	▽	–	–	–

Retailer	Reader Score	Price Paid	Selection	In-Store Service	Checkout Ease	Website Usability	Shipping	Installation	Haul-Away
SMALL APPLIANCES (Continued)									
Target	84	❶	⌄	⌄⌄	❶	⌄	–	–	–
HHGregg	84	❶	❶	❶	❶	–	–	–	–
Sams Club	84	⌃	⌄⌄	⌄⌄	❶	⌄	–	–	–
Home Depot	84	❶	⌄	⌄	⌃	❶	–	–	–
Menards	82	❶	⌄	⌄	⌃	⌄	–	–	–
Best Buy	82	❶	❶	❶	❶	❶	–	–	–
Sears	82	❶	❶	❶	❶	⌄	–	–	–
Kmart	81	❶	⌄	⌄⌄	❶	–	–	–	–
Walmart	80	❶	⌄	⌄⌄	–	⌄	–	–	–

Guide to the Ratings

APPLIANCE RETAILERS. The chart is based on 21,115 subscribers who reported on 80,052 appliance-purchase experiences between Fall 2014 and Fall 2015. (Respondents may not be representative of the U.S. population.) **Reader Score** reflects readers' assessments of their overall buying experience and is not limited to factors under **Survey Results.** A score of 100 would mean that all respondents had been completely satisfied; 80, very satisfied, on average; 60, fairly well satisfied. Differences of fewer than 4 points aren't meaningful. Retailers are listed in order of precise reader score. **Price, Selection, Service, Checkout Ease, Website Usability, Shipping, Installation,** and **Haul-Away** were rated on a scale from excellent to very poor. Small-appliance and major-appliance results aren't directly comparable because of differences in methodology. A dash (—) means not applicable or insufficient sample size.

Electronics Retailers

In order of highest reader score, within types.

⌄⌄ ⌄ ❶ ⌃ ⌃⌃
WORSE ————— BETTER

Retailer	Reader Score	Product Quality	Customer Service	Price Paid	Selection	Checkout Ease	Website Usability	Walk-in Retailer Buying Ease	Walk-in Retailer Web Customer Support
ONLINE STORES									
BHPhotoVideo.com	96	⌃⌃	⌃⌃	⌃	⌃⌃	⌃⌃	⌃⌃	NA	NA
Crutchfield.com	96	⌃⌃	⌃⌃	⌃	⌃	⌃⌃	⌃⌃	NA	NA
Abt.com	95	⌃⌃	⌃⌃	⌃	⌃⌃	⌃⌃	⌃⌃	NA	NA
Adorama.com	94	⌃⌃	⌃	⌃⌃	⌃⌃	⌃⌃	⌃⌃	NA	NA
Apple.com	94	⌃⌃	⌃⌃	⌄	❶	⌃⌃	⌃⌃	NA	NA
Amazon.com	94	⌃	⌃⌃	⌃	⌃⌃	⌃⌃	⌃⌃	NA	NA

Retailer	Reader Score	Survey Results							
		Product Quality	Customer Service	Price Paid	Selection	Checkout Ease	Website Usability	Walk-in Retailer Buying Ease	Walk-in Retailer Web Customer Support
ONLINE STORES (Continued)									
Costco.com	93	⌃	⌃	⌃⌃	⌄	⌃⌃	⌃⌃	NA	NA
Shopmyexchange.com	93	⌃⌃	⌃	⌃⌃	①	⌃⌃	⌃⌃	NA	NA
Bose.com	93	⌃⌃	⌃	⌄	①	⌃⌃	⌃⌃	NA	NA
Newegg.com	92	⌃	⌃	⌃	⌃	⌃	⌃⌃	NA	NA
MacMall.com	92	⌃⌃	—	⌃	⌃⌃	⌃	⌃	NA	NA
Target.com	91	⌃	①	⌃	①	⌃	⌃	NA	NA
SamsClub.com	91	⌃	①	⌃⌃	⌄	⌃	⌃	NA	NA
BJs.com	91	⌃	—	⌃⌃	⌄	⌃	⌃⌃	NA	NA
QVC.com	90	⌃	⌃	⌃	⌄	⌃⌃	⌃	NA	NA
Independent websites	90	⌃	⌃	⌃	①	⌃	⌃	NA	NA
Sears.com	90	⌃	—	⌃	①	⌃	①	NA	NA
BestBuy.com	89	⌃	①	⌃	⌃	⌃	⌃	NA	NA
TigerDirect.com	89	⌃	①	⌃	⌃	⌃	⌃	NA	NA
Staples.com	88	⌃	①	⌃	①	⌃	⌃	NA	NA
Microsoft.com	88	⌃	①	①	①	⌃	⌃	NA	NA
Frys.com	88	⌃	①	⌃	①	①	①	NA	NA
Walmart.com	88	⌃	①	⌃	①	⌃	①	NA	NA
Groupon.com	87	①	①	⌃	⌄⌄	⌃	⌃	NA	NA
HSN.com	87	⌃	⌃	⌃	⌄	⌃	⌃	NA	NA
hhgregg.com	87	—	—	⌃	—	—	—	NA	NA
HP.com	85	①	①	①	①	⌃	①	NA	NA
OfficeDepot.com	85	①	—	①	①	⌃	⌃	NA	NA
Dell.com	84	①	①	①	①	①	①	NA	NA
Lenovo.com	84	①	①	①	①	①	①	NA	NA
WALK-IN STORES									
Abt Electronics	95	⌃⌃	⌃⌃	⌃	⌃⌃	⌃⌃	⌃⌃	⌃⌃	⌃⌃
B&H Photo	93	⌃⌃	⌃⌃	⌃	⌃⌃	⌃⌃	⌃⌃	⌃	—
Navy Exchange	93	⌃⌃	⌃	⌃⌃	⌃	⌃	①	①	—
Nebraska Furniture Mart	93	⌃⌃	⌃	⌃	⌃⌃	⌃	⌃	⌃	—
Bose	92	⌃⌃	⌃	⌄	①	⌃⌃	⌃	⌃⌃	⌃
Video Only	92	⌃⌃	⌃⌃	⌃	⌃⌃	⌃⌃	—	⌃	—
Apple Store	92	⌃⌃	⌃⌃	⌄⌄	⌃	⌃	⌃⌃	⌃	⌃⌃
Costco	92	⌃	①	⌃	⌄	①	⌃	①	⌃
Independent Stores	91	⌃⌃	⌃⌃	①	⌃	⌃⌃	①	⌃	⌃

Electronics Retailers (Continued)

In order of highest reader score, within types.

Retailer	Reader Score	Product Quality	Customer Service	Price Paid	Selection	Checkout Ease	Website Usability	Walk-in Retailer Buying Ease	Walk-in Retailer Web Customer Support
WALK-IN STORES (Continued)									
Simply Mac	90	⇑	⇑	↓	—	⇑	—	↑	—
Army & Air Force Exchange	90	⇑	●	↑	●	↑	●	●	●
Meijer	89	↑	↓	↑	↓	↑		●	—
P.C. Richard & Son	88	↑	↑	↑	↑	↑	↑	●	↑
Microsoft	88	↑	↑	↓	●	⇑	↑	↑	↑
BJ's	88	↑	⇓	↑	↓	●	●	●	↓
GameStop	88	↑	↑	●	↑	↑	↑	●	—
Sam's Club	88	↑	↓	↑	↓	●	●	●	●
Micro Center	88	↑	↑	●	↑	●	↑	↓	↑
Fred Meyer Stores	88	●	●	●	↓	↑	—	●	—
Barnes & Noble	87	↑	●	●	↓	↑	↑	●	●
HHGregg	87	↑	●	●	↑	↑	●	●	●
Target	86	↑	↓	●	↓	●	●	↓	●
Best Buy	85	↑	●	●	●	●	●	●	●
BrandsMart USA	85	↑	●	↑	↑	●	—	⇓	—
Staples	85	↑	●	●	↓	↑	●	↓	●
Sears	85	↑	●	●	●	●	●	↓	●
RadioShack	85	●	●	●	⇓	↑	—	●	—
Office Depot/Office Max	84	●	●	●	↓	↑	●	↓	●
Fry's Electronics	83	↑	↓	●	↑	●	↓	⇓	↓
Walmart	82	●	⇓	●	↓	↓	●	⇓	↓
Kmart	81	●	—	●	—	●	—	⇓	—

Guide to the Ratings

ELECTRONICS RETAILERS. Ratings are based on 156,999 purchases of electronic products purchased by 94,983 Consumer Reports' subscribers between January 2015 and June 2016. The Reader Score represents overall satisfaction with the shopping experience and is not exclusively determined by factors under the survey results. A reader score of 100 would mean all respondents are completely satisfied; 80, that respondents are "very satisfied" on average. Differences of less than 5 points are not meaningful in comparing walk-in retailers while differences of less than 6 points are not meaningful in comparing online retailers. Each rating category under Survey Results (other than walk-in retailer buying ease) reflects average scores on a scale from very poor to excellent. Ratings are based on CR subscribers who may not be representative of the general U.S. population. A dash (—) indicates that we lacked sufficient data.

Product Ratings & Brand Reliability

The Quick Guides, product ratings, and brand-reliability information that follow are designed to help you zero in on the model you want to buy. See the buying advice highlights in the Quick Guides to help you decide what you want from a product. Then go to the ratings charts to get the big picture on performance.

For some products, you'll find full ratings that include every currently available model we tested. For others, the ratings charts include only models recommended for most people, and to models designated as CR Best Buys.

To obtain ratings, we put all models within a category through weeks of testing, side by side, so that test results can be compared. We rank products by performance; products with equal scores are listed alphabetically.

Consumer Reports checked that the products rated in this Buying Guide were still available at press time. But depending on how long after publication you use this book, you may find a rating for a product that's no longer available. Or you may not find a rating for a model that's available because it hadn't been tested as of publication.

In addition to checking for similar models, you can also refer to the brand reliability charts for some products.

Every year we survey readers about breakages and other problems they encounter with household products. From their responses, we estimate the percentage of a brand's products that are likely to break in given time period. The reliability charts that accompany the ratings give brand-breakage rates for many of our product categories. Our findings have been dependable over the more than 30 years we've surveyed brand reliability, though they're not infallible predictors.

A brand's reliability estimate includes data on many models, some of which may have been more or less reliable than others. And surveys of a brand's past models can't anticipate design or manufacturing changes. Still, you can improve your chances of getting a trouble-free product by going with a brand that has a lower estimated breakage rate.

Action Camcorders

Action camcorders are small, light, and rugged, and have fewer features than full-sized cams, which are dwindling in number. Most action cams have Wi-Fi for easy sharing of videos, and some can shoot in 4K.

What to Look For

- An LCD with very good quality. Most models don't have a viewfinder, and you must compose on the display.
- Long battery life.
- A model that can be charged via a computer's USB port.
- Image stabilization, which can reduce blurriness due to hand shake, a big plus when you're moving around.
- A model with a good score for audio if sound quality matters to you.
- 4K recording if you want to display video and photos on an ultra high-definition TV or a 4K computer display.

What to Skip

- Digital zoom, which degrades image quality. Look for optical zoom instead.

What You'll Pay

Expect to spend $100 to $400 for an HD action cam and up to $600 for a 4K model.

BUYING ADVICE

If you're into outdoor activities, look for an action cam that's waterproof or that comes with a waterproof case.

For more buying advice, go to ConsumerReports.org/camcorders

All tested models in performance order.

Recommended	Rank	Brand & Model	Price	Score	Picture Quality	Ease of Use	Audio Quality	Image Stabilizer	Display Quality	Versatility	Still Camera	Battery Life, WiFi Off (min.)
✓	1	**Sony** HDR-AS100V	$300	69	⌃	⌄	◑	⌃	NA	◑	◑	130
$	2	**Kodak** PixPro SP1	$180	67	◑	◑	◑	◑	◑	◑	◑	130
$	3	**Sony** HDR-AS50	$200	67	◑	⌃	◑	⌃	NA	◑	⌄	100
✓	4	**Sony** HDR-AS50R	$350	67	◑	⌃	◑	⌃	NA	◑	⌄	100
✓	5	**Sony** FDR-X1000V	$400	66	◑	⌄	◑	⌃	NA	◑	⌃	110
✓	6	**Sony** HDR-AS200V	$300	66	◑	⌄	◑	⌃	NA	◑	◑	105

Recommended	Rank	Brand & Model	Price	Score	Picture Quality	Ease of Use	Audio Quality	Image Stabilizer	Display Quality	Versatility	Still Camera	Battery Life, WiFi Off (min.)
✓	7	**GoPro** HERO4 Silver Standard Edition	$400	65	Good	Good	Good	NA	Good	Good	Good	110
✓	8	**GoPro** Hero3+ Silver Edition	$300	65	Fair	Good	Good	NA	NA	Very Good	Good	135
$	9	**Garmin** VIRB	$200	64	Good	Good	Fair	Very Good	Fair	Fair	Good	101
$	10	**Sony** HDR-AS20	$160	63	Good	Fair	Good	Very Good	NA	Good	Good	130
✓	11	**Ricoh** WG-M2	$300	63	Good	Very Good	Fair	Very Good	NA	Good	Fair	140
$	12	**Activeon** CX Gold	$200	62	Good	Good	Good	Good	Good	Very Good	Good	80
✓	13	**Kodak** PixPro SP360	$260	61	Fair	Fair	Good	NA	NA	Very Good	Good	160
	14	**GoPro** HERO	$130	60	Fair	Fair	Fair	NA	NA	Fair	Good	165
	15	**Drift** Ghost S	$300	60	Fair	Good	Poor	NA	Good	Good	Very Good	145
	16	**Panasonic** HX-A500	$350	60	Good	Fair	Fair	NA	Good	Fair	Good	80
	17	**Activeon** CX	$100	60	Fair	Good	Good	NA	Good	Very Good	Good	120
	18	**iON** SnapCam	$100	59	Fair	Very Good	Fair	NA	NA	Poor	Fair	105
	19	**iON** CAMOCAM	$210	59	Fair	Fair	Poor	NA	NA	Fair	Good	240
	20	**iON** AirPro2 WiFi	$150	58	Fair	Fair	Good	Poor	Poor	Good	Fair	120
	21	**Vivitar** DVR914 4K	$130	58	Good	Very Good	Good	Very Good	NA	Very Good	Poor	110
	22	**Drift** Stealth2	$100	58	Good	Excellent	Fair	NA	NA	Good	Poor	60
	23	**GoPro** Hero+ LCD	$270	57	Fair	Good	Poor	NA	Good	Fair	Good	120
	24	**GoPro** HERO4 Session	$200	57	Fair	Fair	Good	NA	NA	Fair	Good	200
	25	**Activeon** DX	$140	57	Good	Very Good	Fair	NA	NA	Very Good	Fair	80
	26	**Liquid Image** Ego LS 800	$350	55	Good	Very Good	Poor	NA	NA	Fair	Fair	110
	27	**TomTom** Bandit	$400	55	Fair	Fair	Good	NA	NA	Fair	Good	110
	28	**Polaroid** Cube	$100	54	Fair	Fair	Good	NA	NA	Poor	Fair	90
	29	**Panasonic** HX-A1	$200	54	Fair	Good	Good	NA	NA	Fair	Fair	75
	30	**Isaw** Edge	$170	54	Fair	Good	Fair	NA	NA	Very Good	Fair	110
	31	**AEE** S71	$250	52	Fair	Very Good	Fair	NA	Good	Good	Good	85

RATINGS KEY ⊗ POOR ⊙ FAIR ● GOOD ⌃ VERY GOOD ⌃⌃ EXCELLENT
$ **CR BEST BUY** These models offer the best combination of performance and price. All are recommended.
✓ **RECOMMENDED** These are high-performing models that stand out.

Recommended	Rank	Brand & Model	Price	Score	Picture Quality	Ease of Use	Audio Quality	Image Stabilizer	Display Quality	Versatility	Still Camera	Battery Life, WiFi Off (min.)
	32	**Nilox** MINI UP	$90	52	Fair	Good	Poor	NA	NA	Fair	Fair	135
	33	**Kitvision** Escape HD5	$60	51	Fair	Good	Good	NA	NA	Good	Excellent	120
	34	**Monoprice** MHD Sport 2.0 Wi-Fi 12570	$160	50	Fair	Fair	Good	NA	NA	Very Good	Good	90
	35	**SJCAM** WIFI SJ5000	$130	49	Fair	Fair	Fair	NA	Good	Good	Good	70
	36	**Garmin** VIRB XE	$400	47	Good	Good	Fair	Good	NA	Good	Good	120
	37	**Garmin** VIRB X	$280	44	Fair	Good	Fair	NA	NA	Good	Good	90
	38	**Polaroid** Cube+	$150	36	Good	Fair	Poor	Good	NA	Poor	Fair	90

Guide to the Ratings

Score mainly reflects picture quality and ease of use. The displayed score is out of a total of 100 points. **Picture Quality** is based on image clarity, color accuracy, and contrast. **Ease of Use** takes into account ergonomics of the controls and displays, and user-manual readability. **Audio Quality** represents accuracy using the built-in microphone, plus freedom from noise. **Image Stabilizer** reflects how well the model reduces the effects of camcorder shake. "NA" indicates that the model lacks this feature. **Display Quality** reflects image clarity, color accuracy, and contrast of the LCD display. **Versatility** indicates features that increase a camcorder's utility or capabilities. **Still Camera** refers to overall quality of the photo functions of the camcorder, which includes picture quality and handling. **Battery Life, Wi-Fi Off (min.)** is how long the camcorder can continuously record images with the LCD viewer in constant use and Wi-Fi off. **Price** is approximate retail.

QUICK GUIDE

Computers, Desktop

Desktops typically offer more performance for the money than laptops and are less expensive to repair. They let you work on a larger screen, and generally come with better speakers.

What to Look For
■ For basic tasks such as browsing the Web and email, a low-end processor such as the Intel Pentium or Celeron, or the AMD E2 or A4 series.
■ Intel Core i7 for improved graphics performance, or AMD's FX series processors for heavy-duty gaming.
■ At least 1TB of storage. If you use the cloud, you can get a faster solid-state drive with 128 or 256GB.

What to Skip
■ Upgrading to over 4GB of memory, unless you're a big multitasker or video editor.

What You'll Pay
You can get a very good all-in-one for $600 to $900, but many fuller-featured models cost more than $1,000.

BUYING ADVICE
Save money on your purchase by using coupon and forum sites such as Ebates, FatWallet .com, and Techbargains .com

For more buying advice, go to ConsumerReports.org/computers

All tested models in performance order.

Rec.	Rank	Brand & Model	Price	Score	Performance	Versatility	Ergonomics	Display	Speakers	Display Size (in.)	Processor	Memory (GB)	Storage (GB)
		ALL-IN-ONE DESKTOPS											
✓	1	**Dell** XPS 27"	$1650	85	⌃	⌃	⌃	⌃	⌃	27	Core i5-4460S	8	1000
✓	2	**Lenovo** Ideacentre AIO 700-27 F0BD002KUS	$1400	84	⌃	⌃	⌃	⌃	⌄	27	Core i5-6400	8	1000
$	3	**Lenovo** Ideacentre AIO 700 24" F0BE006SUS	$900	83	⌃	⌃	⌃	⌃	⌄	23.8	Core i5-6400	8	1000
✓	4	**HP** ENVY 27-p020qe	$1580	80	⌃	⌃	⌃	⌃	●	27	Core i5-6400T	8	1000
✓	5	**Dell** Inspiron 24 7000	$1000	78	⌃	⌃	⌃	⌃	●	23.8	Core i5-6300Q	12	1000

Rec.	Rank	Brand & Model	Price	Score	Performance	Versatility	Ergonomics	Display	Speakers	Display Size (in.)	Processor	Memory (GB)	Storage (GB)
		ALL-IN-ONE DESKTOPS (Continued)											
✓	6	**HP** ENVY 34-a010	$1650	77	Very Good	Very Good	Very Good	Excellent	Very Good	34	Core i5-6400T	12	1000
✓	7	**HP** Pavilion 24-b040qe	$850	76	Very Good	Very Good	Very Good	Very Good	Good	23.8	Core i5-6400T	12	1000
✓	8	**Asus** Zen Z240IC-GT-09S	$1150	76	Very Good	Very Good	Excellent	Very Good	Good	23.8	Core i5-6400T	8	1000
✓	9	**Apple** iMac w/ Retina 5K display MF886LL/A	$1800	76	Very Good	Very Good	Good	Excellent	Very Good	27	Core i5 3.5GHz	8	1128
✓	10	**Dell** Inspiron 24 5000	$900	76	Good	Excellent	Excellent	Very Good	Good	23.8	Core i5-6400T	12	1000
✓	11	**HP** ENVY 27-p014	$900	75	Very Good	Very Good	Excellent	Very Good	Very Good	27	Core i5-6400T	12	1000
✓	12	**Apple** 27-inch iMac with Retina 5K display MK472LL/A	$1900	74	Excellent	Very Good	Good	Excellent	Very Good	27	Core i5 3.2GHz	8	1032
$	13	**Lenovo** Ideacentre AIO 300-23" F0BY0041US	$600	73	Good	Excellent	Excellent	Very Good	Good	23	Core i3-6100U	8	1000
✓	14	**Dell** Inspiron 24 3000 (Intel)	$730	72	Good	Very Good	Excellent	Very Good	Good	23.8	Core i5-6200U	8	1000
✓	15	**Acer** Aspire AZ3-710-UR55	$700	70	Good	Very Good	Very Good	Very Good	Good	23.8	Core i3-4170T	6	1000
✓	16	**Apple** iMac with Retina 4K display MK452LL/A	$1380	69	Excellent	Good	Good	Very Good	Excellent	21.5	Core i5 3.1GHz	8	1000
✓	17	**Apple** 21.5-inch iMac MK442LL/A	$1300	69	Excellent	Good	Good	Very Good	Excellent	21.5	Core i5 2.8GHz	8	1000
✓	18	**HP** Pavilion 27-n220	$850	69	Very Good	Excellent	Very Good	Very Good	Good	27	Core i3-6100T	8	1000
✓	19	**Lenovo** Yoga Home 900	$1200	65	Excellent	Good	Very Good	Very Good	Good	27	Core i5-5200U	8	256
	20	**Lenovo** AIO 300 22" F0BX00AHUS	$480	62	Good	Very Good	Very Good	Very Good	Good	21.5	Pentium 4405U	4	500
	21	**Dell** Inspiron I3455-10041WHT	$600	60	Fair	Very Good	Excellent	Very Good	Good	23.8	A8-7410	8	1000
	22	**Lenovo** Ideacentre AIO 300-20"	$430	60	Good	Good	Very Good	Very Good	Good	20	Pentium G4400T	4	500
	23	**Dell** Inspiron 20 3000 Intel	$500	39	Poor	Very Good	Very Good	Good	Good	19.5	Pentium N3700U	4	1000
	24	**HP** All-in-One 22-3110	$375	37	Poor	Very Good	Excellent	Very Good	Good	21.5	E1-6015	4	1000

RATINGS KEY ⊘ POOR ⊘ FAIR ➊ GOOD ⌃ VERY GOOD ⌃ EXCELLENT

$ CR BEST BUY These models offer the best combination of performance and price. All are recommended.

✓ RECOMMENDED These are high-performing models that stand out.

Rec.	Rank	Brand & Model	Price	Score	Performance	Versatility	Ergonomics	Display	Speakers	Display Size (in.)	Processor	Memory (GB)	Storage (GB)
		COMPACT DESKTOPS											
✓	1	**Dell** Inspiron I3647-3538BK	$375	71	⌃	⌃⌃	⌃	NA	NA	NA	Core i3-4160	4	1000
	2	**Apple** Mac Mini MGEM2LL/A	$450	53	⊖	⊖	NA	NA	◉	NA	Core i5 1.4GHz	4	500
	3	**Intel** Compute Stick 2nd Gen	$150	36	⌄	⌄	NA	NA	NA	NA	Atom x5-Z8300	2	32
	4	**Intel** Compute Stick	$100	30	⌄	⌄	NA	NA	NA	NA	Atom Z3735F	2	32
		FULL-SIZE DESKTOPS											
✓	1	**Dell** XPS 8900	$700	90	⌃⌃	⌃⌃	⌃⌃	NA	NA	NA	Core i5-6400	8	1000
✓	2	**HP** ENVY Phoenix 850qe (Win 10)	$900	83	⌃⌃	⌃⌃	⌃	NA	NA	NA	Core i7-4790	16	2000
✓	3	**HP** ENVY 750-114	$550	81	⌃	⌃⌃	⌃	NA	NA	NA	Core i5-6400	12	2000
✓	4	**Lenovo** Erazer X315	$500	81	⌃	⌃⌃	⌃	NA	NA	NA	A8-7600	12	1000
✓	5	**Dell** Inspiron Desktop (Win 10)	$575	79	⌃	⌃⌃	⌃	NA	NA	NA	Core i5-4460	8	1000
✓	6	**HP** Pavilion 510xt	$550	72	⌃	⌃	⌃	NA	NA	NA	Core i5-6400T	8	1000
✓	7	**Dell** Inspiron Desktop AMD	$400	66	⊖	⌃	⌃	NA	NA	NA	A8-8600P	8	1000
	8	**HP** 251-a120	$300	53	⌄	⌃	⌃	NA	NA	NA	A6-6310	4	1000

Guide to the Ratings

Score reflects all of the Ratings factors. Displayed scores are rounded; models are listed in order of precise score out of a total of 100. Scores are comparable between the full-size and compact categories. Scores for the all-in-one category are not comparable to any other category. **Performance** reflects speed while running productivity applications, multimedia applications, and 3D games. **Versatility** includes hardware, such as memory-card slots and A/V connections; software, such as security programs and productivity applications; and tech support and warranty provisions. **Ergonomics** represents the quality of the keyboard and pointing device, and accessibility of features. For all-in-ones, **Display** is our judgment of clarity, color, brightness, and viewing angle. **Speakers** covers fidelity, bass response, and loudness. **Price** is approximate retail.

Our Readers Rate Technical Support

At some point in its life your computer will probably break down or you'll run into some technical difficulty installing or removing software. So it helps to know which companies offer the after-sale support that matches your needs.

Many free technical-support policies end after a year or less. Apple's phone support ends after 90 days, but it offers unlimited free support at its Apple Stores after that. Sales staff often pitch an extra-cost "extended" service plan. Our advice is to skip such pricey extended service warranties unless you really need the handholding or you travel everywhere with your laptop.

Tech Support
In order of reader score.

Rec.	Rank	Manufacturer	Reader Score	Phone Support	Online Support	Problem Solved (%)
	1	**Apple**	82	⏫	🔼	79
	2	**Microsoft**	68	🅘	🔽	74
	3	**Dell**	56	⏬	⏬	57
	4	**Lenovo**	54	⏬	⏬	51
	5	**HP**	53	⏬	⏬	50
	6	**Asus**	52	⏬	⏬	46
	7	**Samsung**	51	⏬	⏬	42
	8	**Acer/Gateway**	50	⏬	⏬	42
	9	**Toshiba**	50	⏬	⏬	46

Guide to the Ratings
Ratings are based on responses from 3,236 owners of 3,800 desktop, laptop, and Chromebook computers. Respondents were CRO subscribers surveyed online in January 2015. Data are based on respondents' most recent experience(s) contacting a manufacturer's technical-support service. **Reader Score** represents overall satisfaction and is not exclusively determined by the factors under survey results. A reader score of 100 designates that respondents were "completely satisfied." A score of 80 indicates that respondents were "very satisfied"; 60, "fairly well satisfied"; and 40, "somewhat dissatisfied." Differences of fewer than 5 points are not meaningful. **Online Support** was rated by those respondents who contacted a manufacturer via a website, e-mail, or an online live-chat or video-chat program. **Problem Solved** indicates whether computer problems were solved by manufacturer-based technical support. Differences of fewer than 8 percentage points between percent of problems solved are not meaningful.

Computers, Laptop

Some laptops offer features and capabilities that rival those of traditional desktops. You'll find more thin-and-light laptops than ever, and touch screens and solid-state drives are becoming more common.

What to Look For

■ A convertible or detachable if you want a laptop/tablet combo.
■ An 11- to 13-inch model if you plan to carry the laptop around with you frequently.
■ A 14- to 16-inch screen for the ideal balance of performance, portability, and price.
■ A 17- to 18-inch model for an entertainment-oriented desk-top replacement.

What to Skip

■ Upgrading to more than 4GB of memory unless you're a heavy multitasker or a video editor.

What You'll Pay

A well-equipped 15-inch laptop in the middle price range should cost you $600 to $700.

BUYING ADVICE

If you want to customize a model, order à la carte from the manufacturer's website.

For more buying advice, go to ConsumerReports.org/computers.

All tested models in performance order.

Rec.	Rank	Brand & Model	Price	Score	Ergonomics	Portability	Performance	Versatility	Display	Battery Life (hr.)	Weight (lb.)	Processor
		10- TO 11-INCH LAPTOPS										
✓	1	**Apple** MacBook Air 11-inch MJVM2LL/A	$900	70	⌃	⌃	⌃	⌄	⌃	13.5	2.4	Intel Core i5 1.6GHz
	2	**Lenovo** Ideapad Yoga 700	$700	64	⌃	⌃	⌃	❶	⌃	10.25	2.4	Intel Core m5-6Y54 1.1GHz
	3	**Microsoft** Surface 3	$500	61	❶	⌃	❶	❶	⌃	10.25	2	Atom x7-Z8700
	4	**Asus** VivoBook E200HA-US01	$200	58	❶	⌃	⌄	❶	❶	14.75	2.1	Intel Atom x5-Z8300 1.44GHz
	5	**Asus** Trans-former Book TP200SADHO4T	$300	57	❶	⌃	⌄	❶	⌃	13	2.6	Intel Celeron N3050 1.6GHz

Rec.	Rank	Brand & Model	Price	Score	Ergonomics	Portability	Performance	Versatility	Display	Battery Life (hr.)	Weight (lb.)	Processor
		10- TO 11-INCH LAPTOPS (Continued)										
	6	**Dell** Inspiron 11 3000	$180	56	◑	◔	◒	◑	◑	12	2.5	Intel Celeron N3050 1.6GHz
	7	**Lenovo** Ideapad Miix 310	$300	53	◑	◔	◒	◑	◑	12.75	2.4	Intel Atom Z8350 1.44GHz
	8	**Lenovo** IdeaPad 100s 80R2001FUS	$150	53	◑	◔	◔	◑	◑	8.25	2.3	Intel Atom Z3735F 1.33GHz
	9	**Asus** Transformer Book T100CHI-C1	$250	50	◒	◔	◒	◑	◔	11.25	2.4	Intel Atom Z3775 1.46GHz
	10	**Toshiba** Satellite Click10 LX0W_C64	$250	50	◔	◑	◒	◑	◔	8.75	2.2	Intel Atom x5-Z8300 1.44GHz
		12- TO 13-INCH LAPTOPS										
✓	1	**Vaio** Z	$1,500	81	◔	◕	◕	◑	◔	22.75	2.6	Intel Core i5-6267U 2.9GHz
✓	2	**Vaio** Flip Z	$1,800	81	◔	◕	◕	◔	◔	14	2.9	Intel Core i5-6267U 2.9GHz
$	3	**Dell** XPS 13 Non-Touch	$1,000	80	◔	◕	◕	◑	◔	17	2.7	Intel Core i5-6200U 2.3GHz
✓	4	**Apple** MacBook 12-inch MF855LL/A	$1,200	77	◔	◕	◔	◒	◔	16.25	2	Intel Core M 1.1GHz
✓	5	**Apple** MacBook 12-inch MLHE2LL/A	$1,300	76	◔	◕	◔	◒	◔	17	2.1	Intel Core m3 1.1GHz
✓	6	**Microsoft** Surface Book	$1,500	76	◕	◔	◔	◑	◔	15.25	3.4	Intel Core i5-6300U 2.4GHz
$	7	**Asus** ZenBook Flip UX360CA	$800	75	◔	◕	◔	◔	◔	14.75	3	Intel Core m3-6Y30 0.9GHz
✓	8	**Lenovo** Yoga 900S	$1,100	75	◔	◕	◔	◑	◔	15.75	2.2	Intel Core m5-6Y54 1.1GHz
✓	9	**Lenovo** YOGA 900 - 80MK002CUS	$1,000	75	◔	◕	◔	◑	◔	13.5	2.8	Intel Core i7-6500U 2.5GHz
$	10	**Asus** Zenbook UX305FA-ASM1	$700	73	◔	◕	◔	◔	◔	14	2.7	Intel Core M-5Y10c 0.8GHz
✓	11	**Apple** MacBook Pro 13-inch with Retina Display MF839LL/A	$1,300	73	◔	◕	◔	◑	◔	19	3.5	Intel Core i5 2.7GHz
✓	12	**Apple** MacBook Air 13-inch MJVE2LL/A	$900	73	◔	◕	◔	◒	◔	18.25	3	Intel Core i5 1.6GHz
$	13	**Acer** Aspire S5-371-52JR	$750	73	◔	◕	◔	◑	◔	13.5	2.9	Intel Core i5-6200U 2.3GHz
✓	14	**Vaio** S	$1,150	72	◔	◔	◕	◔	◔	10.75	2.2	Intel Core i5-6200U 2.3GHz
✓	15	**HP** Spectre 13-v011dx	$1,250	69	◑	◔	◕	◑	◑	11.5	2.4	Intel Core i7-6500U 2.5GHz

Rec.	Rank	Brand & Model	Price	Score	Ergonomics	Portability	Performance	Versatility	Display	Battery Life (hr.)	Weight (lb.)	Processor
		12- TO 13-INCH LAPTOPS (Continued)										
✓	16	**Lenovo** ThinkPad X260	$1,100	69	Very Good	Very Good	Excellent	Very Good	Very Good	13	3.1	Intel Core i5-6200U 2.3GHz
✓	17	**HP** Spectre x360 13-4103dx	$1,150	68	Very Good	Good	Very Good	Very Good	Very Good	11	3.3	Intel Core i7-6500U 2.5GHz
✓	18	**Samsung** Notebook 9 NP900X3L-K06US	$950	67	Very Good	Very Good	Very Good	Very Good	Excellent	7.75	1.9	Intel Core i5-6200U 2.3GHz
✓	19	**LG** gram 13Z950	$800	66	Very Good	Very Good	Very Good	Good	Good	8.5	2.2	Intel Core i5-5200U 2.2GHz
✓	20	**Acer** Aspire R7-372T-54TM	$900	66	Very Good	Good	Excellent	Very Good	Very Good	10.75	3.5	Intel Core i5-6200U 2.3GHz
✓	21	**Samsung** ATIV Book 9 NP930X2K-K02US	$830	66	Very Good	Very Good	Very Good	Good	Very Good	10	2.1	Intel Core M-5Y31 0.9GHz
✓	22	**Microsoft** Surface Pro 3	$830	66	Very Good	Very Good	Very Good	Good	Very Good	10	2.4	Intel Core i5-4300U 1.9GHz
✓	23	**Samsung** Notebook 9 spin NP940X3L-K01US	$1,200	66	Excellent	Good	Very Good	Very Good	Very Good	8	2.8	Intel Core i7-6500U 2.5GHz
✓	24	**Samsung** ATIV Book 9 Plus NP940X3K-K03US	$1,200	66	Excellent	Good	Very Good	Very Good	Very Good	9.5	3.1	Intel Core i5-5200U 2.2GHz
✓	25	**Lenovo** Ideapad Miix 700	$650	65	Very Good	Very Good	Very Good	Good	Very Good	10.75	2.5	Intel Core m3-6Y30 0.9GHz
✓	26	**Microsoft** Surface Pro 4	$930	65	Very Good	Very Good	Very Good	Good	Excellent	9	2.4	Intel Core m3-6Y30 0.9GHz
	27	**Asus** Transformer Book T300CHI-F1-DB	$500	64	Very Good	Very Good	Very Good	Good	Good	7.25	3.2	Intel Core M-5Y10c
	28	**Dell** Inspiron 13 7000 3rd Gen	$750	64	Excellent	Good	Very Good	Very Good	Good	10	3.5	Intel Core i5-6200U 2.3GHz
	29	**Dell** XPS 13 Touch	$1,450	63	Excellent	Good	Very Good	Very Good	Very Good	7.5	2.8	Intel Core i5-6200U 2.3GHz
	30	**Dell** XPS 12 2in1	$975	63	Very Good	Good	Very Good	Very Good	Very Good	8.75	2.8	Intel Core m5-6Y54 1.1GHz
	31	**Acer** Switch Alpha 12 SA5-271-594J	$750	62	Very Good	Good	Very Good	Good	Very Good	8.75	2.8	Intel Core i5-6200U 2.3GHz

RATINGS KEY ⊗ POOR ⊘ FAIR ❶ GOOD ⌄ VERY GOOD ⌄⌄ EXCELLENT
🅢 **CR BEST BUY** These models offer the best combination of performance and price. All are recommended.
✓ **RECOMMENDED** These are high-performing models that stand out.

Rec.	Rank	Brand & Model	Price	Score	Ergonomics	Portability	Performance	Versatility	Display	Battery Life (hr.)	Weight (lb.)	Processor
14-INCH LAPTOPS												
✓	1	**Lenovo** ThinkPad X1 Yoga	$1,900	79	⌃⌃	⌃	⌃⌃	⌃	⌃⌃	12.5	3	Intel Core i7-6500U 2.5GHz
✓	2	**Lenovo** Yoga 710 14"	$1,000	75	⌃	⌃	⌃⌃	!	⌃	13.5	3.5	Intel Core i5-6200U 2.3GHz
✓	3	**Lenovo** ThinkPad X1 Carbon 4th Gen	$1,150	73	⌃	⌃	⌃⌃	!	⌃	14.75	2.6	Intel Core i5-6200U 2.3GHz
✓	4	**Lenovo** ThinkPad X1 Carbon Ultrabook (3rd Gen)	$1,150	71	⌃	⌃	⌃	!	⌃	14.25	2.9	Intel Core I5-5200u 2.2GHz
✓	5	**Lenovo** YOGA 700 14 - 80QD003YUS	$640	69	⌃	⌃	⌃⌃	!	⌃	10.75	3.6	Intel Core i5-6200U 2.3GHz
✓	6	**LG** gram 14Z950	$900	68	⌃	⌃	⌃	!	⌃	9.25	2.1	Intel Core i5-5200U 2.2GHz
✓	7	**Lenovo** Ideapad 500S	$750	66	⌃	⌃	⌃⌃	⌃	⌃	8.5	3.7	Intel Core i7-6500U 2.5GHz
✓	8	**Lenovo** Flex 4	$680	66	⌃⌃	⌃	!	⌃	!	11.75	4	Intel Core i5-6200U 2.3GHz
	9	**Lenovo** Ideapad 510s	$650	63	⌃	⌃	!	!	!	9.75	3.7	Intel Core i5-6200U 2.3GHz
	10	**Asus** VivoBook E403SA-US21	$375	62	⌃	⌃	⊘	!	!	15.25	3.2	Intel Pentium N3700 1.6GHz
	11	**Lenovo** Ideapad 300S	$530	60	⌃	⌃	!	⌃	⌃	9.75	3.6	Intel Core i5-6200U 2.3GHz
15- TO 16-INCH LAPTOPS												
✓	1	**Apple** MacBook Pro 15-inch with Retina Display MJLQ2LL/A	$1,800	77	⌃	⌃	⌃⌃	!	⌃	16.5	4.4	Intel Core i7 2.2GHz
✓	2	**Samsung** Notebook 9 NP900X5L-K02US	$1,200	77	⌃	⌃	⌃⌃	⌃	⌃	10.5	2.8	Intel Core i7-6500U 2.5GHz
$	3	**Lenovo** Yoga 710 15"	$980	76	⌃⌃	⌃	⌃⌃	!	⌃	14	4.1	Intel Core i5-6200U 2.3GHz
✓	4	**HP** Spectre x360-15t	$1,150	75	⌃	⌃	⌃⌃	⌃	⌃	13.75	4.2	Intel Core i5-6200U 2.3GHz
✓	5	**Samsung** Notebook 9 pro NP940Z5L-X01US	$1,400	75	⌃⌃	!	⌃⌃	⌃	⌃	8.25	4.4	Intel Core i7-6700HQ 2.6GHz
✓	6	**Asus** ZenBook Pro UX501VW-DS71T	$1,500	74	⌃	⌃	⌃⌃	⌃	⌃	11	5	Intel Core i7-6700HQ 2.6GHz
✓	7	**Dell** XPS 15 Touch 6th-Gen	$1,700	72	⌃⌃	!	⌃⌃	⌃	⌃	8.25	4.5	Intel Core i5-6300HQ 2.3GHz

15- TO 16-INCH LAPTOPS (Continued)

Rec.	Rank	Brand & Model	Price	Score	Ergonomics	Portability	Performance	Versatility	Display	Battery Life (hr.)	Weight (lb.)	Processor
$	8	Acer Aspire V5-591G-55PV	$700	71	Very Good	Very Good	Excellent	Very Good	Good	10	4.7	Intel Core i5-6300HQ 2.3GHz
✓	9	Dell XPS 15 Non-Touch	$1,200	70	Very Good	Very Good	Very Good	Very Good	Excellent	10.25	4.3	Intel Core i5-6300HQ 2.3GHz
$	10	Dell Inspiron 15 5000 3rd-Gen	$700	69	Excellent	Very Good	Excellent	Very Good	Very Good	10.25	4.6	Intel Core i5-6200U 2.3GHz
✓	11	Dell Inspiron 15 7000 3rd-Gen	$750	68	Excellent	Very Good	Very Good	Very Good	Very Good	9.25	4.7	Intel Core i5-6200U 2.3GHz
✓	12	Acer Aspire Nitro VN7-592G-77	$1,200	67	Very Good	Good	Excellent	Very Good	Very Good	5.75	5.1	Intel Core i7-6700HQ 2.6GHz
✓	13	LG gram 15Z960	$1,100	67	Very Good	Very Good	Excellent	Good	Very Good	8	2.1	Intel Core i5-6200U 2.3GHz
✓	14	Lenovo Ideapad Y700 80NW000PUS	$1,000	67	Excellent	Good	Good	Excellent	Good	9.25	6.4	Intel Core i7-6700HQ 2.6GHz
✓	15	Asus Q503UA-BHI5T16	$680	67	Excellent	Very Good	Good	Excellent	Very Good	11.25	5.1	Intel Core i5-6200U 2.3GHz
✓	16	Acer Aspire VN7-572G-53E7	$650	66	Very Good	Good	Good	Very Good	Excellent	9.5	5.2	Intel Core i5-6200U 2.3GHz
✓	17	Lenovo Ideapad 700 15"	$850	65	Very Good	Good	Very Good	Very Good	Very Good	8.75	4.9	Intel Core i5-6300HQ 2.3GHz
✓	18	Samsung Notebook 7 740U5LE	$1,000	65	Excellent	Good	Good	Very Good	Very Good	9.25	5	Intel Core i7-6500U 2.5GHz
✓	19	Acer Aspire R5-571T-59DC	$600	65	Excellent	Good	Good	Very Good	Very Good	9.25	4.8	Intel Core i5-6200U 2.3GHz
✓	20	Asus Q524UQ-BBI7T14	$1,050	64	Excellent	Good	Good	Very Good	Very Good	8	5.1	Intel Core i7-6500U 2.5GHz
✓	21	HP Pavilion 15 i5	$920	63	Very Good	Good	Very Good	Very Good	Good	9.5	5.3	Intel Core i5-6300HQ 2.3GHz
✓	22	Toshiba Satellite S55-C5138	$600	61	Very Good	Good	Good	Very Good	Very Good	7	4.8	Intel Core i7-6500U 2.5GHz
✓	23	HP Pavilion x360 15.6	$660	61	Excellent	Very Good	Good	Very Good	Fair	9.5	4.8	Intel Core i5-6200U 2.3GHz
✓	24	HP Pavilion 15-ab220nr	$650	60	Excellent	Good	Good	Very Good	Very Good	8.5	4.9	Intel Core i5-6200U 2.3GHz

17- TO 18-INCH LAPTOPS

Rec.	Rank	Brand & Model	Price	Score	Ergonomics	Portability	Performance	Versatility	Display	Battery Life (hr.)	Weight (lb.)	Processor
✓	1	**Lenovo** Ideapad 700 17"	$1,100	75	Very Good	Good	Excellent	Very Good	Excellent	9.75	6	Intel Core i7-6700HQ 2.6GHz
✓	2	**Lenovo** Ideapad Y700 80Q0008WUS	$1,175	74	Very Good	Good	Excellent	Very Good	Excellent	10.75	7.6	Intel Core i7-6700HQ 2.6GHz
✓	3	**Lenovo** Z70- 80FG00DCUS	$900	69	Very Good	Good	Very Good	Excellent	Excellent	6.75	6.2	Intel Core i7-5500U 2.4GHz
✓	4	**HP** Pavilion 17 Gaming	$770	65	Very Good	Good	Good	Excellent	Excellent	10.25	6.9	Intel Core i5-6300HQ 2.3GHz
✓	5	**Dell** Inspiron 17 7000 3rd-Gen	$900	64	Excellent	Good	Good	Very Good	Excellent	9.75	6.3	Intel Core i5-6200U 2.3GHz
✓	6	**Dell** Inspiron i5759-5306SLV	$800	61	Excellent	Fair	Good	Excellent	Excellent	6.5	7.6	Intel Core i5-6200U 2.3GHz
	7	**Asus** X751LXDH71WX	$800	59	Very Good	Fair	Good	Very Good	Very Good	4.75	5.8	Intel Core i7-5500U 2.4GHz
	8	**HP** ENVY 17t	$900	58	Very Good	Fair	Good	Excellent	Very Good	5.5	7	Intel Core i7-5500U 2.4GHz
	9	**Dell** Inspiron 17 5000 Intel 6th Gen	$850	58	Excellent	Fair	Good	Excellent	Very Good	6.5	7.6	Intel Core i5-6200U 2.3GHz
	10	**Toshiba** Satellite L75-C7136	$500	57	Very Good	Good	Good	Very Good	Good	6	5.9	Intel Core i5-6200U 2.3GHz
	11	**HP** Laptop 17.3	$790	55	Excellent	Good	Good	Very Good	Good	6	5.7	Intel Core i5-6200U 2.3GHz
	12	**Lenovo** 300-17ISK 80QH008MUS	$330	53	Very Good	Good	Good	Very Good	Good	8.5	5.8	Intel Core i3-6100U 2.3GHz
	13	**HP** Pavilion 17-g148dx	$380	51	Excellent	Good	Fair	Very Good	Good	5.75	5.8	Intel Core i3-5020U 2.2GHz
	14	**HP** Pavilion 17z	$600	49	Excellent	Fair	Fair	Excellent	Good	5	6.6	AMD A10-8700P 1.8GHz
	15	**Lenovo** G70-80Q5004QUS	$330	47	Very Good	Good	Fair	Very Good	Good	6.75	6.1	AMD A8-6410 2GHz
	16	**HP** 17-p110nr	$400	43	Very Good	Good	Fair	Very Good	Good	6	5.9	AMD A6-6310 1.8GHz

RATINGS KEY ⊗ POOR   ⌄ FAIR   ● GOOD   ⌃ VERY GOOD   ⌃⌃ EXCELLENT
Ⓢ **CR BEST BUY** These models offer the best combination of performance and price. All are recommended.
✓ **RECOMMENDED** These are high-performing models that stand out.

Most & Least Reliable
Percentage of models that had problems.

DESKTOPS

Apple	15%
Lenovo	23%
Samsung	25%
Dell	27%
Gateway	27%
HP	27%
Acer	28%
Asus	29%

LAPTOPS

Apple	17%
Gateway	25%
Samsung	27%
Dell	29%
HP	30%
Acer	30%
Lenovo	31%
Asus	33%

Desktops Our conclusion is based on breakage rate estimates for laptops between 2012 and 2016, from 64,001 subscribers who purchased a new laptop in that time period. We estimate failure rates for 3-year-old desktops not covered by a service contract, accounting for the number of hours they're used per week. Differences of fewer than 5 points aren't meaningful.

Laptops Our conclusion is based on breakage rate estimates for laptops between 2012 and 2016, from 82,927 subscribers who purchased a new laptop in that time period. We estimate failure rates for 3-year-old laptops not covered by a service contract, accounting for the number of hours they're used per week. Differences of fewer than 3 points aren't meaningful.

Source 2016 Spring Product Reliability Survey, Consumer Reports National Research Center.

Cooktops

Cooktops can be placed wherever counter space allows, including an island. Gas and smoothtop electric cooktops dominate, but prices are dropping for electric induction, which speeds heating using an electromagnetic field.

What to Look For

■ If you have a choice in fuel, and you want the visual confirmation of a flame, a gas cooktop is for you; a smoothtop electric makes for easy cleaning.

■ An induction model for quick heating; some now cost around $1,200, though you can still pay far more.

■ At least one high-powered gas burner or electric element for quick heating.

What to Skip

■ Buying by Btu. Short for British thermal unit, the measurement merely indicates gas used and heat generated and doesn't guarantee better or faster cooking.

■ Models with recipe databases and other pricey features if you just want good cooking.

What You'll Pay

A cooktop and wall oven will cost $2,000 or more; some high-performing electric and gas ranges sell for less than half of that.

BUYING ADVICE

More 30-inch gas cooktops have five burners instead of four, though using all five at once may require some maneuvering.

For more buying advice, go to ConsumerReports.org/cooktops.

All tested models in performance order.

Rec.	Rank	Brand & Model	Price	Score	High Heat	Low Heat	High-Power Burners	Medium-Power Burners	Low-Power Burners	Stainless Steel	Glass Ceramic	Porcelain Enamel	Continuous Grates
30-INCH GAS													
✓	1	**Whirlpool** WCG97USODS	$900	80	Good	Excellent	1	3	1	•			•
	2	**GE** PGP953SETSS	$990	64	Good	Very Good	1	3	1	•			•
	3	**Kenmore** 32683	$990	62	Very Good	Good	2	2	1	•			•
36-INCH GAS													
✓	1	**Thermador** SGSX365FS	$1900	81	Very Good	Excellent	3	2	0	•			•
✓	2	**GE** Monogram ZGU385NSMSS	$1500	80	Good	Excellent	3	2	0	•			•
✓	3	**Kenmore** 32713	$1215	79	Very Good	Excellent	2	2	1	•			•
✓	4	**GE** Café CGP650SETSS	$1440	77	Good	Excellent	1	3	1	•			•
✓	5	**LG** LSCG366ST	$1100	74	Very Good	Very Good	2	2	1	•			•
	6	**Wolf** CG365P/S	$2000	64	Very Good	Good	2	3	0	•			•
	7	**Miele** KM3474GSS	$1750	62	Very Good	Good	3	2	0	•			•
	8	**Frigidaire** Professional FPGC3677RS	$1350	60	Good	Good	2	2	1	•			•
	9	**KitchenAid** KCGS556ESS	$1100	54	Very Good	Fair	1	2	2	•			•
	10	**Jenn-Air** JGD3536BS	$2000	38	Very Good	Poor	3	1	1	•			•
36-INCH GAS RANGETOPS													
	1	**Kenmore** Pro Slide-in 34913	$1920	44	Very Good	Poor	3	2	1	•	•		•

Guide to Ratings

Score reflects cooktop performance at high and low heat. The displayed score is out of a total of 100 points. **High Heat** reflects how quickly the highest-powered element heated water to near-boiling. **Low Heat** reflects how well the lowest-powered element held a low heat as for melting chocolate and how the most powerful element, set to low, held tomato sauce below a boil. **Price** is approximate retail.

RATINGS KEY ⊘ POOR ⌄ FAIR ❶ GOOD ⌃ VERY GOOD ✦ EXCELLENT
Ⓢ CR BEST BUY These models offer the best combination of performance and price. All are recommended.
✓ RECOMMENDED These are high-performing models that stand out.

Rec.	Rank	Brand & Model	Price	Score	Test Results		Features				
					High Heat	Low Heat	High-Power Elements	Medium-Power Elements	Low-Power Elements	Expandable Elements	Touch Controls
		30-INCH ELECTRIC SMOOTHTOPS									
✓	1	**KitchenAid** KECC604BBL	$900	94	⌃	⌃	2	0	2	•	
✓	2	**Jenn-Air** JEC4430BS	$1400	94	⌃	⌃	2	0	2	•	•
✓	3	**GE** Profile PP9030SJSS	$1260	92	⌃	⌃	2	2	1	•	•
✓	4	**Kenmore** Turbo-boil 45313	$1200	91	⌃	⌃	2	0	3	•	•
✓	5	**Bosch** NETP066SUC	$1200	88	⌃	⌃	1	1	3	•	•
$	6	**Whirlpool** G7CE3034XP	$700	86	⌃	⌃	2	0	2	•	
$	7	**Frigidaire** FFEC3024LB	$500	85	⌃	⌃	2	0	2		
	8	**Thermador** CES304FS	$1500	75	⌵	⌃	1	2	1	•	•
		36-INCH ELECTRIC SMOOTHTOPS									
✓	1	**KitchenAid** KECC664BSS	$1080	93	⌃	⌃	2	1	1	•	
✓	2	**Viking** VEC5366BSB	$2150	88	⌃	⌃	1	3	2	•	
		30-INCH ELECTRIC INDUCTION									
✓	1	**GE** Café CHP9530	$1800	99	⌃	⌃	3	1	0		•
✓	2	**Kenmore** 43820	$1440	99	⌃	⌃	3	1	0		•
✓	3	**Bosch** NIT5066UC	$1440	98	⌃	⌃	2	2	0		•
✓	4	**Kenmore** 43800	$1200	97	⌃	⌃	3	1	0		•
✓	5	**Frigidaire** FGIC3067MB	$1260	95	⌃	⌃	3	1	0		•
✓	6	**KitchenAid** KICU500XB	$1395	95	⌃	⌃	2	2	0		•
✓	7	**Whirlpool** GCI3061XB	$1215	95	⌃	⌃	2	0	2		•
		36-INCH ELECTRIC INDUCTION									
✓	1	**Thermador** CIT36XKB [1]	$5000	92	⌃	⌃	2	1	1	•	•
	2	**Jenn-Air** JIC4536XS	$2100	90	⌃	⌃	5	0	0	•	•

[1] Unique model with a full cooking surface rather than individual elements. In practical use with four pots it allows for two large, high-power cooking areas, and two medium or low-power areas.

Most & Least Reliable

Percentage likely to break by third year of ownership.

ELECTRIC

Kenmore	3%
GE	4%
Whirlpool	4%
Frigidaire	5%
Jenn-Air	7%
KitchenAid	8%

GAS

Bosch	4%
GE	5%
Kenmore	5%
Whirlpool	6%
Wolf	7%
Jenn-Air	7%
Thermador	8%
KitchenAid	8%

The chart shows the estimated failure rates for cooktops purchased new and not covered by a service contract, by the third year of ownership. Differences of fewer than 5 percentage points aren't meaningful. Results are based on a survey of 5,967 owners of electric and gas cooktops. Note that models within a brand may vary.

Source 2015 Summer Product Reliability Survey, Consumer Reports National Research Center

Digital Cameras

Consumers are placing increasing demands on cameras, and manufacturers are meeting those needs by adding more capabilities, especially wireless connectivity.

What to Look For

■ A zoom range with a wide-angle option as low as 28mm, 24mm, or wider for more expansive panoramic landscapes or large group portraits.

■ An LCD that can swivel for hard-to-reach shots.

■ A touch screen for easy interaction with menus.

■ An optical or electronic viewfinder, which can help you conserve battery power or compose photos when bright light washes out your LCD.

■ An easily accessible video mode, which lets you record video while shooting photos.

■ Extended zoom ranges from 5x to 83x.

■ An SLR or mirrorless model with interchangeable lenses for the most versatility.

■ Wi-Fi features for quickly uploading images and video.

What to Skip

■ Buying a camera solely based on its megapixel count, because higher resolution alone doesn't guarantee better photographs.

■ An extended warranty; digital cameras have been very reliable overall in our subscriber surveys.

What You'll Pay

For basic point-and-shoots, expect to spend $90 to $400. For advanced point-and-shoots, $330 to $1,300. For mirrorless cameras, $300 to $3,700. For SLRs, $400 to $3,700.

BUYING ADVICE

If you don't intend to change the lens on your camera, consider an advanced point-and-shoot, which has a fixed lens. Some models have large image sensors with excellent optics and lots of features.

For more buying advice, go to ConsumerReports.org/cameras.

All tested models in performance order.

ADVANCED POINT-AND-SHOOT

Rec.	Rank	Brand & Model	Price	Score	Megapixels	Weight (oz.)	Image Quality	Flash Photos	Video Quality	Ease of Use	LCD Quality	Viewfinder	Test Lens
✓	1	**Sony** Cyber-shot DSC-RX10 II	$1,200	79	20	30	●	●	●	●	●	●	24-200mm
✓	2	**Canon** Power-Shot G1 X Mark II	$650	78	13	20	●	●	●	●	●	NA	24-120mm
✓	3	**Canon** Power-Shot G7 X Mark II	$700	77	20	11	●	●	●	●	●	NA	24-100mm
✓	4	**Panasonic** Lumix DMC-FZ1000	$800	77	20	31	●	●	●	●	●	●	25-400mm
✓	5	**Sony** Cyber-shot DSC-RX100 IV	$950	77	20	10	●	●	●	●	●	●	24-70mm
✓	6	**Canon** Power-Shot G7 X	$580	75	20	11	●	●	●	●	●	NA	24-100mm
✓	7	**Canon** Power-Shot G3 X	$850	75	20	27	●	●	●	●	●	NA	24-600mm
✓	8	**Leica** D-Lux (Typ 109)	$1,100	73	13	16	●	●	●	●	●	●	24-75mm
✓	9	**Panasonic** Lumix DMC-LX100	$700	72	13	16	●	●	●	●	●	●	24-75mm
✓	10	**Sony** Cyber-shot DSC-RX10	$800	72	20	30	●	●	●	●	●	●	24-200mm
✓	11	**Sony** Cyber-shot DSC-RX100 III	$750	72	20	10	●	●	●	●	●	●	24-70mm
✓	12	**Panasonic** Lumix DMC-ZS100	$700	72	20	11	●	●	●	●	●	●	27-270mm
$	13	**Canon** Power-Shot G9 X	$400	71	20	7	●	●	●	●	●	NA	28-84mm
✓	14	**Fujifilm** X100T	$1,300	71	16	17	●	●	●	●	●	●	35mm
	15	**Fujifilm** X30	$500	70	12	16	●	●	●	●	●	●	28-112mm
	16	**Fujifilm** X70	$700	69	16	13	●	●	●	●	●	NA	28mm
	17	**Ricoh** GR II	$600	68	16	9	●	●	●	●	●	NA	28mm
	18	**Canon** Power-Shot G16	$380	68	12	14	●	●	●	●	●	●	28-140mm
	19	**Canon** Power-Shot G5 X	$700	67	20	14	●	●	●	●	●	●	24-100mm
	20	**Panasonic** Lumix DMC-FZ200	$300	60	12	22	●	●	●	●	●	●	25-600mm
	21	**Leica** X-E (Typ 102)	$1,580	59	16	14	●	●	NA	●	●	NA	36mm
	22	**Panasonic** Lumix DMC-ZS60	$450	57	18	10	●	●	●	●	●	●	24-720mm
	23	**Canon** Power-Shot SX60 HS	$450	57	16	24	●	●	●	●	●	●	21-1365mm
	24	**Fujifilm** XQ2	$300	53	12	7	●	●	●	●	●	NA	25-100mm

Rec.	Rank	Brand & Model	Price	Score	Megapixels	Weight (oz.)	Image Quality	Flash Photos	Video Quality	Ease of Use	LCD Quality	Viewfinder	Test Lens
		MIRRORLESS											
✓	1	**Panasonic** Lumix DMC-GH4	$2,200	77	16	21	●	●	●	●	●	●	14-140mm (2.0)
✓	2	**Panasonic** Lumix DMC-GX8	$1,380	77	20	18	●	NA	●	●	●	●	14-42mm (2.0)
✓	3	**Sony** a7S	$3,300	76	12	18	●	NA	●	●	●	●	24-70mm (1.0)
✓	4	**Fujifilm** X-Pro2	$2,400	75	24	18	●	NA	●	●	●	●	18-55mm (1.5)
✓	5	**Panasonic** Lumix DMC-G7K	$800	75	16	16	●	●	●	●	●	●	14-42mm (2.0)
$	6	**Canon** EOS M10	$500	73	18	11	●	●	●	●	●	NA	15-45mm (1.6)
✓	7	**Sony** a7	$1,300	73	24	18	●	NA	●	●	●	●	28-70mm (1.0)
✓	8	**Fujifilm** X-T1	$1,700	73	16	17	●	●	●	●	●	●	18-55mm (1.5)
✓	9	**Olympus** OM-D E-M5 Mark II	$1,400	73	16	19	●	●	●	●	●	●	12-50mm (2.0)
✓	10	**Panasonic** Lumix DMC-GX85	$800	72	16	16	●	●	●	●	●	●	12-32mm (2.0)
✓	11	**Fujifilm** X-T10	$800	72	16	14	●	●	●	●	●	●	16-50mm (1.5)
✓	12	**Fujifilm** X-E2	$1,100	71	16	13	●	●	●	●	●	●	18-55mm (1.5)
	13	**Sony** a7R	$3,000	70	36	17	●	NA	●	●	●	●	24-70mm (1.0)
	14	**Canon** EOS M3	$600	69	24	14	●	●	●	●	●	NA	18-55mm (1.6)
	15	**Fujifilm** X-A2	$550	69	16	13	●	●	●	●	●	NA	16-50mm (1.5)
	16	**Olympus** Pen-F	$1,450	69	20	18	●	●	●	●	●	●	14-42mm (2.0)
	17	**Olympus** OM-D E-M10 Mark II	$650	69	16	15	●	●	●	●	●	●	14-42mm (2.0)
	18	**Sony** a5100	$500	69	24	10	●	●	●	●	●	NA	16-50mm (1.5)
	19	**Sony** a6300	$1,150	68	24	15	●	●	●	●	●	●	16-50mm (1.5)
	20	**Sony** a5000	$400	68	20	10	●	●	●	●	●	NA	16-50mm (1.5)
	21	**Fujifilm** X-E2S	$1,400	67	16	13	●	●	●	●	●	●	18-55mm (1.5)
	22	**Olympus** Pen E-PL7	$450	67	16	14	●	●	●	●	●	NA	14-42mm (2.0)
	23	**Sony** a6000	$650	65	24	12	●	●	●	●	●	●	16-50mm (1.5)
	24	**Pentax** Q-S1	$350	62	12	8	●	●	●	●	●	NA	5-15mm (5.5)
	25	**Nikon** 1 J5	$500	62	21	10	●	●	●	●	●	NA	10-30mm (2.7)

Rec.	Rank	Brand & Model	Price	Score	Megapixels	Weight (oz.)	Image Quality	Flash Photos	Video Quality	Ease of Use	LCD Quality	Viewfinder	Test Lens
		MIRRORLESS (Continued)											
	26	**Nikon** 1 AW1	$800	60	14	13	○	○	○	○	○	NA	11-27.5mm (2.7)
	27	**Olympus** OM-D E-M10	$500	60	16	15	○	○	○	○	○	○	14-42mm (2.0)
	28	**Nikon** 1 V3	$1,200	56	18	11	○	○	○	○	○	NA	10-30mm (2.7)
		SLR											
✓	1	**Nikon** D500	$3,070	79	21	31	○	NA	○	○	○	○	16-80mm (1.5)
✓	2	**Nikon** D750	$2,300	77	24	31	○	○	○	○	○	○	24-120mm (1.0)
✓	3	**Canon** EOS 5D Mark III	$3,500	76	22	34	○	NA	○	○	○	○	24-105mm (1.0)
✓	4	**Nikon** D810	$3,000	74	36	35	○	○	○	○	○	○	24-120mm (1.0)
✓	5	**Nikon** D7200	$1,400	74	24	26	○	○	○	○	○	○	18-105mm (1.5)
$	6	**Canon** EOS Rebel T5i	$600	73	18	30	○	○	○	○	○	○	18-55mm (1.6)
✓	7	**Canon** EOS 70D	$1,100	73	20	28	○	○	○	○	○	○	18-55mm (1.6)
✓	8	**Canon** EOS Rebel T6s	$1,050	72	24	22	○	○	○	○	○	○	18-135mm (1.6)
✓	9	**Canon** EOS 6D	$1,800	72	20	29	○	NA	○	○	○	○	24-105mm (1.0)
✓	10	**Nikon** D7100	$1,100	72	24	44	○	○	○	○	○	○	18-105mm (1.5)
$	11	**Nikon** D3300	$450	71	24	17	○	○	○	○	○	○	18-55mm (1.5)
$	12	**Canon** EOS Rebel SL1	$500	71	18	23	○	○	○	○	○	○	18-55mm (1.6)
	13	**Nikon** D5500	$850	70	24	17	○	○	○	○	○	○	18-55mm (1.5)
	14	**Canon** EOS 80D	$1,350	70	24	28	○	○	○	○	○	○	18-55mm (1.6)
	15	**Canon** EOS Rebel T6	$500	70	18	18	○	○	○	○	○	○	18-55mm (1.6)
	16	**Canon** EOS Rebel T6i	$750	69	24	21	○	○	○	○	○	○	18-55mm (1.6)
	17	**Canon** EOS Rebel T5	$400	69	18	18	○	○	○	○	○	○	18-55mm (1.6)
	18	**Canon** EOS 7D Mark II	$1,850	68	20	34	○	○	○	○	○	○	18-135mm (1.6)
	19	**Nikon** D5300	$600	67	24	20	○	○	○	○	○	○	18-55mm (1.5)

Rec.	Rank	Brand & Model	Price	Score	Megapixels	Weight (oz.)	Image Quality	Flash Photos	Video Quality	Ease of Use	LCD Quality	Viewfinder	Test Lens
		SLR (Continued)											
	20	**Pentax** K-3 II	$990	67	24	29	⌃	NA	●	⌃	⌃	≪	18-135mm (1.5)
	21	**Sony** SLT-A77 II	$1,650	65	24	27	●	⌃	≪	⌃	⌃	≪	16-50mm (1.5)
	22	**Pentax** K-S2	$540	65	20	25	⌃	●	●	⌃	⌃	≪	18-50mm (1.5)
	23	**Nikon** D610	$1,700	65	24	32	●	≪	●	⌃	≪	≪	24-85mm (1.0)
	24	**Pentax** K-50	$380	64	16	24	⌃	⌃	●	⌃	⌃	≪	18-55mm (1.5)
	25	**Sony** SLT-A68	$700	64	24	25	●	⌃	⌃	⌃	●	≪	18-55mm (1.5)
	26	**Sony** SLT-A58K	$500	63	20	30	●	●	●	⌃	●	≪	18-55mm (1.5)

Recommended	Rank	Brand & Model	Price	Score	Megapixels	Weight (oz.)	Image Quality	Flash Photos	Video Quality	Ease of Use	LCD Quality	Widest Angle (mm)	Battery Life (shots)
		POINT AND SHOOT											
✓	1	**Canon** PowerShot N100	$350	67	12	10	⌃	⌃	⌃	●	⌃	24	330
✓	2	**Nikon** Coolpix S7000	$200	62	16	6	⌃	●	●	●	●	25	210
✓	3	**Canon** PowerShot N2	$300	62	16	7	⌃	⊘	⌃	●	⌃	28	200
	4	**Canon** PowerShot SX610 HS	$200	60	20	7	⌃	●	●	●	⌃	25	270
	5	**Sony** Cyber-shot DSC-WX350	$270	60	18	6	⌃	●	●	●	●	25	470
	6	**Canon** PowerShot ELPH 350 HS	$160	59	20	5	⌃	●	●	●	●	25	185
	7	**Canon** PowerShot N	$200	56	12	7	⌃	⊘	●	●	⌃	28	200
	8	**Canon** PowerShot ELPH 170	$120	52	20	5	●	●	⊘	●	●	25	200
	9	**Canon** PowerShot ELPH 160	$100	47	20	5	●	●	⊘	●	●	28	220

Recommended	Rank	Brand & Model	Price	Score	Megapixels	Weight (oz.)	Image Quality	Flash Photos	Video Quality	Ease of Use	LCD Quality	Widest Angle (mm)	Battery Life (shots)
		POINT AND SHOOT (Continued)											
	10	**Sony** Cyber-shot DSC-W830	$130	45	20	4	Good	Fair	Good	Fair	Good	25	210
	11	**Nikon** Coolpix S3700	$120	41	20	4	Good	Good	Fair	Good	Fair	25	240
		SUPERZOOM											
✓	1	**Nikon** Coolpix P900	$600	67	16	33	Very Good	Very Good	NA	Very Good	Very Good	24	360
✓	2	**Nikon** Coolpix S9900	$260	67	16	10	Very Good	Good	Good	Very Good	Very Good	25	300
✓	3	**Nikon** Coolpix P610	$360	66	16	21	Very Good	Very Good	Good	Very Good	Very Good	24	360
✓	4	**Canon** PowerShot SX710 HS	$280	65	20	9	Very Good	Very Good	Very Good	Good	Very Good	25	230
✓	5	**Canon** PowerShot SX720 HS	$380	63	20	9	Very Good	Very Good	Good	Good	Very Good	24	250
	6	**Canon** PowerShot SX540 HS	$400	59	20	17	Very Good	Very Good	Good	Good	Very Good	24	205
	7	**Sony** Cyber-shot DSC-WX500	$300	59	18	8	Good	Good	Very Good	Good	Good	24	400
	8	**Canon** PowerShot SX530 HS	$250	58	16	17	Very Good	Very Good	Good	Good	Good	24	210
	9	**Nikon** Coolpix L840	$200	58	16	21	Very Good	Good	Good	Good	Very Good	22.5	590
	10	**Fujifilm** FinePix S9800	$220	58	16	26	Very Good	Very Good	Fair	Good	Very Good	24	300
	11	**Sony** Cyber-shot DSC-HX80	$350	58	18	9	Good	Good	Very Good	Very Good	Good	24	390
	12	**Fujifilm** FinePix S9900W	$200	57	16	26	Very Good	Very Good	Fair	Good	Very Good	24	300
	13	**Canon** PowerShot SX420 IS	$300	55	20	12	Very Good	Good	Fair	Good	Good	24	195
	14	**Canon** PowerShot SX410 IS	$180	55	20	12	Very Good	Good	Fair	Good	Good	24	185
	15	**Nikon** Coolpix B500	$300	54	16	21	Good	Very Good	Good	Good	Very Good	22.5	600
	16	**Sony** Cyber-shot DSC-H400	$250	48	20	24	Good	Good	Fair	Good	Good	24.5	300
	17	**Sony** Cyber-shot DSC-HX90V	$430	45	18	9	Fair	Good	Very Good	Very Good	Good	24	390

RATINGS KEY ⊘ POOR ⊙ FAIR ● GOOD ⌃ VERY GOOD ⌃⌃ EXCELLENT

$ CR BEST BUY These models offer the best combination of performance and price. All are recommended.

✓ RECOMMENDED These are high-performing models that stand out.

Recommended	Rank	Brand & Model	Price	Score	Megapixels	Weight (oz.)	Image Quality	Flash Photos	Video Quality	Ease of Use	LCD Quality	Widest Angle (mm)	Battery Life (shots)
		RUGGED/WATERPROOF POINT-AND-SHOOT											
✓	1	**Olympus** Stylus TG-4	$330	66	16	9	⌃	◐	⌄	⌃	⌃⌃	25	NA
✓	2	**Nikon** Coolpix AW130	$300	62	16	8	⌃	◐	◐	◐	⌃	24	370
✓	3	**Canon** PowerShot D30	$300	57	12	8	⌃	◐	◐	◐	⌃	28	300
$	4	**Sony** Cyber-shot DSC-TX30	$230	56	18	5	◐	⌃	⌃	◐	◐	26	250
$	5	**Olympus** Stylus TG-860	$230	53	16	8	◐	◐	⌄	◐	⌃	21	NA
✓	6	**Olympus** Stylus Tough TG-870	$280	52	16	8	◐	◐	⌄	◐	⌃	21	NA
$	7	**Fujifilm** FinePix XP90	$200	52	16	7	◐	◐	◐	◐	⌃	28	210
	8	**Panasonic** Lumix DMC-TS30	$140	50	16	5	◐	⌄	⌄	◐	◐	25	250
	9	**Ricoh** WG-5 GPS	$260	49	16	9	◐	◐	◐	◐	⌃	25	240
	10	**Nikon** Coolpix S33	$110	46	13	6	◐	◐	◐	⌄	◐	30	220
	11	**Ricoh** WG-30W	$225	44	16	7	⌄	◐	◐	◐	◐	28	300
	12	**Fujifilm** FinePix XP80	$150	38	16	6	⌄	⌄	⌄	◐	◐	28	210

Guide to the Ratings

Score is based mainly on image quality, ease of use, and versatility, plus LCD, flash, and video quality. **Megapixels** is the number of pixels, in millions, on the sensor. **Weight (oz.)** is with battery, memory card, and strap. **Image Quality** combines several tests, including regular photos, low-light photos, and flash photos as well as color tests, among others. **Flash Photos** tests the quality of the built-in flash's light output and evenness of illumination. **Video Quality** mostly reflects footage shot in regular and low light, with audio quality and macro (close-up) capability also considered. **Ease of Use** is our evaluation of the camera's controls, manual, response time, and focusing. **LCD Quality** is a judgment of images viewed under various lighting conditions. For **Widest Angle (mm)**, the lower the number, the broader the vista the camera can capture. **Battery Life (Shots)** is as the manufacturer states. **Price** is approximate retail.

Most & Least Reliable

Percentage likely to break by third year of ownership.

POINT-AND-SHOOT

Pentax/Ricoh	3%
Canon	4%
Sony	5%
Panasonic	5%
Olympus	5%
Fujifilm	5%
Nikon	6%

INTERCHANGEABLE LENS

Fujifilm	3%
Canon	3%
Nikon	4%
Sony	4%
Panasonic	5%
Pentax/Ricoh	6%
Olympus	8%

The conclusions in this chart are based on our failure rate estimates for digital cameras by the third year of ownership. Our data are gathered from 69,976 subscribers who purchased a new digital camera between 2011 and 2016 not covered by a service contract. Differences of fewer than 4 points aren't meaningful. Models within a brand may vary, and changes in design or manufacturer might affect future reliability. Still, choosing a brand with a good reliability estimate can improve your odds of getting a dependable model.

Source 2016 Spring Product Reliability Survey, Consumer Reports National Research Center.

Dishwashers

New dishwashers use less energy and water, though cycle times can exceed 2 hours. Those we recommend aced our washing tests and are quiet.

What to Look For

■ Adjustable racks and other loading aids for flexibility.
■ A soil sensor to adjust the cycle's time and water use, improving efficiency.
■ A rinse/hold option to prevent soil from setting while you wait for a full load.

What to Skip

■ Drawer models, which are expensive and tend to use more energy and water than regular models.

■ Stainless-steel tubs, which can add to the cost. Hybrid stainless/plastic and gray-speckled plastic tubs cost less and also resist stains.

What You'll Pay

A dishwasher with hidden controls, interactive digital displays, and special grime-fighting cycles can cost $1,500 or more. But for clean dishes, sparkling performance starts around $500.

BUYING ADVICE

The three basic cycles—light, normal, and heavy—should be enough for most chores, even for baked-on food.

For more buying advice, go to ConsumerReports.org/dishwashers.

All tested models in performance order.

Rec.	Rank	Brand & Model	Price	Score	Washing	Drying	Energy Use	Noise	Ease of Use	Cycle Time (min.)	Ample Flatware Slots	Adjustable Upper Rack	Self-Cleaning Filter	Interior Material
							Test Results						Features	
✓	1	**KitchenAid** KDTM354DSS	$860	85	⌃⌃	⌃⌃	⌃⌃	⌃	⌃	125	•	•	•	SS
✓	2	**Kenmore** Elite 12793	$980	85	⌃⌃	①	⌃⌃	⌃⌃	⌃	145	•	•		SS
✓	3	**KitchenAid** KDTM704ESS	$1620	83	⌃⌃	①	⌃⌃	⌃	⌃⌃	110	•	•	•	SS
✓	4	**Kenmore** Elite 14833	$1115	82	⌃⌃	①	⌃⌃	⌃	⌃⌃	115	•	•	•	SS
✓	5	**Kenmore** Elite 14763	$750	82	⌃⌃	①	⌃⌃	⌃	⌃⌃	115	•	•		SS
$	6	**Bosch** Ascenta SHX3AR7[5]UC	$630	81	⌃⌃	⌃	⌃⌃	⌃	⌃⌃	95	•	•		SS/P

Rec.	Rank	Brand & Model	Price	Score	Washing	Drying	Energy Use	Noise	Ease of Use	Cycle Time (min.)	Ample Flatware Slots	Adjustable Upper Rack	Self-Cleaning Filter	Interior Material
✓	7	**KitchenAid** KDFE454CSS	$1350	81	Excellent	Good	Excellent	Excellent	Good	140	•	•		SS
	8	**GE** Profile PDF820SSJSS	$900	80	Excellent	Good	Excellent	Very Good	Very Good	150	•	•		SS
	9	**Thermador** Topaz Series DWHD640JFM	$1500	80	Excellent	Excellent	Excellent	Very Good	Very Good	125	•	•		SS
	10	**Bosch** 800 Plus Series SHX7PT55UC	$1300	80	Excellent	Excellent	Excellent	Very Good	Very Good	125	•	•		SS
	11	**Kenmore** Elite 14793	$850	80	Excellent	Good	Very Good	Very Good	Very Good	145	•	•		SS
	12	**Bosch** 500 Series SHP65T55UC	$810	80	Excellent	Excellent	Excellent	Very Good	Very Good	125	•	•		SS
	13	**Bosch** 300 Series DLX SHX53TL5UC	$760	80	Excellent	Excellent	Excellent	Good	Very Good	125	•	•		SS
	14	**KitchenAid** KDTM404ESS	$1170	80	Excellent	Good	Excellent	Very Good	Very Good	110	•	•	•	SS
	15	**KitchenAid** KDTE254ESS	$900	80	Excellent	Good	Excellent	Very Good	Very Good	145	•	•		SS
	16	**Kenmore** Elite 14753	$750	80	Excellent	Good	Excellent	Very Good	Very Good	145	•	•		SS
	17	**GE** Profile PDT855SSJSS	$1400	79	Excellent	Good	Excellent	Very Good	Very Good	155	•	•		SS
	18	**GE** Profile PDT846SSJSS	$1100	79	Excellent	Good	Excellent	Very Good	Very Good	155	•	•		SS
	19	**Bosch** 800 Series SHE68T55UC	$850	79	Excellent	Excellent	Excellent	Very Good	Very Good	125	•	•		SS
	20	**Equator** ST6501	$760	79	Excellent	Good	Excellent	Very Good	Excellent	135	•	•		SS
	21	**GE** Profile PDT750SSFSS	$1100	79	Excellent	Good	Excellent	Very Good	Very Good	140	•	•		SS
	22	**Blomberg** DWT55300SS	$800	79	Excellent	Excellent	Excellent	Good	Very Good	130	•	•		SS
	23	**Viking** 100 Series FDW101	$880	79	Excellent	Excellent	Excellent	Good	Very Good	130	•	•		SS
	24	**GE** Profile PDT760SSFSS	$1500	78	Excellent	Good	Excellent	Very Good	Very Good	140	•	•		SS
	25	**Bertazzoni** DW24XT	$1050	78	Excellent	Good	Excellent	Very Good	Very Good	135	•	•		SS

RATINGS KEY ⊘ POOR ⊙ FAIR ❶ GOOD ⌄ VERY GOOD ⊗ EXCELLENT

🅢 **CR BEST BUY** These models offer the best combination of performance and price. All are recommended.
✓ **RECOMMENDED** These are high-performing models that stand out.

Rec.	Rank	Brand & Model	Price	Score	Washing	Drying	Energy Use	Noise	Ease of Use	Cycle Time (min.)	Ample Flatware Slots	Adjustable Upper Rack	Self-Cleaning Filter	Interior Material
	26	**Blomberg** DWT54100SS	$750	78	⌃	○	⌃	○	○	85	•	•		SS
	27	**Maytag** MDB8979SEZ	$850	78	⌃	○	○	○	⌃	155	•	•	•	SS
	28	**Miele** Futura Classic Plus G4925US	$1000	78	⌃	○	⌃	○	○	150	•	•		SS
	29	**Thermador** Emerald Series DWHD440MFM	$1300	78	○	⌃	⌃	○	○	130	•	•		SS
	30	**KitchenAid** Architect Series II KDTE554CSS	$1080	78	⌃	○	⌃	○	○	145	•	•		SS
	31	**Miele** Futura Crystal G6165SCVISF	$1400	78	⌃	⌃	⌃	○	○	150	•	•		SS
	32	**Kenmore** 13693	$600	78	⌃	⌃	⌃	○	○	160		•		SS
	33	**Blomberg** DWT25502SS	$530	77	⌃	○	⌃	○	○	110	•	•		SS
	34	**Beko** DUT25400X	$550	77	⌃	○	⌃	○	○	110	•	•		SS
	35	**Kenmore** 13223	$300	77	⌃	⌃	⌃	○	○	160	•	•		SS
	36	**Viking** 300 Series FDW300	$1100	77	⌃	○	⌃	○	○	115	•	•		SS
	37	**GE** Cafe CDT725SSFSS	$1000	77	○	○	⌃	○	○	145	•	•		SS
	38	**Kucht** K6502D	$750	77	⌃	○	⌃	○	○	140	•	•		SS
	39	**Blomberg** DWT56502SS	$650	77	⌃	○	⌃	○	○	110	•	•		SS
	40	**Beko** DDT25400X	$550	77	⌃	○	⌃	○	○	110	•	•		SS
	41	**GE** GDT580SSFSS	$720	76	⌃	⌃	⌃	○	○	155	•	•		SS
	42	**Thermador** DWHD651JFP	$2200	76	○	⌃	○	○	○	120	•	•		SS
	43	**Bosch** 800 Series SHXN8U55UC	$1080	75	⌃	○	⌃	⌃	○	130	•	•		SS
	44	**KitchenAid** KDTE104ESS	$600	75	○	○	⌃	○	○	135	•	•		SS
	45	**Kenmore** 13209	$500	75	⌃	⌃	⌃	○	○	155	•	•		P
	46	**Bosch** 300 Series SHP53U55UC	$720	75	⌃	○	⌃	○	○	160	•	•		SS

Rec.	Rank	Brand & Model	Price	Score	Washing	Drying	Energy Use	Noise	Ease of Use	Cycle Time (min.)	Ample Flatware Slots	Adjustable Upper Rack	Self-Cleaning Filter	Interior Material
	47	**Bosch** 800 Plus Series SHE9PT55UC	$1900	75	Very Good	Excellent	Excellent	Excellent	Excellent	130	•	•		SS
	48	**Whirlpool** WDT720PADM	$400	75	Excellent	Excellent	Very Good	Very Good	Very Good	155	•	•		P
	49	**LG** LDS5040ST	$590	75	Very Good	Excellent	Very Good	Very Good	Very Good	110	•	•	•	SS
	50	**Samsung** DW80F800UWS	$720	75	Excellent	Excellent	Very Good	Very Good	Excellent	140	•	•	•	SS
	51	**Bosch** 500 Series SHE65U55UC	$850	74	Excellent	Very Good	Excellent	Excellent	Very Good	160	•	•		SS
	52	**GE** Monogram ZDT870SPFSS	$1700	74	Very Good	Good	Excellent	Excellent	Very Good	150	•	•		SS
	53	**Samsung** Chef Collection DW80H9970US	$1350	74	Excellent	Good	Excellent	Very Good	Very Good	155	•	•		SS
	54	**Miele** Futura Lumen G6595SCViK2O	$1800	73	Excellent	Excellent	Very Good	Very Good	Very Good	155	•	•		SS
	55	**Kenmore** 13473	$400	73	Excellent	Excellent	Excellent	Good	Good	160		•		P
	56	**GE** GDT680SSHSS	$810	73	Excellent	Good	Very Good	Good	Very Good	155	•	•		SS
	57	**GE** GDT545PSJSS	$450	73	Excellent	Good	Very Good	Good	Very Good	150	•	•		P
	58	**Amana** ADB1700ADS	$500	72	Excellent	Good	Good	Good	Good	145				SS
	59	**GE** GDT635HSJSS	$640	72	Very Good	Good	Excellent	Good	Very Good	155	•	•		SS/P
	60	**LG** LDS5540ST	$630	71	Very Good	Good	Very Good	Very Good	Excellent	145	•	•	•	SS
	61	**Dacor** Renaissance RDW24S	$1700	71	Excellent	Good	Very Good	Good	Very Good	150				SS
	62	**Bosch** 300 Series DLX SHS63VL5UC	$720	71	Excellent	Fair	Excellent	Very Good	Very Good	125	•	•		SS
	63	**Whirlpool** WDT920SADM	$720	70	Very Good	Good	Excellent	Very Good	Very Good	160	•	•		SS
	64	**Jenn-Air** TriFecta JDB9000CWS	$1200	70	Excellent	Fair	Very Good	Excellent	Very Good	140	•	•		SS
	65	**Maytag** MDB8969SDM	$650	70	Excellent	Excellent	Very Good	Good	Excellent	170	•	•	•	SS

RATINGS KEY POOR FAIR GOOD VERY GOOD EXCELLENT

$ CR BEST BUY These models offer the best combination of performance and price. All are recommended.

RECOMMENDED These are high-performing models that stand out.

Rec.	Rank	Brand & Model	Price	Score	Washing	Drying	Energy Use	Noise	Ease of Use	Cycle Time (min.)	Ample Flatware Slots	Adjustable Upper Rack	Self-Cleaning Filter	Interior Material
	66	**GE** GDT655SSJSS	$600	69	⬆⬆	⬇	⬆⬆	⬆	⬆	155	•	•		SS
	67	**GE** GDT695SSJSS	$700	69	⬆⬆	⬇	⬆⬆	⬆	⬆	155	•	•		SS
	68	**GE** Monogram ZDT800SSFSS	$1500	69	⬆⬆	⊖	⬆⬆	⬆	⬆	165	•	•		SS
	69	**Maytag** MDB4949SDM	$450	69	⬆⬆	⬆⬆	⬆	⊖	⬆	170	•	•	•	SS
	70	**Jenn-Air** TriFecta JDB9200CWS	$1400	69	⬆⬆	⬇	⬆⬆	⬆	⬆	140	•	•		SS
	71	**Bosch** Ascenta SHX5AV55UC	$630	68	⬆⬆	⬇	⬆⬆	⬆	⬆	120	•	•		P
	72	**LG** LDF8874ST	$850	67	⬆	⊖	⬆	⬆	⬆	150	•	•		SS
	73	**Whirlpool** WDT780SAEM	$500	67	⬆⬆	⬇	⬆⬆	⊖	⬆	155	•	•		SS
	74	**Samsung** DW80J3020US	$450	67	⬆⬆	⬇	⬆	⬆	⊖	145	•		•	SS
	75	**Whirlpool** WDF540PADM	$500	66	⬆⬆	⬆⬆	⬆⬆	⊖	⊖	115	•			P
	76	**Haier** HDBL655AFS	$650	66	⬆	⬇	⬆⬆	⊖	⬆	115	•	•		SS
	77	**Jenn-Air** TriFecta JDB9800CWS	$1600	66	⬆	⬇	⬆⬆	⬆	⊖	155	•	•		SS
	78	**Haier** HDBL865ATS	$800	66	⬆	⬇	⬆⬆	⊖	⊖	120	•	•		SS
	79	**Frigidaire** Professional FPID2497RF	$700	66	⬆⬆	⬇	⬆	⬆	⬆⬆	135	•			SS
	80	**Scholtes** LFDS3XL60HZ	$1400	66	⬆	⊖	⊖	⬆⬆	⬆⬆	105	•	•		SS
	81	**Frigidaire** Gallery FGBD2445N[F]	$500	65	⬆	⬆	⬆	⊖	⬆⬆	120		•	•	P
	82	**Samsung** DW80J7550US	$700	65	⬆⬆	⬇	⬆	⬆⬆	⬆⬆	195	•	•		SS
	83	**Amana** ADB1500ADS	$450	64	⬆⬆	⬇	⬆⬆	⊖	⊖	140				P
	84	**Asko** XL Series D5436XLS	$1100	62	⬆	⬇	⬆⬆	⊖	⊖	115	•	•		SS
	85	**LG** LDT9965BD	$950	62	⬆⬆	⬇⬇	⬆⬆	⬆	⬆⬆	140	•	•		SS
	86	**Smeg** ST8646XU	$1100	62	⬆⬆	⬇⬇	⬆⬆	⊖	⬆	100		•		SS
	87	**Asko** XXL Series D5636XXLSHI	$1300	62	⬆	⬇	⬆⬆	⊖	⊖	115	•			SS

DISHWASHERS

Rec.	Rank	Brand & Model	Price	Score	Washing	Drying	Energy Use	Noise	Ease of Use	Cycle Time (min.)	Ample Flatware Slots	Adjustable Upper Rack	Self-Cleaning Filter	Interior Material
	88	Frigidaire FFBD2406NW	$270	60						125			•	P
	89	Frigidaire FFBD2411NS	$300	60						130			•	P
	90	Frigidaire FFID2423RS	$380	60						120			•	P
	91	Electrolux Wave-Touch EW24ID80QS	$980	60						200	•	•		SS
	92	Electrolux Wave-Touch EWDW6505G[S]	$1025	59						135	•	•	•	SS
	93	Frigidaire Gallery FGID2474QF	$550	58						120	•	•		SS
	94	Frigidaire Gallery FGCD2456QF	$670	58						120	•	•		SS
	95	Summit DW2433SSX	$625	58						145	•	•		SS
	96	Electrolux IQ-Touch EI24ID30QS	$730	58						120	•	•		SS
	97	Electrolux IQ-Touch EI24ID50QS	$900	57						120	•	•		SS
	98	Frigidaire Gallery FGBD2438PF	$400	57						130				P
	99	LG LDF7774ST	$700	57						140	•	•		SS
	100	Samsung DW80J9945US	$1000	56						195	•	•		SS
	101	Frigidaire Gallery FGBD2434PF	$400	55						125				P
	102	Amana ADB1100AWW	$300	54						160				P
	103	Electrolux Icon EDW7505HP[S]	$1500	54						125	•	•	•	SS
	104	GE GDF510PSJSS	$430	52						205				P
	105	Whirlpool WDF110PABW	$280	51						160				P
	106	GE GSD3301JWW	$360	49						110			•	P
	107	Fagor LFA75IT	$700	43						135	•	•		SS
	108	Frigidaire FBD2400KS	$250	34						90				P

Guide to the Ratings

Score is mostly washing performance and includes noise, energy and water use, and loading. The displayed score is out of a total of 100 points. **Washing** is the result of a normal cycle with a very dirty full load, and high-temperature and heated-dry options selected when available. **Drying** is our assessment of how thoroughly a model dries plastic items, the most stubborn in any load. We evaluate drying performance using the same cycle we use for our Washing test. As directed by manufacturers, we use rinse aid in every load. **Energy Use** is energy and water use for a normal cycle. **Noise** covers listener judgments during fill, wash, and drain. **Ease of Use** considers convenience of controls and the ability to hold extra place settings and oversized items. **Cycle Time (min.)** is based on a cycle used for washing test. Under **Brand & Model,** bracketed letters or numbers mean color code. Under Features, in **Interior Materials**, SS= stainless steel, P=plastic. **Price** is approximate retail.

Most & Least Reliable
Percentage likely to break by third year of ownership.

DISHWASHERS

Bosch	10%
Whirlpool	11%
Miele	12%
LG	14%
Kenmore	14%
KitchenAid	15%
Maytag	16%
GE	17%
Frigidaire	18%
Samsung	23%

Our findings are based on estimated failure rates for dishwashers by the third year of ownership by brand that were purchased new and not covered by a service contract. Differences of fewer than 5 points are not meaningful. Models within a brand can vary, and design or manufacture changes might affect future reliability. Still, choosing a brand with a lower estimated failure rate can improve your odds of getting a dependable model.

Source 2016 Winter Product Reliability Survey, Consumer Reports National Research Center.

QUICK GUIDE

Dryers

Electric and gas dryers perform similarly, our years of testing show. Increasing capacities let you do more laundry at once. An excellent capacity score means the dryer can hold about 25 or more pounds of laundry.

What to Look For

■ A moisture sensor to cut down on energy costs and avoid overdrying clothes.
■ An extended-tumble setting without heat to prevent wrinkles when you can't remove clothes immediately.

What to Skip

■ Steam settings, which left some wrinkles in our heavily wrinkled shirts, though it did remove odors. They did remove odors better than regular dryers, though.
■ Unnecessary specialty cycles, which up the price. A choice of heat level, timed dry and auto-dry, and a few fabric types should do.

What You'll Pay

Gas dryers cost about $50 to $150 more than comparable electric models, but the likely savings in fuel costs should more than make up the difference in the long run.

BUYING ADVICE

Look for a dryer that scored very good or excellent for noise if it will be near a bedroom.

For more buying advice, go to ConsumerReports.org/dryers.

All tested models in performance order.

Recommended	Rank	Brand & Model	Price	Score	Drying Performance	Capacity	Convenience	Noise	Stainless-Steel Drum	Porcelain Top	Drying Rack	Custom Programs	Steam Option
ELECTRIC													
✓	1	**Samsung** DV56H9100EG	$1450	86	⌃	⌃	⌃	⌃	•		•	•	•
✓	2	**Samsung** DV56H9000EP	$1200	84	⌃	⌃	⌃	⌃	•		•	•	•
✓	3	**LG** DLEX8500V	$1450	84	⌃	⌃	⌃	⌃	•	•	•	•	•
✓	4	**Whirlpool** WED92HEFW	$750	80	⌃	⌃	⌃	⌃	•		•		•

① Energy star dryer.

Recommended	Rank	Brand & Model	Price	Score	Drying Performance	Capacity	Convenience	Noise	Stainless-Steel Drum	Porcelain Top	Drying Rack	Custom Programs	Steam Option
		ELECTRIC (Continued)											
✔	5	**LG** DLEX7700VE	$1100	80	Very Good	Excellent	Very Good	Excellent	•			•	•
	6	**Maytag** MED8200FW	$1150	79	Excellent	Very Good	Very Good	Excellent	•		•	•	•
	7	**LG** DLEX9000V	$1350	79	Very Good	Excellent	Excellent	Excellent	•			•	•
	8	**Samsung** DV42H5600EW (Lowe's)	$720	79	Excellent	Very Good	Excellent	Very Good	•		•	•	•
	9	**LG** DLEY1701V	$700	79	Very Good	Very Good	Excellent	Very Good	•		•	•	•
	10	**Maytag** Maxima MED8100DC ⓘ	$1400	79	Excellent	Very Good	Very Good	Excellent	•				•
	11	**Maytag** Bravos MEDB855DW	$1000	79	Very Good	Excellent	Very Good	Excellent				•	
	12	**LG** DLEX3570W	$900	78	Excellent	Very Good	Excellent	Very Good	•		•	•	•
	13	**Kenmore** 81382	$650	78	Very Good	Very Good	Excellent	Very Good	•		•	•	
	14	**GE** GFDR485EFMC	$1260	78	Very Good	Very Good	Excellent	Very Good	•		•	•	•
	15	**LG** DLE1001W	$650	78	Very Good	Very Good	Very Good	Very Good				•	
	16	**GE** GFDR270EHWW	$990	77	Very Good	Very Good	Excellent	Very Good			•	•	•
	17	**LG** DLHX4072V ⓘ	$1200	77	Very Good	Very Good	Excellent	Very Good	•		•	•	•
	18	**Kenmore** Elite 81592	$1200	77	Very Good	Very Good	Very Good	Very Good	•		•	•	•
	19	**Samsung** DV52J8700EP ⓘ	$1080	77	Excellent	Very Good	Very Good	Very Good	•		•	•	•
	20	**Maytag** Maxima MED7100DW ⓘ	$1000	77	Excellent	Very Good	Very Good	Very Good	•				•
	21	**Kenmore** 81182	$550	76	Very Good	Very Good	Excellent	Very Good				•	
	22	**Whirlpool** Cabrio WED8500DW	$1000	76	Very Good	Excellent	Very Good	Very Good					•
	23	**Kenmore** 69132 ⓘ	$800	76	Very Good	Excellent	Very Good	Very Good					•
	24	**Samsung** DV45H7200EW	$800	76	Very Good	Very Good	Very Good	Very Good					
	25	**LG** DLE3170W	$720	76	Very Good	Very Good	Excellent	Excellent				•	
	26	**LG** DLEX5680V	$900	76	Excellent	Very Good	Very Good	Very Good	•		•	•	•

ⓘ Energy star dryer.

RATINGS KEY ⊝ POOR ⊙ FAIR ❶ GOOD ⌃ VERY GOOD ⌃⌃ EXCELLENT
❺ **CR BEST BUY** These models offer the best combination of performance and price. All are recommended.
✔ **RECOMMENDED** These are high-performing models that stand out.

Recommended	Rank	Brand & Model	Price	Score	Drying Performance	Capacity	Convenience	Noise	Stainless-Steel Drum	Porcelain Top	Drying Rack	Custom Programs	Steam Option
		GAS											
✓	1	**Samsung** DV56H9100GG	$1400	86	◉	◉	◉	◉	•		•	•	•
✓	2	**Samsung** DV56H9000GP	$1300	84	◉	◉	◉	◉	•		•	•	•
✓	3	**LG** DLGX8501V	$1550	84	◉	◉	◉	◉	•	•	•	•	•
✓	4	**Whirlpool** WGD90HEFW	$1000	80	◉	◉	◉	◉	•			•	•
✓	5	**Whirlpool** WGD92HEFW	$850	80	◉	◉	◉	◉	•			•	
✓	6	**LG** DLGX7701VE	$1200	80	◉	◉	◉	◉	•			•	•
	7	**Maytag** MGD8200FW	$1250	79	◉	◉	◉	◉	•			•	•
	8	**LG** DLGX9001V	$1400	79	◉	◉	◉	◉	•			•	•
	9	**Samsung** DV42H5600GW (Lowe's)	$1000	79	◉	◉	◉	◉			•	•	•
	10	**LG** DLGY1702V	$800	79	◉	◉	◉	◉	•			•	
	11	**Maytag** Maxima MGD8100DC [1]	$1500	79	◉	◉	◉	◉	•				•
	12	**Maytag** MGDB855DW	$1150	79	◉	◉	◉	◉				•	
	13	**LG** DLGX3571W	$990	78	◉	◉	◉	◉			•	•	•
	14	**GE** GFDR485GFMC	$1350	78	◉	◉	◉	◉	•		•	•	•
	15	**LG** DLG1002W	$750	78	◉	◉	◉	◉				•	
	16	**GE** GFDR270GHWW	$1080	77	◉	◉	◉	◉	•			•	
	17	**Samsung** DV52J8700GP	$1170	77	◉	◉	◉	◉	•		•	•	•
	18	**Kenmore** 91182	$650	76	◉	◉	◉	◉				•	
	19	**Whirlpool** Cabrio WGD8500DW	$1100	76	◉	◉	◉	◉					•
	20	**Kenmore** 79132	$900	76	◉	◉	◉	◉					•
	21	**Samsung** DV45H7200GW	$900	76	◉	◉	◉	◉					
	22	**LG** DLG3171W	$810	76	◉	◉	◉	◉				•	
	23	**Kenmore** Elite 71522	$1100	76	◉	◉	◉	◉	•		•	•	•

[1] Energy star dryer.

Guide to Ratings

Drying Performance combines performance on three types of laundry loads of different sizes and fabric mixes: A 6-lb. load, predominantly cotton, which includes jeans and towels; an 8-lb. load of cotton/polyester blend clothing; and a 3-lb. load of synthetic delicates, women's pajamas, nightgowns, bras and underwear. **Capacity** among the models we tested, drum volume was approximately 4 cu. ft. **Convenience** was judged on controls and ergonomics, such as ease of loading and unloading, servicing the lint filter, whether the door could clear a tall basket, and whether the machine has a raised edge to contain spills. **Noise** was determined by a panel of judges who listened while machines dried a 6-pound load, judging both sound quality and volume. **Price** is approximate retail.

Most & Least Reliable

Percentage likely to break by fifth year of ownership.

ELECTRIC

LG	8%
Speed Queen	12%
Whirlpool	13%
Kenmore	13%
Maytag	14%
Bosch	14%
Amana	17%
GE	17%
Samsung	18%
Frigidaire	18%
Electrolux	19%

GAS

LG	9%
Samsung	14%
Whirlpool	15%
Kenmore	16%
Maytag	17%
GE	18%
Frigidaire	20%

The conclusions in this chart are based on our failure rate estimates for dryers by fifth year of ownership. Our data are gathered from 54,690 subscribers who purchased a new dryer between 2008 and 2016 not covered by a service contract. We also adjust for the usage of the dryer, measured by the number of loads typically done in one week. Differences of fewer than 6 points aren't meaningful. Models within a brand may vary, and changes in design or manufacture may affect future reliability. Still, choosing a brand with a lower estimated failure rate can improve your odds of getting a dependable model.

Source 2016 Winter Product Reliability Survey, Consumer Reports National Research Center.

QUICK GUIDE
Fitness Trackers

Fitness trackers range from simple to sophisticated with price points to match. Here's how to find the right tracker to fit your budget, fitness, lifestyle, and fashion sense.

What to Look For

■ Look for a greater variety of materials, shapes, and colors—and some models created in collaboration with bona fide fashion designers.
■ Preview the tracker's companion app to make sure it lives up to your expectations.
■ Battery life can stretch from one day to several months, depending on the sophistication of the device. But not all trackers are rechargeable.
■ If you're going to wear your tracker in the pool,

it should be waterproof.
■ Make sure it's comfortable; you're going to be wearing it 24/7.
■ Make sure the device is simpatico with your cell phone or computer.

What to Skip
■ GPS. You can get the same benefit by carrying your smartphone and activating a free app, such as RunKeeper.

What You'll Pay
Expect to pay $20 for a basic model and $250 for a fully featured model.

BUYING ADVICE

If you simply want to know how many steps your taking each day, look for an all-day tracker.

For more buying advice, go to ConsumerReports.org/fitness-trackers.

All tested models in performance order.

Recommended	Rank	Brand & Model	Price	Score	Ease of Use	Heart-Rate Monitor Accuracy	Step Count Accuracy	Battery Life (days)	Step Counting	Floors Climbed	GPS Tracking	Sleep Tracking	Food Tracking	Notifications
		BUILT-IN DATA READOUT												
✓	1	**Fitbit** Surge	$250	87	⌃	⌃	⌃	7	•	•	•	•	•	•
✓	2	**TomTom** Spark Cardio+Music	$250	84	⌃	⌃	⌃	0.5	•		•	•		•
$	3	**Garmin** Vivosmart HR	$150	83	⌃	⌃	⌃	5	•	•		•		•
✓	4	**Basis** Peak	$200	82	⌃	⌃	⌃	4	•			•		•

BUILT-IN DATA READOUT (Continued)

Recommended	Rank	Brand & Model	Price	Score	Ease of Use	Heart-Rate Monitor Accuracy	Step Count Accuracy	Battery Life (days)	Step Counting	Floors Climbed	GPS Tracking	Sleep Tracking	Food Tracking	Notifications
$	5	**Fitbit** Blaze	$200	82	⌃⌃	⌃	⌃⌃	5	•	•		•		•
$	6	**Fitbit** ChargeHR	$150	82	⌃⌃	⌃⌃	⌃⌃	5	•	•		•		•
✓	7	**Garmin** Vivosmart HR+	$220	79	⌃	⌃⌃	⌃⌃	5	•	•	•	•		•
$	8	**Samsung** Gear Fit	$130	79	⌃⌃	⌃	⌃⌃	3.5	•					
✓	9	**Fitbit** Alta	$130	78	⌃⌃	NA	⌃⌃	5	•			•		•
$	10	**Fitbit** One	$100	77	⌃⌃	NA	⌃⌃	14	•	•		•	•	
✓	11	**Garmin** Vivoactive HR	$250	77	⌃	⌃⌃	⌃	8	•	•	•	•		•
✓	12	**Samsung** Gear Fit2	$180	76	⌃	⌃⌃	⌃⌃	4	•	•	•	•		•
✓	13	**Microsoft** Band 2	$175	74	⌃	●	⌃⌃	2	•	•	•	•		•
✓	14	**Under** Armour Band	$120	74	⌃	NA	⌃⌃	5	•			•		•
✓	15	**Mio** Fuse	$100	72	⌃	⌃⌃	⌃⌃	6	•					
	16	**Polar** Loop 2	$120	70	⌃	NA	⌃⌃	8	•			•		•
	17	**Polar** A300	$100	69	⌃	NA	⌃	28	•			•		
	18	**Garmin** Vivofit 3	$100	68	⌃	NA	⌃⌃	365	•			•		
	19	**Garmin** Vivosmart	$90	66	⌃	NA	⌃⌃	7	•			•		•
	20	**Polar** A360	$200	66	⌃	⌃⌃	⊙	12	•			•		•
	21	**Garmin** Vivoactive	$220	65	●	NA	⌃⌃	21	•		•	•		•
	22	**LifeTrak** Zone C410	$90	61	●	⌃⌃	⌃⌃	365	•			•		
	23	**Adidas** Fit Smart	$130	57	⌃⌃	⌃⌃	⊙	4.5	•		•			•
	24	**LifeTrak** Zone R420	$100	56	●	NA	⌃	365	•			•		
	25	**Garmin** Vivofit 2	$80	50	●	NA	●	365	•			•		

DATA READOUT VIA APP ONLY

Recommended	Rank	Brand & Model	Price	Score	Ease of Use	Heart-Rate Monitor Accuracy	Step Count Accuracy	Battery Life (days)	Step Counting	Floors Climbed	GPS Tracking	Sleep Tracking	Food Tracking	Notifications
	1	**Withings** Activite' Pop	$125	71	⌃	NA	⌃⌃	240	•			•		
	2	**Garmin** Vivomove	$150	64	⌃	NA	⌃⌃	365	•			•		
	3	**Withings** Go	$80	64	⌃	NA	⌃⌃	240	•			•	•	

Recommended	Rank	Brand & Model	Price	Score	Ease of Use	Heart-Rate Monitor Accuracy	Step Count Accuracy	Battery Life (days)	Step Counting	Floors Climbed	GPS Tracking	Sleep Tracking	Food Tracking	Notifications
		DATA READOUT VIA APP ONLY (Continued)												
	4	**Jawbone** Up Move	$50	61	◔	NA	⊗	180	•			•	•	
	5	**Misfit** Shine 2	$100	60	◑	NA	⊗	180	•			•		•
	6	**Misfit** Shine	$70	56	◑	NA	⊗	180	•			•	•	
	7	**Jawbone** Up3	$75	55	◑	NA	◔	7	•			•	•	
	8	**Fossil** Q Reveler	$95	54	◔	NA	◔	7	•					•
	9	**Misfit** Ray	$100	54	◑	NA	⊗	180	•			•		•
	10	**Fossil** Q Dreamer	$95	51	◔	NA	◑	7	•					•
	11	**Fitbit** Flex	$100	44	◒	NA	⊗	5	•			•	•	
	12	**Xiaomi** Mi Band Pulse	$20	41	◑	NA	◒	30	•			•		•
	13	**Moov** Now	$60	40	◒	NA	NA	180	•					

Guide to Ratings

Ease of Use is composite score of ergonomics, ease of interaction, syncing, pairing, and readability of the display in bright light, and low light. **Ease of Interaction** is the ease of accessing core functions, performing key tasks such as: accessing messages, calendars, alarms, etc., interacting with the device menu and app interface, taking activity measurements, reading activity results from the display, responsiveness of touchscreen or other control interaction methods. **Ease of Pairing** is an assessment of the steps necessary for pairing the tracker with another device for the first time. **Heart-rate Monitor Accuracy** measures how accurately the fitness tracker measured our testers actual heart rate. **Step Count Accuracy** measures how accurately the fitness tracker counted our testers actual steps. **Price** is approximate retail.

RATINGS KEY ⊝ POOR ◒ FAIR ◑ GOOD ◔ VERY GOOD ⊗ EXCELLENT
$ CR BEST BUY These models offer the best combination of performance and price. All are recommended.
✓ RECOMMENDED These are high-performing models that stand out.

Gas Grills

You don't have to spend a fortune to get great-tasting grilled food. Many midpriced grills now have side burners and other perks once found only on the priciest of grills.

What to Look For
■ Burners made of high-quality stainless steel, cast iron, or cast brass, which usually carry a 10-year or longer warranty.
■ Stainless-steel and coated cast-iron grates for sturdiness and rust-resistance.
■ A battery-powered electronic igniter.
■ Side burners to handle the veggies as the burgers cook.

What to Skip
■ Buying by Btu/hr., because more doesn't guarantee faster preheating or better searing and cooking.

What You'll Pay
Figure on $300 to $600 for a grill that can handle most of your cooking needs. Several midsized grills that cost less than $600 outcooked models that cost hundreds of dollars more.

BUYING ADVICE

Large grills fit 28 burgers or more and a medium fits 18 to 28, based on our measurements of the main cooking area.

For more buying advice, go to ConsumerReports.org/grills.

All tested models in performance order.

Rec.	Rank	Brand & Model	Price	Score	Preheat Performance	Evenness Performance	Indirect Cooking	Temperature Range	Convenience
		MIDSIZE (room for 18 to 28 burgers)							
$	1	**Nexgrill** 720-0830H (Home Depot)	$270	77	✪	✪	⌃	⌃	❶
	2	**Member's Mark** 720-0882D (Sam's Club)	$400	76	✪	⌃	⌃	❶	⌃
$	3	**Backyard Grill** BY16-101-003-05 / GBC1646WS (Walmart)	$150	76	✪	⌃	⌃	⌃	❶
$	4	**Char-Broil** 463433016 (Walmart)	$170	74	✪	⌃	⌃	❶	❶
✓	5	**Weber** Spirit SP-320 46700401	$600	74	❶	✪	✪	❶	✪

RATINGS KEY ⊗POOR ⊙FAIR ❶GOOD ⌃VERY GOOD ✪EXCELLENT
$ **CR BEST BUY** These models offer the best combination of performance and price. All are recommended.
✓ **RECOMMENDED** These are high-performing models that stand out.

Rec.	Rank	Brand & Model	Price	Score	Preheat Performance	Evenness Performance	Indirect Cooking	Temperature Range	Convenience
		MIDSIZE (Continued)							
	6	**Kenmore** Elite 33577	$1000	73	●	●	●	●	●
	7	**BHG** BH15-101-099-04 (Walmart)	$350	73	●	●	●	●	●
	8	**Nexgrill** Deluxe 720-0896B (Home Depot)	$400	73	●	●	●	●	●
	9	**Kenmore** Elite 33586	$550	72	●	●	●	●	●
	10	**Landmann** 42172	$460	71	●	●	●	●	●
	11	**Char-Broil** Advantage 463344116 [Item #748080] (Lowe's)	$270	71	●	●	●	●	●
	12	**Napoleon** Legend LA400 Series LA400RSIBPSS	$1000	71	●	●	●	●	●
	13	**Weber** Spirit E-320 46710001	$550	70	●	●	●	●	●
	14	**Member's Mark** Dual Lid 720-0839 (Sam's Club)	$500	70	●	●	●	●	●
	15	**Weber** Genesis S-330	$970	70	●	●	●	●	●
		LARGE (room for 28 or more burgers)							
	1	**Kenmore** 16136	$600	72	●	●	●	●	●
✓	2	**Napoleon** Prestige Pro 665RSIB	$2600	72	●	●	●	●	●
	3	**Kenmore** Elite 700 Series 3358	$1400	71	●	●	●	●	●
	4	**Kenmore** PG-40611SOL	$300	70	●	●	●	●	●
		SMALL (room for 18 or fewer burgers)							
$	1	**Huntington** 630124	$140	74	●	●	●	●	●
✓	2	**Weber** Spirit E-220 46310001	$450	71	●	●	●	●	●
$	3	**Broil-Mate** 165154	$200	71	●	●	●	●	●
$	4	**Huntington** 665154 (Home Depot)	$190	71	●	●	●	●	●

Guide to Ratings

Evenness Performance is the evenness of heating over the grill's surface at the highest and lowest setting using all main burners plus the evenness after a 10-minute preheat, using thermocouples. **Preheat Performance** evaluates the temperature after a 10-minute preheat using thermocouples. It also gives an indication how quickly the grill reaches its maximum temperature. **Temperature Range** reflects how wide a temperature span the grill offers by comparing temperatures at the high setting and low setting using all the main burners. **Indirect Cooking** indicates grill temperature when only one or two of the burners are on, to represent a cooking task where the food is placed between or alongside the direct flame. **Convenience** includes grate material, wheels or casters for moving the grill, and useful features such as electronic igniter. **Price** is approximate retail.

Generators

The best portable generators can power your fridge and other essentials for as little as $600. Stationary models add powering an electric oven, a dryer, central air conditioning, and more—plus extended run time and automatic starting when the power goes out.

What to Look For

■ Enough wattage for your needs. Figure on 5,000 to 7,000 watts for most home items; 10,000 watts or more for central A/C, a washer and dryer, and an electric range.

■ A propane or natural-gas hookup. It saves the storage and potential sourcing hassles of gasoline and is found on all stationary models and some portables, sometimes via add-on kits (about $200).

■ Automatic low-oil shutoff, which protects the engine from internal damage.

■ Electric start (portables).
■ Smartphone monitoring on some stationary models.

What to Skip

■ Big surge claims; the best units handled the extra watts that some appliances draw when they cycle on.

What You'll Pay

Figure on $600 to $1,500 for most 5,000- to 7,000-watt portables; $1,800 to $3,200 for a similar-wattage stationary model, plus installation; $3,500-plus for higher-wattage models.

BUYING ADVICE

Factor in an additional $500 to $900 for a transfer switch to safely power your home's electrical box.

For more buying advice, go to ConsumerReports.org/generators.

All tested models in performance order.

Recommended	Rank	Brand & Model	Price	Score	Power Delivery	Power Quality	Noise	Ease of Use	Claimed Output (watts)	Fuel Type	Electric Start	Fuel Gauge
		PORTABLE										
✓	1	Honda EU7000is	$4000	79	⌃	⌃	⌃	⌃	5500	gas	•	•
✓	2	Kohler PRO7.5E	$1400	73	⌃	⌃	◑	⌃	6300	gas	•	•
$	3	Generac RS7000E	$900	72	⌃	⌃	○	⌃	7000	gas	•	•
$	4	Troy-Bilt XP7000 30477A	$900	72	⌃	◑	○	⌃	7000	gas	•	•
✓	5	Honda EM6500SXK2	$2800	70	⌃	⌃	◑	⌃	5500	gas	•	•

Recommended	Rank	Brand & Model	Price	Score	Power Delivery	Power Quality	Noise	Ease of Use	Claimed Output (watts)	Fuel Type	Electric Start	Fuel Gauge
		PORTABLE (Continued)										
✓	6	**BlackMax** BM90700B	$1000	70	⤒	∧	∨	∧	7000	gas	•	
$	7	**Briggs & Stratton** 30470	$900	69	⤒	∧	∨	∧	7000	gas	•	•
✓	8	**Briggs & Stratton** 30549	$1100	69	⤒	∧	∨	∧	7500	gas	•	•
✓	9	**Westinghouse** WH7500E	$1000	69	⤒	∧	◑	∧	7500	gas	•	•
✓		**DeWalt** DXGNR7000	$1000	69	⤒	∧	∨	∧	7000	gas	•	
$	10	**Predator** 68530 [1][2]	$600	68	⤒	∧	∨	∧	7000	gas	•	•
$	11	**Generac** GP5500 5939	$700	67	⤒	∧	∨	∧	5500	gas		•
✓	12	**NorthStar** 165603 [1]	$1500	66	⤒	◑	◑	∧	6600	gas		
✓	13	**Champion** 41537	$1000	66	⤒	∧	∨	∧	7500	gas	•	•
✓	14	**Yamaha** EF7200DE	$1350	65	⤒	◑	◑	∧	6000	gas	•	•
		Ryobi RY905500	$600	65	⤒	∧	∨	∧	5000	gas		
✓	15	**Powermate** PM0146500	$850	65	⤒	∧	∨	∧	6500	gas	•	•
		LARGE STATIONARY										
✓	1	**Cummins** 13GSBA-6722B	$4300	93	⤒	⤒	∧	⤒	NG 11040 LPG 12750	LPG/NG	•	
✓	2	**Kohler** 14RESAL [3]	$3700	93	⤒	⤒	∧	⤒	NG 12000 LPG 14000	LPG/NG	•	
✓	3	**Generac** 6241 [3]	$3500	91	⤒	⤒	◑	⤒	NG 13000 LPG 14000	LPG/NG	•	
✓	4	**Briggs & Stratton** 040401 [3]	$4300	86	⤒	∧	∧	⤒	NG 13600 LPG 16000	LPG/NG	•	
		SMALL STATIONARY										
$	1	**Generac** 6237 [3]	$2250	91	⤒	⤒	◑	⤒	NG 7000 LPG 8000	LPG/NG	•	

[1] Price includes optional wheel kit. [2] Has electric start but requires optional battery (usually about $50).
[3] Comes with a transfer switch.

Guide to the Ratings

Score is based on power delivery, power quality, run time, noise, and ease of use. **Ease of Use** includes starting, transport (for portables), and helpful features such as fuel shutoff. **Power Delivery** indicates how much wattage models delivered and how well they handled surges in power demand over various loads. **Noise** was measured at 23 and 50 feet from the generator. **Power Quality** evaluates a generator's ability to deliver power smoothly, with consistent voltage. Under **Claimed Output (watts)** and **Fuel Type,** LPG=propane and NG=natural gas. **Price** is approximate retail. **Note:** Portables have a run time of approximately 7 to 12 hours; stationary models run on natural gas indefinitely.

Headphones

Headphones come in all sizes and types, from tiny earbuds to big, over-the-ear, DJ-style models. They're indispensable for listening to music on the go or for watching videos on a tablet, laptop, or phone.

What to Look For
- Clear, accurate sound with sufficient volume.
- A comfortable fit.
- If you don't want to be disturbed by outside noise, an isolating design that physically blocks sound or headphones with noise canceling.
- Wireless headphones if you don't want cords tangling or flapping as you exercise.
- A model that doubles as a headset if you want the ability to answer or place calls without taking the phone out of your pocket or backpack.

What to Skip
- Paying a high price just to get a big-brand name.

What You'll Pay
You can find decent earbuds for as little as $20. Decent over-ear and on-ear models generally cost $80 and more. Expect to pay more for wireless headphones and models with active noise canceling.

BUYING ADVICE

If you want the best sound, especially for serious music listening, we recommend one of the better-rated corded models in our ratings.

For more buying advice, go to ConsumerReports.org/headphones.

All tested models in performance order.

Recommended	Rank	Brand & Model	Price	Score	Sound Quality	Noise Reduction	Sensitivity	Type	Design
		HOME/STUDIO STYLE NOISE-REDUCING							
✓	1	**Bose** QuietComfort 25	$300	75	⌃	⊛	Medium high/ Medium	Over-ear	Closed
✓	2	**PSB** Speakers M4U 2	$400	73	⌃	⊛	Very High/ Very High/ Medium high	Over-ear	Closed

Rec.	Rank	Brand & Model	Price	Score	Sound Quality	Sensitivity	Type	Design
		PORTABLE STEREO						
✓	1	**1MORE** E1001 Triple Driver	$100	86	⊗	Medium	Ear-insert	Isolating
✓	2	**PSB** Speakers M4U 4	$300	86	⊗	Medium high	Ear-insert	Isolating
✓	3	**Klipsch** X12i	$350	80	⌃	High	Ear-insert	Isolating
✓	4	**Westone** ADV Alpha	$150	80	⌃	Medium high	Ear-insert	Isolating
$	5	**AKG** by Harman Y23	$40	76	⌃	High	Ear-insert	Isolating
$	6	**Scosche** SportClip 3	$30	76	⌃	Very High	Ear-insert	Isolating
✓	7	**Bose** SoundTrue Ultra in-ear	$130	71	⌃	Medium	Ear-insert	Isolating
✓	8	**Marshall** Mode EQ	$100	71	⌃	Medium	Ear-insert	Isolating
✓	9	**NAD** Electronics VISO HP20	$170	71	⌃	High	Ear-insert	Isolating
$	10	**Phiaton** MS 100 BA	$80	71	⌃	High	Ear-insert	Isolating
✓	11	**Sennheiser** Momentum In-Ear	$80	71	⌃	High	Ear-insert	Isolating
$	12	**Shure** SE112	$50	71	⌃	Very High	Ear-insert	Isolating
✓	13	**Bowers** & Wilkins C5 series 2	$180	66	⌃	High	Ear-insert	Isolating
$	14	**Denon** Music Maniac AH-C50MA	$40	66	⌃	High	Ear-insert	Isolating
$	15	**Optoma** NuForce NE750M	$80	66	⌃	High	Ear-insert	Isolating
$	16	**Panasonic** RP-TCM125	$20	66	⌃	Medium high	Ear-insert	Isolating
$	17	**Philips** Action-Fit Sport SHQ2305/27	$40	66	⌃	Medium high	Ear-insert	Isolating
$	18	**Razer** Adaro In Ear	$60	66	⌃	Very High	Ear-insert	Isolating
$	19	**Sennheiser** CX 215	$30	66	⌃	High	Ear-insert	Isolating
$	20	**Sennheiser** CX 300-II Precision	$40	66	⌃	High	Ear-insert	Isolating
$	21	**Skullcandy** Strum	$50	66	⌃	High	Ear-insert	Isolating

RATINGS KEY ⊗ POOR ⊘ FAIR ⏺ GOOD ⌃ VERY GOOD ⊗ EXCELLENT
$ CR BEST BUY These models offer the best combination of performance and price. All are recommended.
✓ RECOMMENDED These are high-performing models that stand out.

Rec.	Rank	Brand & Model	Price	Score	Sound Quality	Sensitivity	Type	Design
		HOME/STUDIO STYLE STEREO						
✓	1	**Grado** Prestige SR325e	$295	91	⊗	Medium high	Over-ear	Open air
✓	2	**Grado** Prestige SR225e	$200	88	⊗	Medium high	Over-ear	Open air
✓	3	**HiFiMan** HE-400i	$450	88	⊗	Low	Over-ear	Open air
✓	4	**HiFiMan** HE-400S	$300	88	⊗	Low	Over-ear	Open air
✓	5	**Bowers** & Wilkins P7	$320	86	⊗	Medium	Over-ear	Closed
$	6	**Grado** Prestige SR80e	$100	86	⊗	Medium high	On-ear	Open air
✓	7	**Oppo** PM-3	$400	86	⊗	Medium	Over-ear	Closed
✓	8	**Audeze** Sine	$450	81	⊗	Low	Over-ear	Closed
✓	9	**Shure** SRH1440	$300	81	⊗	Low	Over-ear	Open air
$	10	**Grado** Prestige SR125e	$150	80	⌃	Medium high	On-ear	Open air
$	11	**Bose** SoundTrue around-ear headphones II	$180	76	⌃	Medium	Over-ear	Closed
$	12	**Grado** Prestige SR60e	$80	76	⌃	Medium high	On-ear	Open air
$	13	**Yamaha** HPH-200	$150	76	⌃	Medium high	On-ear	Open air
$	14	**Audio-Technica** ATH-M50x	$170	71	⌃	Medium	Over-ear	Closed
✓	15	**Blue** Microphones Mo-Fi	$350	71	⌃	Very High/ Medium high	Over-ear	Closed
✓	16	**NAD** Electronics VISO HP50	$250	71	⌃	Medium high	Over-ear	Closed
$	17	**Phaz** P2	$100	71	⌃	Very High/ Medium high	Over-ear	Closed
✓	18	**Sennheiser** Momentum On-Ear M2 (Wired)	$230	66	⌃	Medium high	On-ear	Closed
$	19	**Skullcandy** Grind	$60	66	⌃	Medium high	On-ear	Closed
✓	20	**Sony** MDR-1A	$300	66	⌃	Medium	Over-ear	Closed

RATINGS KEY ⊗ POOR ⊘ FAIR ● GOOD ⌃ VERY GOOD ⊗ EXCELLENT
$ CR BEST BUY These models offer the best combination of performance and price. All are recommended.
✓ RECOMMENDED These are high-performing models that stand out.

Rec.	Rank	Brand & Model	Price	Score	Sound Quality	Sensitivity	Type	Design
WIRELESS HOME/STUDIO STYLE STEREO								
✓	1	**Sony** MDR-1ABT	$400	76	⌃	Medium	Over-ear	Closed
✓	2	**AKG** by Harman K845BT	$300	71	⌃	Low	Over-ear	Closed
✓	3	**Bose** SoundLink around-ear headphones II	$280	71	⌃	Medium high	Over-ear	Closed
✓	4	**Bowers & Wilkins** P5 Wireless	$400	71	⌃	Medium high	On-ear	Closed
✓	5	**Pendulumic** Stance S1+	$200	71	⌃	High/Medium	Over-ear	Closed
✓	6	**Audio-Technica** ATH-SR5BT	$200	66	⌃	Medium	On-ear	Closed
✓	7	**beats** by dre solo2 wireless	$200	66	⌃	High	On-ear	Closed
$	8	**Plantronics** BackBeat Sense	$180	66	⌃	Low	On-ear	Closed
$	9	**Polk** Audio Hinge Wireless	$200	66	⌃	High	On-ear	Closed
✓	10	**Sennheiser** Urbanite XL Wireless	$250	66	⌃	Medium high	Over-ear	Closed
$	11	**Skullcandy** Grind Wireless	$90	66	⌃	Medium	On-ear	Closed

Guide to the Ratings

Score is based mainly on sound quality, which considers tonal accuracy, clarity, detail, ambience, and dynamics. The displayed score is out of a total of 100 points. **Sound Quality** represents the tonal accuracy, clarity, detail, ambience and dynamics of the audio reproduced by the headphones. **Noise Reduction** represents how well the headphones reduce ambient noise when the active noise cancellation feature is activated. **Sensitivity** assesses how loudly wire-connected headphones will play for a given audio input signal level; for wireless models, we judge sensitivity using the optional wired connection. An isolating design blocks some outside noise. **Price** is approximate retail.

House & Deck Stains

Some exterior stains can lighten your workload by lasting longer before they need to be reapplied. The best we tested not only kept their looks for at least three years on a deck, but they also resisted cracking, dirt, and mildew.

What to Look For

■ A mildew-resistant stain for shady areas and a fade-resistant one for sunny spots.
■ Opaque, or solid, stains for a long-lasting finish.
■ Clear finishes to show off natural color and grain—if you're willing to reapply them each year.
■ Semi-transparent stains for a reasonable compromise.

What to Skip

■ Buying strictly by brand; different products from the same manufacturer often perform differently.

What You'll Pay

You'll need about a gallon of solid stain ($30 to $45) for 350 square feet of a house, fence, or deck that's been previously stained. Expect to need twice as much for two coats on fresh wood. Double the amounts for semi-transparent stains ($29 to $45) or clear sealers ($18 to $34), both of which tend to soak into the wood.

BUYING ADVICE

Need to buy 5 gallons? Buy the stain in a 5-gallon bucket. You'll save as much as $30 and get more consistent color.

For more buying advice, go to ConsumerReports.org/stains.

Guide to the Ratings

Score is the weighted average of each year's appearance for two coats over pine-clapboard siding. Fully tested finishes have undergone accelerated outdoor weathering for up to three years; each year approximates three years on vertical surfaces, one year on decks. Displayed scores are rounded; products are listed by precise overall score. Scores for previously tested products may have changed because of changes in tabulations. **Appearance** indicates performance after years indicated. **Resists** means a score of at least good for that attribute at the end of testing. **VOCs** is maximum grams per liter as stated on can. **Price** is approximate retail per gallon.

RATINGS KEY ⊘POOR ⊖FAIR ❶GOOD ⊙VERY GOOD ⊛EXCELLENT
Ⓢ **CR BEST BUY** These models offer the best combination of performance and price. All are recommended.
✓ **RECOMMENDED** These are high-performing models that stand out.

Recommended	Rank	Brand & Model	Price	Score	After 1 Year	After 2 Years	After 3 Years	Cracking	Color Change	Dirt	Resists Mildew	Claimed VOCs
		SOLID WOOD STAINS										
✓	1	**Benjamin Moore** Arborcoat Solid Deck & Siding	$46	74	⊗	⊗	⊗	•	•		•	100
❶	2	**Behr** Solid Color Waterproofing Wood Stain (Home Depot)	$29	74	⊗	⊗	⊗	•	•	•	•	100
	3	**Olympic** Maximum Solid (Lowe's)	$37	68	⊗	⊗	⊗	•	•		•	169
	4	**Cabot** Solid Acrylic Siding	$36	68	⊗	⊗	⊙	•	•	•		100
	5	**Thompson's** WaterSeal Deck & House Solid Latex	$26	67	⊗	⊗	⊙	•	•	•		100
	6	**Wolman** DuraStain Solid	$33	60	⊗	⊗	⊙	•	•			100
	7	**Sherwin-Williams** Woodscapes Solid	$48	57	⊗	⊙	⊙	•	•			136
	8	**Behr** Premium Solid Color Weatherproofing Wood Stain (Home Depot)	$37	56	⊗	⊗	⊙	•	•		•	100
	9	**Flood** SWF-SOLID Solid Wood Stain	$29	48	⊗	⊗	⊙	•				250
	10	**Cabot** Solid Color Decking Stain	$38	46	⊗	⊙	⊙		•			100
	11	**Woodsman** Solid Color Deck Stain	$30	19	⊙	⊙	⊙					250
	12	**Thompson's** WaterSeal Waterproofing Solid (Home Depot)	$29	12	⊙	⊙	⊙					100
		SEMI-TRANSPARENT WOOD STAINS										
✓	1	**Behr** Premium Semi-Transparent Weatherproofing Wood Stain (Home Depot)	$37	65	⊗	⊗		•	•	•	•	100
	2	**Cabot** Semi-Transparent Deck & Siding	$38	46	⊗	⊙		•			•	250
	3	**Behr** Semi-Transparent Waterproofing Wood Stain (Home Depot)	$29	41	⊗	⊙						100
	4	**Olympic** Elite Advanced Stain + Sealant in One Semi-Transparent (Lowe's)	$42	41	⊗	⊙					•	100
	5	**Benjamin Moore** Arborcoat Semi-Transparent Deck & Siding	$46	40	⊗	⊙					•	100
	6	**Flood** TWF-SEMI Semi-Transparent Wood Stain	$29	38	⊗	⊙						250

Recommended	Rank	Brand & Model	Price	Score	After 1 Year	After 2 Years	After 3 Years	Cracking	Color Change	Dirt	Resists Mildew	Claimed VOCs
					Appearance			Resists				

SEMI-TRANSPARENT WOOD STAINS (Continued)

Recommended	Rank	Brand & Model	Price	Score	After 1 Year	After 2 Years	After 3 Years	Cracking	Color Change	Dirt	Resists Mildew	Claimed VOCs
	7	**Olympic** Maximum Semi-Transparent (Lowe's)	$37.	36	⌃	⌄						98
	8	**Ace** Wood Royal Semi-Transparent Deck & Siding	$31	35	⌃	⌄					•	100
	9	**Sikkens** Cetol SRD Semi-Transparent	$43	33	⌃	⌄⌄					•	100
	10	**Thompson's** WaterSeal Deck & House Semi-Transparent Latex	$25	32	⌃	⌄					•	100
	11	**Olympic** Wood Protector Semi-Transparent (Lowe's)	$29	32	⌃	⌄					•	100
	12	**Wolman** DuraStain Semi-Transparent	$30	32	⌄	⌄						250
	13	**Cabot** Express Deck Wood Stain Semi-Transparent	$37	22	●	⌄⌄						250
	14	**Sherwin-Williams** Woodscapes Semi-Transparent	$46	21	⌄	⌄⌄						79
	15	**Thompson's** WaterSeal Waterproofing Semi-Transparent (Home Depot)	$27	12	⌄⌄	⌄⌄						100

CLEAR SEALER WOOD STAINS

Recommended	Rank	Brand & Model	Price	Score	After 1 Year	After 2 Years	After 3 Years	Cracking	Color Change	Dirt	Resists Mildew	Claimed VOCs
	1	**Olympic** Maximum Sealant (Lowe's)	$34	28	⌄						•	98
	2	**Thompson's** WaterSeal Advanced Waterproofer	$23	27	⌄						•	100
	3	**Wolman** RainCoat Clear Water Repellent	$18	25	⌄				•			250
	4	**Olympic** Wood Protector Waterproofing Sealant (Lowe's)	$25	17	⌄						•	78
	5	**Thompson's** WaterSeal Waterproofing Wood Protector Clear (Home Depot)	$15	12	⌄⌄						•	100
	6	**Thompson's** WaterSeal Waterproofer Plus Clear Wood Protector	$19	9	⌄⌄						•	100
	7	**Benjamin Moore** Waterproofer (320)	$24	5	⌄⌄							250
	8	**Olympic** WaterGuard for Wood (Lowe's)	$14	5	⌄⌄						•	79

QUICK GUIDE

Lawn mowers

Most people buy self-propelled gas mowers; the best start at just $300. Cordless electrics save on gas and tune-ups for only bit more—and you'll spend even less if you can live with a cord.

What to Look For

■ An electric push-type mower for small, level lawns.
■ A gas-powered mower for larger lawns and high or thick grass and weeds.
■ Side-discharge capability for when grass is too high to mulch or bag effectively.
■ Rear-wheel drive for slopes.
■ A blade-brake clutch, which stops only the blade when you release the handlebar lever, for safety.
■ A washout port that accepts a hose for easy cleaning.

What to Skip

■ Larger engines, which don't guarantee better mowing, and high rear wheels.

What You'll Pay

About $300 to $600 for top-scoring gas self-propelled mowers, $350 to $500 for battery models, and $200 to $300 for capable push gas or corded electric mowers.

BUYING ADVICE

Mowers with multiple drive speeds cost little more than single-speed mowers, and the time-savings are well worth the slightly higher price

For more buying advice, go to ConsumerReports.org/mowers.

All tested models in performance, within types.

Recommended	Rank	Brand & Model	Price	Deck Size (in.)	Engine Size	Score	Mulching	Bagging	Side Discharging	Handling	Ease of Use
		GAS MULTIPLE SPEEDS SELF-PROPELLED									
✓	1	**Honda** HRX217K5VLA	$680	21	190	89	⊗	⊗	⊗	⊙	⊗
✓	2	**Honda** HRX2175VYA	$700	21	190	88	⊗	⊗	⊗	⊙	⊗
✓	3	**Honda** HRX2175VKA	$600	21	190	87	⊗	⊗	⊗	⊗	⊙
✓	4	**Honda** HRX217VKA	$600	21	190	83	⊗	⊗	⊙	⊗	⊙
✓	5	**Honda** HRR2169VLA	$500	21	160	83	⊗	⊗	⊙	⊗	⊗

Recommended	Rank	Brand & Model	Price	Deck Size (in.)	Engine Size	Score	Mulching	Bagging	Side Discharging	Handling	Ease of Use
GAS MULTIPLE SPEEDS SELF-PROPELLED (Continued)											
✓	6	**Toro** 20381	$520	21	159	82	◈	◈	◈	◈	◈
✓	7	**Honda** HRR2169VYA	$500	21	160	82	◈	◈	◈	◈	◈
$	8	**Honda** HRR2169VKA	$430	21	160	81	◈	◈	◈	◈	◈
$	9	**Toro** Recycler Smart Stow 20340	$400	22	190	77	◈	◈	◈	◈	◈
$	10	**Toro** 20353	$400	22	163	75	◈	◈	◈	◈	◈
✓	11	**Toro** Recycler 20333	$400	22	190	75	◈	◈	◈	◈	◈
✓	12	**Cub Cadet** SC500EZ 12ATC6A	$500	21	190	74	◈	◐	◈	◈	◈
$	13	**Troy-Bilt** TB-280ES 12AGA26G	$340	21	190	73	◈	◈	◈	◈	◈
$	14	**Toro** Recycler 20332	$360	22	190	73	◈	◈	◈	◈	◐
$	15	**Cub Cadet** SC300HW 12ABB22J	$300	21	159	71	◈	◐	◈	◈	◈
✓	16	**Husqvarna** HU725AW-DEX 961430120	$450	22	163	71	◈	◈	◐	◈	◈
✓	17	**Ariens** 911177	$460	21	159	71	◈	◈	◐	◈	◈
✓	18	**Snapper** SP105 12ALC3	$400	21	175	70	◈	◐	◈	◈	◈
GAS SINGLE SPEED SELF-PROPELLED											
✓	1	**Toro** 20339	$350	22	190	67	◈	◈	◈	◒	◈
$	2	**Toro** 20370	$280	22	149	66	◈	◈	◈	◒	◐
$	3	**Toro** 20371	$300	22	149	65	◈	◈	◈	◒	◐
✓	4	**Lawn-Boy** 10739	$340	21	149	63	◈	◈	◈	◐	◐
✓	5	**Lawn-Boy** 10734	$330	21	149	60	◈	◐	◐	◐	◈
✓	6	**Snapper** 12BA23Z	$280	21	163	60	◈	◐	◈	◒	◐
ELECTRIC-BATTERY SELF-PROPELLED											
✓	1	**EGO** LM2102SP	$600	21	56 volts	79	◈	◈	◈	◈	◈
WIDE DECK MULTIPLE SPEEDS SELF-PROPELLED											
$	1	**Troy-Bilt** TB WC28	$850	28	223	79	◈	◈	◈	◈	◈
✓	2	**Toro** 20199	$1000	30	190	71	◐	◈	◈	◈	◈

Recommended	Rank	Brand & Model	Price	Deck Size (in.)	Engine Size	Score	Mulching	Bagging	Side Discharging	Handling	Ease of Use
GAS PUSH											
$	1	**Cub Cadet** SC100 11A-A92J	$250	21	159	71	Very Good	Very Good	Very Good	Very Good	Very Good
$	2	**Craftsman** 37432	$220	21	149	67	Very Good	Good	Very Good	Very Good	Very Good
$	3	**Husqvarna** LC121P 961350002	$250	21	163	67	Very Good	Very Good	Good	Very Good	Very Good
✓	4	**Yard Machines** 11A-B9A9	$240	21	190	67	Very Good	Very Good	Excellent	Very Good	Good
✓	5	**Craftsman** 37237	$250	21	163	66	Very Good	Good	Very Good	Very Good	Very Good
✓	6	**Lawn-Boy** 17734	$240	21	149	65	Very Good	Good	Good	Very Good	Very Good
✓	7	**Ariens** Razor 911173	$400	21	159	65	Very Good	Excellent	Good	Fair	Very Good
ELECTRIC-BATTERY PUSH											
$	1	**EGO** LM2101	$500	21	56 volts	75	Very Good	Very Good	Very Good	Excellent	Excellent
✓	2	**Black+Decker** CM 2040	$400	20	40 volts	64	Good	Very Good	Good	Excellent	Very Good
$	3	**EGO** LM2000	$400	20	56 volts	62	Good	Good	Good	Excellent	Excellent
✓	4	**Worx** WG771	$500	19	56 volts	60	Good	Good	Good	Excellent	Very Good

Guide to the Ratings

Score, overall, is mostly based on mulching, bagging, side-discharging, handling, and ease of use. Scores for previously tested models may have changed. Display scores are rounded; models are listed by precise overall score. **Mulching** is how evenly clippings were cut and distributed. **Bagging** is filling evenness and capacity with full bag(s), including clogged chutes. **Side-Discharge** is how evenly clippings were dispersed. **Handling** is ease of using drive controls, pushing, pulling, U-turns, and other maneuvers. **Ease of Use** is ease of starting, using blade-stopping controls, changing speeds, and adjusting cut height. **Price** is approximate retail for mowers and attachments.

Most & Least Reliable
Self-Propelled
Percentage likely to break by fourth year of ownership.

GAS

Honda	15%
Lawn-Boy	19%
Troy-Bilt	20%
Toro	23%
Craftsman	24%
Husqvarna	29%
Snapper	29%

Most & Least Reliable
Push mowers
Percentage likely to break by fourth year of ownership.

ELECTRIC

Black + Decker	11%
Green Works	15%

GAS

Murray	13%
Troy-Bilt	13%
Yard Machines	14%
Lawn-Boy	14%
Honda	15%
Craftsman	15%
Husqvarna	16%
Cub Cadet	17%
Toro	21%

The chart shows what we found when we asked 13,854 readers who bought a new walk-behind gas-powered lawn mower between 2009 and 2015 about their experiences. These conclusions are based on our failure rate estimates for walk-behind lawn mowers by the fourth year of ownership. Our statistical model estimates failure rates for lawn mowers not covered by a service contract and accounts for the number of hours they're used annually. Differences of less than 8 points aren't meaningful. Models within a brand may vary, and changes in design or manufacturer may affect future reliability. Still, choosing a brand with a good reliability estimate can improve your odds of getting a dependable model.

Source 2015 Fall Product Reliability Survey, Consumer Reports National Research Center.

QUICK GUIDE

Lawn Tractors

Easier handling is helping zero-turn-radius riders rival lawn tractors as the riding mower of choice. But they're pricier, and most are harder to control on slopes. In our tests, their faster ground speeds also haven't yielded better mowing.

What to Look For

■ A high-back seat for added comfort and support.
■ Variable drive speeds that you control with a foot pedal.
■ A washout port that accepts a hose for cleaning beneath.
■ Electric power takeoff to engage and disengage the blades without a lever.
■ A visible fuel gauge.

What to Skip

■ Zero-turn-radius riders for steep slopes, where riders can be hard to steer and stop.
■ Small rear-engine riders, which usually take a 30-inch bite but can cost as much as a wider-cutting lawn tractor.
■ Pricey bagging systems; mulch kits cost far less and often yield comparable results.

What You'll Pay

About $1,300 to $1,800 for tractors; $2,300-plus for many zero-turn-radius riders.

BUYING ADVICE

Check our scores for the mowing mode you prefer before deciding on any tractor or riding mower.

For more buying advice, go to ConsumerReports. org/tractors.

All tested models in performance, within types.

Rec.	Rank	Brand & Model	Price	Score	Side Discharging	Mulching	Bagging	Handling	Ease of Use	Deck Size (in.)	Engine Power (hp)
		Test Results								**Specs**	
		LAWN TRACTORS ZTR									
$	1	**Troy-Bilt** Mustang 42" 17WFCACS	$2300	82	⊗	⊗	⊗	⌃	⊗	42	22.0
$	2	**Cub Cadet** RZT L42	$2500	82	⊗	⊗	⊗	⌃	⊗	42	22.0
$	3	**Troy-Bilt** Mustang Pivot 17ARCBDT	$2900	81	⌃	⊗	⊗	⊗	⌃	46	22.0
✓	4	**Cub Cadet** RZT L50	$2900	79	⌃	⊗	NA	⌃	⊗	50	23.0
$	5	**Troy-Bilt** Mustang 50" 17WFCACP	$2800	79	⌃	⊗	NA	⌃	⊗	50	25.0
✓	6	**Cub Cadet** RZT L54	$3000	79	⊗	⌃	⊗	⌃	⊗	54	24.0
✓	7	**Cub Cadet** RZT46 fab	$3300	78	⊗	⌃	⌃	⌃	⊗	46	ns

Rec.	Rank	Brand & Model	Price	Score	Side Discharging	Mulching	Bagging	Handling	Ease of Use	Deck Size (in.)	Engine Power (hp)
LAWN TRACTORS ZTR (Continued)											
✓	8	**Cub Cadet** RZT-S42	$4000	77	Very Good	NA	NA	Excellent	Excellent	42	48 Volts
✓	9	**Cub Cadet** RZT-S 46 17WF2BDT	$3000	75	Very Good	Very Good	Good	Very Good	Excellent	42	22.0
✓	10	**John Deere** Z235	$2500	73	Very Good	Very Good	Excellent	Very Good	Excellent	42	20.0
✓	11	**John Deere** Z335E	$2500	73	Very Good	Very Good	Excellent	Very Good	Excellent	42	20.0
✓	12	**Toro** SW4200 74784	$2900	72	Very Good	Very Good	Very Good	Very Good	Excellent	42	24.5
✓	13	**Toro** TimeCutter SS4235 74627	$2600	71	Very Good	Very Good	Very Good	Very Good	Excellent	42	20.0
LAWN TRACTORS											
✓	1	**John Deere** X350	$3200	78	Very Good	Very Good	Excellent	Excellent	Excellent	42	18.5
$	2	**Craftsman** 20442	$2200	78	Very Good	Excellent	Excellent	Excellent	Excellent	46	24.0
✓	3	**Husqvarna** YT46LS	$2300	76	Very Good	Very Good	Excellent	Excellent	Excellent	46	24
✓	4	**John Deere** X310	$4000	75	Very Good	Very Good	Excellent	Excellent	Excellent	42	18.5
✓	5	**John Deere** X304 ①	$3600	75	Very Good	Very Good	Excellent	Excellent	Excellent	42	18.5
✓	6	**John Deere** S240 Sport	$2500	75	Very Good	Very Good	Excellent	Very Good	Excellent	42	18.5
$	7	**John Deere** D125	$1800	75	Very Good	Very Good	Good	Very Good	Excellent	42	20.0
$	8	**Snapper** 960440007	$1600	74	Very Good	Very Good	Very Good	Excellent	Very Good	46	20.0
✓	9	**Troy-Bilt** XP LT Fab46	$1900	73	Very Good	Very Good	Very Good	Excellent	Very Good	46	ns
$	10	**Craftsman** 20390 ①	$1700	72	Very Good	Very Good	Excellent	Excellent	Very Good	42	22.0
✓	11	**John Deere** D110	$1700	71	Very Good	Very Good	Very Good	Excellent	Very Good	42	19.0
✓	12	**Husqvarna** YTH22V46	$1700	70	Very Good	Very Good	Very Good	Very Good	Very Good	46	22.0
$	13	**Craftsman** 20374	$1400	70	Very Good	Very Good	Very Good	Very Good	Good	46	19.0
LAWN TRACTORS WIDE DECK											
✓	1	**Craftsman** 20445	$3500	77	Very Good	Very Good	Excellent	Very Good	Excellent	54	26.0
$	2	**Troy-Bilt** Super Bronco 50	$1900	74	Very Good	Very Good	Excellent	Excellent	Very Good	50	24.0
✓	3	**John Deere** D155	$2200	74	Very Good	Very Good	Very Good	Excellent	Excellent	48	24.0

Rec.	Rank	Brand & Model	Price	Score	Side Discharging	Mulching	Bagging	Handling	Ease of Use	Deck Size (in.)	Engine Power (hp)
		LAWN TRACTORS WIDE DECK (Continued)									
✓	4	John Deere D140	$2000	73	⌃	⌃	⌄	⌄	⌃	48	24.0
$	5	Husqvarna YTH24K48FT	$1900	69	◐	⌃	⌃	⌄	⌃	48	24.0
✓	6	Craftsman 20403 ①	$3000	68	◐	◐	⌄	⌄	⌃	54	24.0
		REAR ENGINE RIDER									
✓	1	Cub Cadet CC30	$1300	61	⌃	⌃	⊙	⊙	⌃	30	ns
$	2	Troy-Bilt TB30R 13BC26JD	$1000	58	⌃	⌃	⊙	⊙	⌃	30	11.5

① Tighter turning than most lawn tractors.

Guide to Ratings

Side Discharging is a combination of evenness, which is how close the mowers came to even, carpet-like mowing, and how evenly clippings were dispersed from the side-discharge chute. **Mulching** reflects a combination of evenness, which is how close the mowers came to even, carpet-like mowing, and how well the mower distributed its clippings over the lawn's surface. **Bagging** denotes how much clippings the bag held either before it filled or the chute clogged. **Handling** includes ease of operating the drive controls (for self-propelled only), pushing and pulling, making U-turns, and maneuvering in tight spots. of use. **Ease of Use** includes ease of starting the engine, operating the blade-stopping controls, shifting speeds (for self-propelled only), and adjusting the cutting height. Bag convenience and ease of changing modes are separate judgments that contribute to the overall score. **Price** is approximate retail.

Most & Least Reliable

Percentage likely to break by fourth year of ownership.

LAWN TRACTORS

John Deere	22%
Husqvarna	28%
Craftsman	30%
Ariens	31%
Troy-Bilt	38%
Cub Cadet	40%

ZERO-TURN RADIUS

John Deere	26%
Toro	27%
Cub Cadet	34%
Husqvarna	36%

These conclusions are based on our failure rate estimates for riding mowers by fourth year of ownership, gathered from 5,833 subscribers who purchased a new mower between 2009 and 2015. Our statistical model estimates failure rates for riding mowers not covered by a service contract and accounts for the number of hours they're used annually. Differences of less than 9 points aren't meaningful. Models within a brand may vary, and changes in design or manufacturer may affect future reliability. Still, choosing a brand with a good reliability estimate can improve your odds of getting a dependable model.

Source 2015 Fall Product Reliability Survey, Consumer Reports National Research Center.

Microwave Ovens

Earlier microwave ovens had just an automatic popcorn setting and perhaps a few others. Many now have auto settings for oatmeal, pasta, stew, and grits, as well as for reheating or defrosting.

What to Look For

■ A sensor, which helps prevent over- or undercooking by measuring emitted steam to gauge when food is done.
■ Convection, speed-cook, and grilling features if you are willing to pay more.

What to Skip

A raft of preprogrammed shortcut keys if you're mostly defrosting and popping corn.

What You'll Pay

Countertop models cost the least, about $80 to $300, and are best for kitchens with ample counter space. Midsized and large models usually have more capacity and features. Midsized models sell the most overall. Over-the-range microwaves, $300 to $900, save space but don't vent as well as a capable range hood.

BUYING ADVICE

More watts usually mean more cooking power. But differences of 100 watts or so don't matter much.

For more buying advice, go to ConsumerReports.org/ microwaves.

All tested models in performance order.

Recommended	Rank	Brand & Model	Price	Score	Heating Evenness	Defrosting Evenness	Speed of Heating	Microwaving Noise	Ease of Use	Venting	Usable Capacity (cu. ft.)	Claimed Capacity (cu. ft.)	Watts
					\multicolumn{5}{c}{Test Results}			\multicolumn{3}{c}{Specs}		
		LARGE COUNTERTOP MICROWAVES											
✔	1	Oster OGG61403	$120	74	⌃	⌃⌃	⌃	⌃	⌃⌃	NA	0.8	1.4	1200
✔	2	Kenmore Elite 74229	$180	74	⌃	⌃	⌃	⌃	⌃⌃	NA	1.3	2.2	1200
✔	3	Panasonic Inverter NN-H965BF	$180	74	⌃	⌃⌃	⌃	❶	⌃⌃	NA	1.4	2.2	1250

Recommended	Rank	Brand & Model	Price	Score	Heating Evenness	Defrosting Evenness	Speed of Heating	Microwaving Noise	Ease of Use	Venting	Usable Capacity (cu. ft.)	Claimed Capacity (cu. ft.)	Watts
		LARGE COUNTERTOP MICROWAVES (Continued)											
⊘	4	**LG** LCRT2010[ST]	$200	73	⌃	⌃	⌃	⌃	⌃	NA	1.2	2.0	1200
⊘	5	**Panasonic** NN-SD975S	$250	73	⌃	⌃	⌃	⌃	⌃	NA	1.5	2.2	1250
		OVER-THE-RANGE MICROWAVES											
⊘	1	**GE** Profile PVM9215SFSS	$550	78	⌃	⌃	●	⌃	⌃	⌃	0.9	2.1	1000
$	2	**GE** JVM3160RFSS	$250	76	⌃	⌃	●	⌃	⌃	⌃	0.9	1.6	1000
⊘	3	**LG** LMV2031ST	$300	75	⌃	⌃	●	⌃	⌃	⌃	0.9	2.0	1000
⊘	4	**GE** JVM7195SFSS	$400	74	⌃	⌃	⌃	⌃	⌃	⌃	0.9	1.9	1100

Guide to Ratings

Score is based mainly on evenness of heating, ease of use, and auto-defrosting ability. The displayed score is out of a total of 100 points. **Heating Evenness** reflects how evenly a model reheated a dish of cold mashed potatoes. **Defrosting Evenness** is based on how well the auto-defrost program defrosted a pound of frozen ground beef. **Speed of Heating** is based on the temperature rise of water heated. **Microwaving Noise** reflects how quiet the oven is while microwaving on high. **Ease of Use** includes how easy it is to set the microwave without referring to the instructions. **Venting (airflow)** is based on the volume of air drawn in by the OTR's internal fan on the highest setting. **Usable Capacity** is the usable space based on our measurements and excludes the corner spaces for models with rotating turntables. Note that most over-the-range models allow you to turn off the rotation to fit large dishes. With the rotation off, measured capacity approximates claimed. But food might require extra tending and stirring. **Price** is approximate retail.

Most & Least Reliable

Percentage likely to break by fifth year of ownership.

OVER-THE-RANGE

Whirlpool	12%
Frigidaire	13%
Kenmore	15%
GE	15%
KitchenAid	16%
Maytag	16%
LG	17%
Bosch	17%
Sharp	18%
Samsung	29%

These conclusions are based on our failure rate estimates for over-the-range microwaves by the fifth year of ownership, gathered from 35,681 subscribers who purchased a new over-the-range microwave between 2008 and 2016. Our statistical model estimates failure rates for over-the-range microwaves not covered by a service contract. Differences of less than 3 points aren't meaningful. Models within a brand may vary, and changes in design or manufacturer may affect future reliability.

Source 2016 Winter Product Reliability Survey, Consumer Reports National Research Center.

Paints, Exterior

Home Depot is the place to go for Behr paints, the top brand in our Ratings. But Ace Hardware's Clark+Kensington, also made our recommended list.

What to Look For
■ Flat and satin finishes for siding. Flat hides flaws; satin adds a touch of gloss.
■ Shinier semigloss for doors, windowsills, trim, and shutters for visual contrast.
■ Mildew resistance for shady spots, fade and color-change resistance for sunny ones, and dirt resistance for urban areas.

What to Skip
■ Economy grades of paints, which don't weather as well as top-of-the-line products from the same brand. Many top paints are low-priced.
■ Buying strictly by brand; manufacturers often reformulate paints in part to comply with tougher regulations.

What You'll Pay
The best values range from about $30 to $40 per gallon. Buying 5-gallon containers can save you even more.

BUYING ADVICE

Paint a sample board with each color you're considering. Observe the paint at different times of the day as the natural light changes.

For more buying advice, go to ConsumerReports.org/paint.

All tested models in performance order.

Rec.	Rank	Brand & Model	Price	Score	After 3 years	After 6 years	After 9 years	Cracking	Color Change	Dirt	Mildew	VOCs (grams/liter)
					Appearance			Resists				
		Completed the equivalent of 9 years' exposure										
✓	1	**Behr** Premium Plus Ultra Exterior (Home Depot)	$39	75	⊛	⌃	⌃	•	•	•	•	50
✓	2	**Clark + Kensington** Exterior (Ace)	$35	75	⊛	⊛	⌃	•	•	•	•	50
	3	**Sherwin-Williams** Emerald Exterior	$72	73	⊛	⌃	⌃	•	•		•	0
	4	**Behr** Premium Plus Exterior (Home Depot)	$30	72	⊛	⊛	⌃	•	•		•	50
	5	**Sherwin-Williams** Duration Exterior	$68	70	⊛	⌃	⌃					92

Completed the equivalent of 9 years' exposure

Rec.	Rank	Brand & Model	Price	Score	Appearance After 3 years	After 6 years	After 9 years	Resists Cracking	Color Change	Dirt	Mildew	VOCs (grams/liter)
	6	**Benjamin Moore** Aura Exterior	$68	70	Excellent	Very Good	Very Good	•	•			67
	7	**Valspar** DuraMax Exterior (Lowe's)	$39	69	Excellent	Very Good	Very Good	•	•	•		100
	8	**Glidden** Spred Exterior ⓘ	$30	69	Excellent	Very Good	Very Good	•	•			100
	9	**California Paints** Fres-Coat Exterior ⓘ	$48	68	Excellent	Very Good	Very Good	•	•	•		100
	10	**Glidden** Premium Exterior (Home Depot) ⓘ	$24	68	Excellent	Very Good	Very Good	•	•			100
	11	**Glidden** High Endurance Plus Exterior (Walmart)	$29	57	Excellent	Very Good	Good	•	•			50
	12	**Sherwin-Williams** Resilience Exterior ⓘ	$63	55	Very Good	Very Good	Good	•	•			48
	13	**Ace** Royal Exteriors Exterior ⓘ	$28	55	Excellent	Very Good	Good	•	•		•	50
	14	**Olympic** Assure Exterior (Lowe's)	$25	53	Excellent	Very Good	Good	•	•		•	50
	15	**Behr** Marquee Exterior (Home Depot)	$48	52	Excellent	Very Good	Good	•	•		•	50

Guide to Ratings

Score is the overall weighted average of each year's appearance for white, blue, and brown based on two coats over primed pine-clapboard siding (for self-priming paints, two coats without primer). Fully tested finishes have undergone accelerated outdoor weathering for up to three years; each year approximates three years on house walls. Displayed scores are rounded; products are listed by precise overall score. Because a brand's flat, eggshell, and semigloss formulations perform similarly overall, we've combined the scores into one to simplify the selection process. Scores for previously tested products may have changed because of changes in tabulations. **Appearance** indicates performance after years indicated. **Resists** means score of at least good for that attribute at the end of testing. **Claimed VOCs** is maximum grams per liter as stated on can. **Price** is approximate retail per gallon.

Printers, All-in-one

All-in-ones are by far the most popular type of printer on the market. The reason? They let you not only print but also copy, scan, and sometimes fax.

What to Look For
■ Low ink costs.
■ An all-in-one inkjet if you want color printing and a model that excels at printing your photos.
■ A black-and-white laser all-in-one for excellent text quality, fast print speed, and a low cost per page—provided you don't need to print in color or scan color photos.

What to Skip
■ An inkjet with a single cartridge for color inks, because separate color cartridges may be more economical, depending on what you print
■ High ink costs, which can make a bargain-price printer a bad deal in the long run.

What You'll Pay
Laser all-in-ones start at a little more than $100. Inkjet all-in-ones cost $60 and up.

BUYING ADVICE

Many all-in-ones have built-in Wi-Fi that enables you to print photos and documents from computers and mobile devices on a home network.

For more buying advice, go to ConsumerReports.org/printers.

All tested models in performance order.

Recommended	Rank	Brand & Model	Price	Score	Ink Cost/Month ($)	Maintenance Ink Use	Photo Quality	Text Quality	Text Speed	Graphics Quality	Convenience	Scan Quality	Copy Quality	Power Saving	Versatility
ALL-IN-ONE BLACK-AND-WHITE LASER															
✔	1	**Canon** image-CLASS MF229DW	$150	81	4.1	NA	⌃	⌃	⌃	⌃	⌃	⌃	⌃	⌃	⌄
✔	2	**Canon** image-CLASS MF6160dw	$490	79	3.7	NA	⌃	⌃	⌃	⌃	⌃	⌃	⌃	⌃	⌄
✔	3	**Samsung** Xpress M2885FW	$250	77	3.3	NA	⌃	⌃	⌃	⌃	⌃	⌃	⌃	⌃	⌄

RATINGS KEY ⌄ POOR ⌄ FAIR ❶ GOOD ⌃ VERY GOOD ⌃ EXCELLENT
$ **CR BEST BUY** These models offer the best combination of performance and price. All are recommended.
✔ **RECOMMENDED** These are high-performing models that stand out.

Recommended	Rank	Brand & Model	Price	Score	Ink Cost/Month ($)	Maintenance Ink Use	Photo Quality	Text Quality	Text Speed	Graphics Quality	Convenience	Scan Quality	Copy Quality	Power Saving	Versatility
		ALL-IN-ONE BLACK-AND-WHITE LASER (Continued)													
✓	4	**Canon** image-CLASS MF6180dw	$525	77	3.5		NA								
✓	5	**Samsung** Xpress M2070FW	$190	76	5		NA								
✓	6	**Dell** S2815dn	$290	76	2.7		NA								
✓	7	**Dell** H815dw	$370	76	2.7		NA								
	8	**Canon** image-CLASS MF212w	$150	75	5		NA								
	9	**Brother** MFC-L5700DW	$300	75	2.4		NA								
	10	**Ricoh** SP 213SFNW	$250	74	4.7		NA								
	11	**Brother** DCP-L5500DN	$300	74	2.4		NA								
	12	**Brother** MFC-L2740DW	$200	74	4.5		NA								
	13	**Brother** MFC-L2700DW	$150	74	4.5		NA								
	14	**HP** LaserJet Pro M127fw	$260	74	5.8		NA								
	15	**Dell** E514dw	$160	71	4		NA								
		ALL-IN-ONE COLOR LASER													
✓	1	**Dell** E525w	$250	76	19										
✓	2	**Dell** S2825cdn	$480	75	9.7										
	3	**Samsung** SL-C480FW	$350	73	20.9										
	4	**Dell** H625cdw	$400	73	13.9										
	5	**Samsung** Xpress C1860FW	$450	71	7.5										
	6	**HP** Color Laserjet Pro M477FDW	$430	68	9.7										
	7	**Samsung** Xpress C460FW	$400	68	13.4										
	8	**Brother** MFC-L8850CDW	$500	67	7.3										
	9	**HP** Color Laserjet Pro MFP M277dw	$380	66	9.5										
	10	**HP** Color LaserJet Pro MFP M177fw	$350	64	11										

		Brand & Model	Price	Score											

Test Results

Recommended	Rank	Brand & Model	Price	Score	Ink Cost/Month ($)	Maintenance Ink Use	Photo Quality	Text Quality	Text Speed	Graphics Quality	Convenience	Scan Quality	Copy Quality	Power Saving	Versatility
		ALL-IN-ONE INKJET													
✓	1	**HP** Officejet Pro 8720	$250	76	4.3										
✓	2	**Epson** Expression Premium XP-830	$160	74	7.7										
✓	3	**Epson** Workforce Pro WF-5690	$360	72	4.7										
✓	4	**Epson** Workforce Pro WF-6530	$450	71	7.3										
✓	5	**Epson** Workforce Pro WF-4630	$200	71	5.6										
✓	6	**HP** Envy 7640	$150	71	10										
$	7	**Brother** MFC-J680DW	$120	71	7.3										
✓	8	**HP** Officejet 5740	$150	71	10.2										
	9	**Canon** Maxify MB5020	$150	70	4.4										
	10	**Canon** Pixma MX532	$150	70	7.4										
	11	**Canon** Maxify MB5320	$200	69	4.5										
	12	**Brother** MFC-J6520DW	$240	69	3.9										
	13	**Epson** Expression Photo XP-960	$230	68	9										
	14	**HP** Envy 4500	$100	68	9.2										
	15	**HP** Envy 5540	$100	68	9.4										
	16	**Brother** MFC-J6720DW	$230	68	4										
	17	**Canon** Maxify MB2320	$150	68	4.9										
	18	**Canon** Pixma MX922	$100	68	6.5										
	19	**Canon** Maxify MB2020	$90	68	4.8										
	20	**Brother** MFC-J5920DW	$280	68	3.4										
	21	**Canon** Pixma MG3620	$60	67	7.4										

ALL-IN-ONE INKJET (Continued)

Recommended	Rank	Brand & Model	Price	Score	Ink Cost/Month ($)	Maintenance Ink Use	Photo Quality	Text Quality	Text Speed	Graphics Quality	Convenience	Scan Quality	Copy Quality	Power Saving	Versatility
	22	**Brother** MFC-J5720DW	$200	67	5.1	Fair	Excellent	Good	Very Good	Very Good	Fair	Good	Very Good	Good	Excellent
	23	**HP** Envy 4520	$80	67	12.4	Good	Very Good	Good	Very Good	Good	Very Good	Very Good	Excellent	Excellent	Good
	24	**HP** Envy 5660	$150	66	9.6	Fair	Good	Very Good	Excellent	Good	Very Good	Very Good	Excellent	Very Good	Very Good
	25	**Canon** Pixma MX492	$70	66	10	Very Good	Very Good	Very Good	Very Good	Very Good	Very Good	Very Good	Very Good	Excellent	Fair
	26	**HP** Officejet 3830	$80	66	11.8	Very Good	Good	Very Good	Excellent	Very Good	Very Good	Very Good	Very Good	Excellent	Fair
	27	**Epson** Workforce WF-3620	$90	66	7.3	Fair	Fair	Very Good	Excellent	Good	Very Good	Very Good	Very Good	Very Good	Very Good
	28	**Brother** MFC-J6925DW	$300	66	3.6	Fair	Very Good	Fair	Very Good	Fair	Good	Excellent	Very Good	Excellent	Excellent
	29	**Epson** Workforce WF-3640	$130	66	7.2	Fair	Fair	Very Good	Excellent	Good	Very Good	Very Good	Very Good	Excellent	Very Good
	30	**Epson** Expression Photo XP-860	$230	66	9.4	Fair	Good	Very Good	Very Good	Very Good	Very Good	Very Good	Very Good	Very Good	Very Good
	31	**Epson** Workforce WF-7620	$200	66	7.2	Fair	Fair	Very Good	Excellent	Good	Very Good	Very Good	Very Good	Very Good	Very Good
	32	**Brother** MFC-J4620DW	$160	65	6.4	Good	Very Good	Good	Very Good	Good	Very Good	Very Good	Good	Very Good	Excellent
	33	**Brother** MFC-J6920DW	$150	65	4	Good	Good	Good	Excellent	Good	Very Good	Very Good	Very Good	Very Good	Excellent
	34	**Canon** Pixma MG7720	$130	65	7.6	Fair	Very Good	Excellent	Very Good	Very Good	Very Good	Excellent	Very Good	Excellent	Excellent
	35	**HP** Deskjet 2540	$70	65	12.2	Very Good	Good	Very Good	Very Good	Very Good	Very Good	Very Good	Very Good	Very Good	Fair
	36	**Canon** Pixma MG6820	$110	65	7.4	Fair	Very Good	Very Good	Very Good	Very Good	Very Good	Excellent	Very Good	Excellent	Very Good
	37	**HP** Officejet 4650	$100	64	11.7	Fair	Very Good	Good	Very Good	Very Good	Very Good	Very Good	Very Good	Excellent	Good
	38	**Kodak** Verite 55SE	$80	64	4.7	Good	Very Good	Very Good	Very Good	Very Good	Very Good	Very Good	Very Good	Fair	Fair
	39	**HP** Officejet Pro 8710	$160	64	4.3	Fair	Excellent	Excellent	Excellent	Good	Very Good	Very Good	Very Good	Excellent	Very Good
	40	**Brother** MFC-J4420DW	$100	63	6.5	Very Good	Fair	Very Good	Excellent	Very Good	Very Good	Very Good	Very Good	Good	Excellent
	41	**Canon** Pixma MG3520	$40	62	7.7	Good	Very Good	Good	Very Good	Very Good	Very Good	Very Good	Very Good	Very Good	Good

RATINGS KEY ⊝ POOR ⊘ FAIR ❶ GOOD ⌃ VERY GOOD ⌃⌃ EXCELLENT
$ **CR BEST BUY** These models offer the best combination of performance and price. All are recommended.
✓ **RECOMMENDED** These are high-performing models that stand out.

Recommended	Rank	Brand & Model	Price	Score	Ink Cost/Month ($)	Maintenance Ink Use	Photo Quality	Text Quality	Text Speed	Graphics Quality	Convenience	Scan Quality	Copy Quality	Power Saving	Versatility
		ALL-IN-ONE INKJET (Continued)													
	42	**Epson** Expression Home XP-430	$70	61	8.8										
	43	**Canon** Pixma MG5720	$80	59	7.3										
	44	**Epson** Workforce ET-4550	$500	57	0.6										
	45	**Epson** Expression ET-2550	$300	54	0.6										
	46	**Epson** Workforce ET-4500	$400	52	0.6										
	47	**Epson** Expression ET-2500	$280	51	0.6										
	48	**Primera** Trio	$300	39	10.4										

Guide to Ratings

Score is based on speed and quality of print, scan, and copy functions, plus ease of use. The displayed score is out of a total of 100 points. **Ink Cost/Month ($)** is estimated cost (in dollars) for ink or toner for the number of pages our readers told us they print in a month of use. For inkjets: 23 text pages, nine graphics pages, 2.4 large photos, 3.6 small photos, and 3.5 photos on plain paper. For lasers: 62 text pages, 24 graphics pages, 1.7 large photos, 1.9 small photos, and 2.3 photos on plain paper. **Maintenance Ink Use** reflects the amount of extra ink used by an inkjet printer to maintain its print heads. "NA" indicates an older model that did not undergo that test. **Photo Quality** reflects a photo's appearance. **Text Quality** assesses clarity and crispness of black text. **Text Speed** reflects how quickly the model can print text on five plain, letter-sized pages. Thirty seconds or less is excellent; 31 to 60 seconds is very good; 61 to 90 seconds is good; 91 to 120 seconds is fair; and longer than 120 seconds is poor. **Graphics Quality** assesses the appearance of color graphics produced by the printer. Black-and-white lasers were judged on black-and-white graphics. **Convenience** measures the ease of carrying out a series of common activities with the printer. **Scan Quality** is for color photos, graphics, and text scanned at each model's default settings. **Copy Quality** is for graphics and text. **Power Saving** indicates how well the printer conserves power between uses. **Versatility** indicates features that increase a printer's utility or capabilities. **Price** is approximate retail.

QUICK GUIDE

Printers, Regular

Inkjet and laser printers have become more affordable and increasingly full-featured.

What to Look For
■ A laser printer if you want fast, low-cost, top-quality black-and-white text.
■ An inkjet if you want the most versatile printer. You can print color photos and graphics as well as text.
■ Wi-Fi if you want to print photos without a computer.

What to Skip
■ Color laser printers, which are costlier than their monochrome counterparts and unsuited for photos.
■ Snapshot printers, most of which didn't provide the photo quality of the best regular inkjets in our tests.

What You'll Pay
Color inkjets can cost as little as $50, and monochrome laser printers less than $100.

BUYING ADVICE

A printer with an Energy Star label will consume very little power when not printing.

For more buying advice, go to ConsumerReports.org/printers.

All tested models in performance order.

Recommended	Rank	Brand & Model	Price	Score	Photo Quality	Text Quality	Text Speed	Graphics Quality	Maintenance Ink Use	Convenience	Power Saving	Versatility	Text Speed (ppm)	Ink Cost/Month ($)
		BLACK-AND-WHITE LASER PRINTERS												
$	1	**Samsung** Xpress M2835DW	$140	82	NA	⊗	⊗	^	⊗	⊗	⊗	⊗	18.8	3.10
✓	2	**Canon** image-CLASS LBP6230DW	$170	77	NA	⊗	⊗	❶	⊗	⊗	⊗	⊙	18.8	6.10
$	3	**Samsung** Xpress M2020W	$120	76	NA	⊗	⊗	❶	⊗	⊗	⊗	⊗	14.3	4.70
	4	**HP** Laserjet Pro M402dn	$200	73	NA	^	⊗	❶	⊗	^	^	⊙	18.8	2.60

Recommended	Rank	Brand & Model	Price	Score	Photo Quality	Text Quality	Text Speed	Graphics Quality	Maintenance Ink Use	Convenience	Power Saving	Versatility	Text Speed (ppm)	Ink Cost/Month ($)

BLACK-AND-WHITE LASER PRINTERS (Continued)

Recommended	Rank	Brand & Model	Price	Score	Photo Quality	Text Quality	Text Speed	Graphics Quality	Maintenance Ink Use	Convenience	Power Saving	Versatility	Text Speed (ppm)	Ink Cost/Month ($)
	5	**Brother** HL-L2360DW	$130	73	NA	⌃	⌃	⌄	⌃	⌃	⌃	⌄	16.7	4.40
	6	**Brother** HL-L5200DW	$220	72	NA	⌃	⌃	!	⌃	⌃	⌃	⌄	23.1	2.40
	7	**Brother** HL-L6250DW	$300	72	NA	⌃	⌃	!	⌃	⌃	⌃	⌄	25	1.60
	8	**Brother** HL-L6200DW	$250	72	NA	⌃	⌃	!	⌃	⌃	⌃	⌄	25	1.60
	9	**Dell** S2810dn	$160	71	NA	⌃	⌃	!	⌃	⌃	⌃	⌄	25	3.00
	10	**HP** Laserjet Pro M201dw	$200	71	NA	⌃	⌃	!	⌃	⌃	⌃	⌄	17.6	4.90
	11	**Dell** E310dw	$110	71	NA	⌃	⌃	!	⌃	⌃	⌃	⌄	15	4.00
	12	**Brother** HL-L2340DW	$100	70	NA	⌃	⌃	⌄	⌃	⌃	⌃	⌄	15	4.60
	13	**Brother** HL-L5100DN	$190	70	NA	⌃	⌃	!	⌃	⌃	⌃	⌄	23.1	2.40
	14	**HP** Laserjet Pro P1102w	$160	70	NA	⌃	⌃	⌄	⌃	⌃	⌃	⌵	13.6	6.60

COLOR LASER PRINTERS

Recommended	Rank	Brand & Model	Price	Score	Photo Quality	Text Quality	Text Speed	Graphics Quality	Maintenance Ink Use	Convenience	Power Saving	Versatility	Text Speed (ppm)	Ink Cost/Month ($)
$	1	**Samsung** ProXpress C2620DW	$350	73	⌃	⌃	⌃	⌃	⌃	⌃	⌃	⌄	13	6.60
✓	2	**Samsung** SL-C430W	$260	68	⌄	⌃	⌃	⌃	⌃	⌃	⌃	⌵	12	20.40
✓	3	**HP** Color LaserJet Pro M452nw	$200	68	⌄	⌃	⌃	⌃	⌃	⌃	⌃	⌵	15	8.70
	4	**HP** Color Laserjet Pro M252dw	$300	67	⌄	⌃	⌃	⌃	⌃	⌃	⌃	!	12	9.20
	5	**Samsung** Xpress C1810W	$270	67	⌄	⌃	⌃	⌃	⌃	⌃	!	⌵	10.3	7.60
	6	**Samsung** Xpress C410W	$230	66	⌄	⌃	⌃	⌃	⌃	⌃	⌃	⌵	11.5	14.30
	7	**HP** Color LaserJet Pro M452dn	$450	64	⌄	⌃	⌃	⌃	⌃	⌃	⌄	⌄	15	8.20
	8	**Brother** HL-L8350CDW	$330	62	⌄	⌃	⌃	⌃	⌃	⌃	⌃	!	15.8	7.70
	9	**Lexmark** CS410dn	$400	61	⌄	⌃	⌃	⌃	⌃	!	⌃	!	15	3.70
	10	**Brother** HL-3140CW	$190	55	⌵	⌃	⌃	⌃	⌃	⌃	⌃	⌵	10.3	13.10

INKJET PRINTERS

Recommended	Rank	Brand & Model	Price	Score	Photo Quality	Text Quality	Text Speed	Graphics Quality	Maintenance Ink Use	Convenience	Power Saving	Versatility	Text Speed (ppm)	Ink Cost/Month ($)
✓	1	**Epson** Workforce Pro WF-5190	$300	70	⌃	⌃	⌃	⌃	⌄	⌃	⌃	⌄	14.3	4.70
✓	2	**Canon** Pixma iP110	$180	66	⌃	⌃	⌃	⌃	⌄	⌃	⌃	⌄	8.3	8.40

Recommended	Rank	Brand & Model	Price	Score	Photo Quality	Text Quality	Text Speed	Graphics Quality	Maintenance Ink Use	Convenience	Power Saving	Versatility	Text Speed (ppm)	Ink Cost/Month ($)
		INKJET PRINTERS (Continued)												
	3	**Canon** Pixma iX6820	$150	65	Very Good	Very Good	Excellent	Excellent	Fair	Very Good	Excellent	Fair	12	6.60
	4	**Canon** Pixma iP8720	$260	65	Very Good	Excellent	Excellent	Excellent	Fair	Very Good	Excellent	Good	11.5	7.10
	5	**HP** Officejet Pro 6230	$100	65	Very Good	Very Good	Excellent	Good	Fair	Very Good	Excellent	Good	11.1	6.40
	6	**Canon** Pixma iP7220	$80	64	Excellent	Excellent	Excellent	Very Good	Fair	Fair	Excellent	Very Good	11.5	6.90
	7	**Canon** Maxify iB4020	$110	63	Very Good	Very Good	Excellent	Good	Fair	Very Good	Excellent	Fair	18.8	4.40
	8	**Epson** Workforce WF-100	$200	63	Very Good	Good	Very Good	Good	Very Good	Very Good	Very Good	Poor	5.2	13.50
	9	**HP** Officejet Pro 8100	$150	62	Good	Very Good	Excellent	Good	NA	Very Good	Very Good	Good	11.5	3.90
	10	**Epson** Workforce WF-7110	$150	60	Fair	Very Good	Excellent	Very Good	Fair	Very Good	Very Good	Fair	13.6	7.20

Guide to Ratings

Score is based on speed and text/photo quality. The displayed score is out of a total of 100 points. **Photo Quality** reflects a photo's appearance. **Text Quality** assesses clarity and crispness of black text. **Text Speed** reflects how quickly the model can print text on five plain, letter-sized pages. Thirty seconds or less is excellent; 31 to 60 seconds is very good; 61 to 90 seconds is good; 91 to 120 seconds is fair; and longer than 120 seconds is poor. **Graphics Quality** assesses the appearance of color graphics produced by the printer, or black-and-white graphics for black-and-white lasers. **Maintenance Ink Use** reflects the amount of extra ink used by an inkjet printer to maintain its print heads. "NA" indicates an older model that did not undergo those tests. **Convenience** measures the ease of carrying out a series of common activities with the printer. **Power Saving** indicates how well the printer conserves power between uses. **Versatility** indicates features that increase a printer's utility or capabilities. **Ink Cost/Month ($)** is estimated cost (in dollars) for ink or toner for the number of pages our readers told us they print in a month of use. For inkjets: 23 text pages, nine graphics pages, 2.4 large photos, 3.6 small photos, and 3.5 photos on plain paper. For lasers: 62 text pages, 24 graphics pages, 1.7 large photos, 1.9 small photos, and 2.3 photos on plain paper. **Price** is approximate retail.

Ranges

Electric radiant smooothtop ranges remain the big sellers, but you have more options than ever, including double-oven ranges for the multitasker in all of us.

What to Look For

■ One or more high-heat burners to heat large quantities of food quickly.
■ Double ovens to simultaneously cook two dishes at different temperatures.
■ Induction, which uses a magnetic field to heat more quickly and precisely. Prices are dropping.
■ At least five oven-rack positions for flexibility.

What to Skip

■ Higher Btu (for British thermal unit) hasn't guaranteed faster heating in our tests. Btu indicates the amount of gas used and the cooktop heat generated.

What You'll Pay

About $400 to $600 for coil, $700 to $1,700 for smoothtop, $600 to $2,000 for gas, or $3,000-plus for pro-style.

BUYING ADVICE

Induction requires magnetic cookware. If a magnet strongly sticks to the bottom of the pot, it will work.

For more buying advice, go to ConsumerReports.org/ranges.

All tested models in performance order.

Recommended	Rank	Brand & Model	Price	Score	Cooktop High	Cooktop Low	Baking	Broiling	Oven Capacity	Self-Cleaning	High-Power Elements	Medium-Power Elements	Low-Power Elements	Convection Mode	Slide-In	Stainless Steel Available
					Test Results						Features					
		SMOOTHTOP double oven (30-inch)														
✔	1	**LG** LDE3037BD	$1620	89	⌃	⌃	⌃	⌃	⌃	⌃	2	0	2	•		•
✔	2	**Samsung** NE58F9710WS	$1800	85	⌃	⌃	⌃	⌃	⌃	⌃	1	2	1	•	•	•
✔	3	**Samsung** NE59J7850WS	$1400	82	⌃	⌃	⌃	⌃	⌃	⌃	1	2	1	•		•

RATINGS KEY ⊘ POOR ⊖ FAIR ● GOOD ⌃ VERY GOOD ⌃ EXCELLENT
🅢 **CR BEST BUY** These models offer the best combination of performance and price. All are recommended.
✔ **RECOMMENDED** These are high-performing models that stand out.

Recommended	Rank	Brand & Model	Price	Score	Cooktop High	Cooktop Low	Baking	Broiling	Oven Capacity	Self-Cleaning	High-Power Elements	Medium-Power Elements	Low-Power Elements	Convection Mode	Slide-in	Stainless Steel Available
SMOOTHTOP double oven (30-inch) (Continued)																
✓	4	**LG** LDE4415ST	$1640	81	●	●	●	●	●	●	2	0	2	•		•
	5	**GE** Profile PB960SJSS	$1530	74	●	●	●	●	●	●	1	2	1	•		•
	6	**Whirlpool** WGE755C0BS	$1600	71	●	●	●	●	●	●	2	0	2	•		•
	7	**Kenmore** 97312	$1700	71	●	●	●	●	●	●	2	1	1	•		•
	8	**Kenmore** 97212	$1600	68	●	●	●	●	●	●	2	0	2	•		•
	9	**Kenmore** 97613	$1400	60	●	●	●	●	●	●	2	0	2			•
SMOOTHTOP single oven (30-inch)																
✓	1	**Kenmore** 95052	$1300	87	●	●	●	●	●	●	2	0	2	•		•
✓	2	**LG** LRE3083SW	$800	86	●	●	●	●	●	●	2	0	2	•		•
✓	3	**Frigidaire** Gallery FGEF3035RF	$870	86	●	●	●	●	●	●	2	0	2	•		•
✓	4	**GE** Café CS980STSS	$2550	86	●	●	●	●	●	●	1	2	2	•		•
✓	5	**GE** Profile PB911SJSS	$1100	85	●	●	●	●	●	●	2	0	2	•		•
✓	6	**Samsung** NE58F9500SS	$1640	83	●	●	●	●	●	●	2	0	2	•	•	•
✓	7	**GE** PS920SFSS	$1800	83	●	●	●	●	●	●	1	2	1	•	•	•
✓	8	**LG** LSE4613ST	$1700	82	●	●	●	●	●	●	2	0	2	•	•	•
✓	9	**Whirlpool** WFE905C0ES	$900	81	●	●	●	●	●	●	2	0	2	•		•
	10	**Frigidaire** FFEF3018LW	$540	79	●	●	●	●	●	●	2	0	2			
	11	**Bosch** HEI8054U	$1800	79	●	●	●	●	●	●	2	0	2	•	•	•
	12	**Kenmore** 94242	$1000	78	●	●	●	●	●	●	2	0	2	•		•
	13	**Samsung** NE59J7630SS	$1000	76	●	●	●	●	●	●	2	0	2	•		•
	14	**Kenmore** 42549	$1440	72	●	●	●	●	●	●	2	0	2	•	•	•
	15	**GE** JB650SFSS	$800	70	●	●	●	●	●	●	2	0	2			•
	16	**Kenmore** 41313	$2200	70	●	●	●	●	●	●	2	0	2	•		•
	17	**Maytag** MER8800DS	$900	68	●	●	●	●	●	●	2	0	2			•

Recommended	Rank	Brand & Model	Price	Score	Cooktop High	Cooktop Low	Baking	Broiling	Oven Capacity	Self-Cleaning	High-Power Elements	Medium-Power Elements	Low-Power Elements	Convection Mode	Slide-in	Stainless Steel Available
		SMOOTHTOP single oven (30-inch) (Continued)														
	18	**Whirlpool** WFE515S0ES	$750	67	VG	VG	VG	F	G	E	2	0	2			•
	19	**Frigidaire** Gallery FGES3065PW	$1600	66	E	E	G	F	G	G	2	0	2	•	•	•
	20	**Frigidaire** FFES3025PW	$1300	66	E	VG	VG	F	G	E	2	0	2		•	•
	21	**KitchenAid** KFEG500ESS	$1350	63	VG	VG	VG	G	E	F	2	0	2			•
	22	**Whirlpool** WFE715H0ES	$900	62	VG	VG	VG	VG	E	F	2	0	2			•
	23	**Samsung** NE59J3420SS	$800	59	VG	G	G	G	E	VG	2	0	2	•		•
	24	**Frigidaire** FFEF3048LS	$700	58	VG	VG	G	G	VG	E	2	0	2			•
	25	**Kenmore** 91312	$500	56	VG	G	G	E	G	NA	1	1	2			•
	26	**Frigidaire** FFEF3013LS	$500	48	VG	E	F	G	G	NA	2	0	2			•
	27	**Amana** AER5630BA	$650	47	VG	VG	G	F	VG	G	1	1	2			•
		ELECTRIC COIL														
$	1	**Kenmore** 94142	$560	81	VG	E	VG	G	E	E	2	0	2			•
	2	**GE** JB250DFWW	$470	69	VG	VG	G	VG	E	E	2	2	0			
	3	**Frigidaire** FFEF3015LS	$600	53	G	VG	G	G	VG	E	2	0	2			•
	4	**Whirlpool** WEC530H0DS	$1200	51	G	G	G	E	E	F	2	0	2			•
	5	**Whirlpool** WFC340S0AW	$700	44	VG	E	VG	F	VG	VG	2	0	2			•
		ELECTRIC INDUCTION														
✓	1	**Kenmore** 95073	$1700	89	E	E	VG	VG	VG	E	2	1	1	•		•
✓	2	**Kenmore** 95103	$1400	88	E	E	VG	E	VG	E	2	1	1	•		•
✓	3	**Samsung** NE58H9970WS	$3400	86	VG	E	VG	E	VG	E	3	1	0	•	•	•
✓	4	**Bosch** HIIP054U	$3200	81	E	E	VG	E	G	G	2	2	0	•	•	•

RATINGS KEY ⊘ POOR   ⊙ FAIR   ❶ GOOD   ⌃ VERY GOOD   ⊛ EXCELLENT

$ **CR BEST BUY** These models offer the best combination of performance and price. All are recommended.

✓ **RECOMMENDED** These are high-performing models that stand out.

Recommended	Rank	Brand & Model	Price	Score	Cooktop High	Cooktop Low	Baking	Broiling	Oven Capacity	Self-Cleaning	High-Power Burners	Medium-Power Burners	Low-Power Burners	Convection Mode	Slide-in	Stainless Steel Available
		ELECTRIC INDUCTION (Continued)														
✓	5	**Frigidaire** Gallery FGIF3061NF	$1540	81	⇑	⇑	↑	●	↑	↑	2	1	1	•		•
	6	**Electrolux** EI30IF40LS	$2000	79	⇑	⇑	↑	↑	↑	↑	3	0	1	•		•
	7	**Samsung** NE595N0PBSR	$1700	77	⇑	⇑	↑	↑	⇑	↑	2	0	2	•		•
		GAS AND DUAL-FUEL double oven (30-inch)														
✓	1	**Samsung** NY58J9850WS	$3300	79	↑	⇑	↑	⇑	↑	●	2	2	1	•		•
✓	2	**LG** LDG4315ST	$1740	73	↑	↑	↑	●	↑	↑	2	2	1	•		•
	3	**GE** Café CGS990SETSS	$3000	57	↑	⇑	●	⌄	⇑	⌄	2	2	1	•		•
	4	**Samsung** NX58J7750SS	$1800	52	↑	●	↑	⌄	↑	⌄	2	2	1	•		•
	5	**Kenmore** 78043	$1275	49	↑	↑	●	⌄	●	↑	2	2	1	•		•
		GAS AND DUAL-FUEL single oven (30-inch)														
✓	1	**Samsung** NX58F5700WS	$1600	79	↑	⇑	⇑	↑	↑	↑	2	2	1	•		•
✓	2	**Samsung** NX58H9500WS	$2000	77	↑	⇑	↑	↑	↑	↑	2	2	1	•	•	•
✓	3	**GE** PGS920SEFSS	$2550	73	↑	⇑	⇑	●	↑	●	1	3	1	•	•	•
✓	4	**Samsung** NX58H5600SS	$1000	73	●	⇑	↑	↑	⇑	●	2	2	1	•		•
✓	5	**Kenmore** 74132	$700	71	↑	↑	↑	●	↑	⇑	2	2	1			•
✓	6	**Samsung** NX58F5500SS	$680	71	●	↑	↑	↑	⇑	●	2	2	1			•
✓	7	**Frigidaire** Gallery FGGF3058RF	$1100	69	↑	↑	↑	●	↑	⇑	2	2	1	•		•
✓	8	**GE** PGB911ZEJSS	$1100	69	↑	⇑	↑	●	↑	●	2	3	0	•		•
	9	**Kenmore** 74332	$1040	68	↑	↑	↑	●	↑	↑	2	2	1			•
	10	**Kenmore** 75232	$1200	68	↑	⇑	↑	●	↑	↑	2	2	1	•		•
	11	**LG** LRG4113ST	$1200	67	↑	⇑	●	●	↑	↑	2	2	1	•		•
	12	**LG** LRG3081ST	$1000	64	●	↑	↑	●	↑	●	2	2	1	•		•
	13	**Bosch** HDI8054U	$2300	63	●	↑	↑	⇑	●	●	2	1	2	•	•	•
	14	**GE** Café CGS985SETSS	$2700	61	↑	⇑	↑	⌄	↑	⌄	2	2	1	•		•

	Rank	Brand & Model	Price	Score	Cooktop High	Cooktop Low	Baking	Broiling	Oven Capacity	Self-Cleaning	High-Power Burners	Medium-Power Burners	Low-Power Burners	Convection Mode	Slide-in	Stainless Steel Available
GAS AND DUAL-FUEL single oven (30-inch) continued																
	15	**Whirlpool** WFG530S0ES	$650	60	Good	Good	Very Good	Fair	Very Good	Very Good	2	2	1	•		•
	16	**LG** LSG4513ST	$2100	60	Very Good	Good	Good	Good	Excellent	Good	2	2	1	•		•
	17	**GE** JGB660SEJSS	$900	59	Very Good	Excellent	Good	Good	Very Good	Very Good	2	2	1			•
	18	**Bosch** HDIP054U	$2800	57	Good	Good	Very Good	Excellent	Good	Good	2	1	2	•	•	•
	19	**KitchenAid** KSGG700ESS	$1900	57	Good	Excellent	Good	Good	Excellent	Fair	2	2	1	•		•
	20	**Frigidaire** FFGF3023LS	$700	53	Good	Excellent	Excellent	Fair	Very Good	Excellent	1	2	1			•
	21	**Maytag** MGR8800DS	$1000	53	Good	Good	Excellent	Fair	Very Good	Fair	2	2	1	•		•
	22	**Amana** AGR5630	$500	52	Good	Excellent	Very Good	Fair	Very Good	Excellent	1	2	1			
	23	**GE** Café C2S985SETSS	$2700	51	Very Good	Excellent	Fair	Good	Very Good	Fair	2	2	1	•		•
	24	**Whirlpool** WEG760H0DS	$1700	48	Good	Good	Very Good	Good	Excellent	Fair	2	2	1	•		•
	25	**Frigidaire** FFGF3017LW	$550	46	Good	Very Good	Good	Fair	Good	NA	1	2	1			
	26	**Whirlpool** WFG715H0ES	$800	45	Good	Fair	Excellent	Fair	Excellent	Fair	2	2	1	•		•
	27	**Frigidaire** FFGS3025PW	$1300	44	Good	Good	Very Good	Fair	Good	Good	1	2	1		•	•
	28	**Frigidaire** Gallery FGGS3065PW	$1500	43	Very Good	Good	Good	Fair	Good	Fair	2	1	1	•	•	•
	29	**Frigidaire** Professional FPGH3077RF	$2250	33	Very Good	Poor	Very Good	Fair	Good	Good	3	1	1	•		•
	30	**Kenmore** 32363	$2000	28	Good	Poor	Good	Good	Good	Good	2	2	1	•		•
PRO-STYLE GAS AND DUAL-FUEL (30-inch)																
✓	1	**KitchenAid** KDRS407VSS	$4140	72	Very Good	Excellent	Very Good	Good	Good	Very Good	3	0	1	•		•
	2	**Wolf** DF304	$6400	68	Good	Very Good	Very Good	Very Good	Good	Fair	3	1	0	•		•

RATINGS KEY ⊘ POOR ⌵ FAIR ❶ GOOD ⌃ VERY GOOD ⌃⌃ EXCELLENT
🅢 CR BEST BUY These models offer the best combination of performance and price. All are recommended.
✅ RECOMMENDED These are high-performing models that stand out.

Recommended	Rank	Brand & Model	Price	Score	Cooktop High	Cooktop Low	Baking	Broiling	Oven Capacity	Self-Cleaning	High-Power Burners	Medium-Power Burners	Low-Power Burners	Convection Mode	Slide-in	Stainless Steel Available
		PRO-STYLE GAS AND DUAL-FUEL (30-inch) continued														
	3	**Dacor** DR30G	$3500	66	(|)	(∧)	(|)	(|)	(∧)	NA	3	1	0	•		•
	4	**GE** Monogram ZGP304NRSS	$4700	65	(|)	(∧)	(∧)	(|)	(∧)	(|)	1	3	0	•		•
	5	**Kenmore** Pro 79523	$2940	65	(∧)	(∧)	(∧)	(∧)	(∧)	(∧)	1	2	1	•		•
	6	**Jenn-Air** JGRP430WP	$4000	62	(|)	(∧)	(∧∧)	(∨)	(|)	(∧)	3	0	1	•		•
	7	**NXR** DRGB3001	$2000	60	(|)	(|)	(|)	(|)	(|)	NA	4	0	0	•		•
	8	**Miele** HR1124	$5000	55	(∧)	(|)	(|)	(∧)	(∧)	(∧)	4	0	0	•		•
	9	**Thermador** PRG304GH	$4150	52	(∧)	(∧)	(∨)	(∨)	(|)	NA	4	0	0	•		•
	10	**Smeg** C30GGXUI	$3000	45	(∧)	(|)	(|)	(∨)	(∨)	NA	1	4	0	•		•
	11	**Wolf** GR304	$4900	45	(|)	(∧)	(∨)	(∨)	(|)	NA	3	1	0	•		•
	12	**Bertazzoni** PRO304GASX	$3100	43	(|)	(|)	(∧)	(|)	(|)	(∨)	1	1	2	•		•
	13	**Viking** RVGR33015BSS	$4600	40	(∧)	(∧)	(∨)	(|)	(∨)	(∨)	3	2	0	•		•
	14	**American** Range ARR304	$3600	32	(∧)	(∨)	(|)	(∨)	(∧)	NA	3	1	0	•		•
		PRO-STYLE GAS AND DUAL-FUEL (36-inch)														
✓	1	**KitchenAid** KDRU763VSS	$7300	74	(∧)	(∧)	(∧)	(∧)	(∧)	(∧)	3	0	1	•		•
✓	2	**GE** Monogram ZDP364NDPSS	$7600	72	(|)	(∧)	(∧)	(|)	(∧)	(∧)	4	0	0	•		•
	3	**Thermador** PRG366JG	$7300	68	(∧)	(∧)	(∧)	(|)	(∧)	(∨)	6	0	0	•		•
	4	**Viking** VGSC536-4G	$7200	68	(∧)	(∧)	(∧)	(∧)	(|)	(∨)	4	0	0	•		•
	5	**Wolf** GR366	$6000	59	(|)	(∧)	(|)	(∨)	(∧)	NA	5	1	0	•		•
	6	**NXR** DRGB3602	$3000	56	(|)	(∧)	(|)	(|)	(|)	NA	6	0	0	•		•
	7	**Jenn-Air** JGRP436WP	$5200	43	(|)	(∧)	(∧)	(∨)	(∧)	(∧)	5	0	1	•		•
	8	**BlueStar** RCS36SBSS	$3600	29	(|)	(∨)	(∨)	(|)	(∧)	NA	5	0	1	•		•
	9	**Verona** VEFSGE365SS	$2500	25	(∧)	(∨)	(∨)	(∨)	(|)	NA	3	0	2	•		•
	10	**Smeg** C36GGXU	$3200	23	(|)	(∨)	(∨)	(∨)	(∨)	NA	1	1	4	•		•

Most & Least Reliable
Percentage likely to break by third year of ownership.

ELECTRIC

GE	5%
Whirlpool	7%
Frigidaire	7%
Kenmore	8%
Maytag	8%
Samsung	10%
LG	10%
KitchenAid	12%

GAS

LG	5%
Frigidaire	6%
Kenmore	7%
GE	7%
Whirlpool	11%
KitchenAid	12%
Maytag	12%

The graph shows what we found when we surveyed more than 6,880 subscribers who bought a new electric range between 2010 and 2015, and 6,114 subscribers who bought a new gas or dual-fuel range during that time frame. The graph shows the estimated failure rates for three-year-old ranges that were purchased new and not covered by a service contract. Differences of less than 5 points aren't meaningful for electric ranges, and differences of less than 4 points aren't meaningful for gas and dual-fuel ranges. Models within a brand can vary, and design or manufacture changes might affect future reliability. Still, choosing a brand with a good repair history can improve your odds of getting a reliable model.

Source 2015 Summer Product Reliability Survey, Consumer Reports National Research Center.

Guide to the Ratings
Score reflects cooktop speed and simmer performance, and oven capacity, baking, broiling, and self-cleaning. The displayed score is out of a total of 100 points. **Cooktop High** is how quickly the most powerful element heated water to near-boil. **Cooktop Low** is how well the lowest-powered element held a low heat, as for melting chocolate, and how well the most powerful element, set on low, held tomato sauce below a boil. **Baking** reflects even browning of cakes and cookies in multirack baking tests. **Broiling** is even browning of a pan of burgers and high-heat searing. **Oven Capacity** is our evaluation of usable space. **Self-Cleaning** is the self-cleaning cycle's effectiveness after the oven is coated with a mixture of eggs, cheese, pie filling, and other ingredients. **Price** is approximate retail.

Refrigerators

Refrigerator design is evolving as Americans buy more fresh food. Four-door models, for example, have a fourth chamber that provides storage flexibility. But everyday performance still matters most, and that's what our tests capture.

What to Look For

■ Fingerprint-resistant stainless steel for busy kitchens. Classic white or black finishes are another option.

■ Temperature-controlled drawers to keep meat, fish, cold cuts, and other food at lower temperatures.

■ Split shelves for taller items as needed.

■ Adjustable door bins and shelves.

What to Skip

■ Fancy climate controls. Many manufacturers claim special freshness technology, but refrigerators that maintain consistent temperatures are best at keeping your food fresh. Dual evaporators help as well by maintaining optimal humidity levels.

What You'll Pay

Four-door models start at $2,500. Three-door French-door models go for $1,500 to $3,000. Top-freezers begin at $600. Side-by-sides start around $900, and cabinet-depth models start at $2,000.

BUYING ADVICE

Width is the key dimension if your new fridge will fill an existing opening. Height matters too if there are cabinets overhead.

For more buying advice, go to ConsumerReports.org/refrigerators

---

All tested models in performance order.

Recommended	Rank	Brand & Model	Price	Score	Temperature Performance	Energy Efficiency	Noise	Ease of Use	Energy Cost/Yr. ($)	Total Usable Capacity (cu. ft.)	Exterior Height (in.)	Exterior Width (in.)	Exterior Depth (in.)
		TOP FREEZERS											
$	1	**LG** LTCS20220S	$870	67	⌃	⌃	⌃	⌄	40	16.7	66	30	33
✓	2	**LG** LTCS24223S	$900	67	⌃	⌃	⌃	⌄	44	19.6	68	33	33
✓	3	**GE** GIE21GSHSS	$1205	67	⌃	⌃	⌃	⌄	47	17.7	67	33	33

Recommended	Rank	Brand & Model	Price	Score	Temperature Performance	Energy Efficiency	Noise	Ease of Use	Energy Cost/Yr. ($)	Total Usable Capacity (cu. ft.)	Exterior Height (in.)	Exterior Width (in.)	Exterior Depth (in.)
TOP FREEZERS (Continued)													
✓	4	**Frigidaire** Gallery FGHI2164QF	$1000	65	⌃	⌃⌃	◐	⌄⌄	39	15.0	69	30	32
✓	5	**Frigidaire** FFHT2021QS	$815	64	⌃	⌃⌃	⌃	⌄⌄	43	16.8	69	30	32
✓	6	**Frigidaire** Gallery FGHT1846QF	$800	64	⌃	⌃⌃	⌃	⌄	45	14.4	67	30	30
$	7	**GE** GTE15CTHRWW	$565	64	⌃	⌃⌃	◐	⌄	40	11.6	62	28	30
✓	8	**Frigidaire** FFHI1831QS	$835	63	⌃	⌃⌃	◐	⌄⌄	43	14.7	66	30	31
✓	9	**Kenmore** 79433	$900	62	◐	⌃⌃	⌃	⌄	54	19.4	69	33	32
✓	10	**GE** GTE18ISHSS	$925	61	⌃	⌃⌃	◐	⌄⌄	43	14.0	67	30	33
✓	11	**Kenmore** 78032	$1370	61	◐	⌃⌃	⌃	⌄	52	19.6	69	33	32
BOTTOM FREEZERS													
✓	1	**Kenmore** Elite 79043	$1400	83	⌃⌃	⌃⌃	⌃⌃	◐	59	17.1	69	33	33
✓	2	**LG** LDC24370ST	$1250	83	⌃⌃	⌃⌃	⌃⌃	◐	59	17.1	69	33	33
✓	3	**Kenmore** Elite 79023	$1300	81	⌃⌃	⌃⌃	⌃⌃	◐	58	15.8	69	30	34
$	4	**Kenmore** 69313	$950	80	⌃⌃	⌃⌃	⌃⌃	⌄	44	13.4	66	30	31
✓	5	**KitchenAid** KRBR102ESS	$1550	77	⌃⌃	⌃⌃	◐	⌄	54	14.9	69	33	31
✓	6	**Maytag** MBF2258DEM	$1300	77	⌃⌃	⌃⌃	◐	⌄	54	14.9	69	33	31
✓	7	**Whirlpool** WRB322DMBM	$1225	77	⌃⌃	⌃⌃	◐	⌄	54	14.9	69	33	31
✓	8	**GE** GDE21ESKSS	$1650	76	⌃⌃	⌃⌃	⌃	◐	49	14.6	70	30	35

Recommended	Rank	Brand & Model	Price	Score	Test Results				Features				
					Temperature Performance	Energy Efficiency	Noise	Ease of Use	Energy Cost/Yr. ($)	Total Usable Capacity (cu. ft.)	Exterior Height (in.)	Exterior Width (in.)	Exterior Depth (in.)
		THREE-DOOR FRENCH-DOOR											
✅	1	**Samsung** RF28HDEDPWW	$2330	87	Excellent	Excellent	Excellent	Very Good	70	20.0	69	36	34
✅	2	**Kenmore** Elite 74093	$2800	85	Excellent	Excellent	Very Good	Very Good	74	21.5	69	36	36
✅	3	**LG** LFXS32766S	$4000	85	Very Good	Excellent	Excellent	Very Good	74	21.5	69	36	36
✅	4	**GE** GFE26GSHSS	$2000	84	Very Good	Excellent	Very Good	Very Good	48	17.1	70	36	35
✅	5	**GE** Profile PWE23KMDES	$2340	84	Excellent	Excellent	Very Good	Very Good	47	16.0	69	36	29
✅	6	**GE** GNE29GSHSS	$1990	83	Very Good	Excellent	Very Good	Very Good	66	20.9	70	36	34
✅	7	**Samsung** RF28HFPDBSR	$2000	83	Excellent	Excellent	Very Good	Very Good	56	20.0	69	36	34
✅	8	**Samsung** RF30HDEDTSR	$3190	83	Excellent	Excellent	Very Good	Very Good	81	20.9	69	36	35
✅	9	**GE** Profile PFH28PSHSS	$2900	82	Very Good	Excellent	Very Good	Very Good	57	19.8	70	36	36
✅	10	**Samsung** RF28HDEDBSR	$2330	82	Excellent	Excellent	Very Good	Very Good	62	20.0	69	36	34
✅	11	**Samsung** RF26HFPNBSR	$2300	82	Excellent	Excellent	Good	Very Good	55	18.3	69	36	33
💲	12	**LG** LFC24770ST	$1500	81	Excellent	Excellent	Very Good	Very Good	55	17.4	69	33	33
✅	13	**Kenmore** Elite 74033	$3100	81	Excellent	Excellent	Very Good	Very Good	68	19.1	69	36	34
✅	14	**LG** LFXS30766S	$2775	81	Excellent	Excellent	Very Good	Very Good	68	19.1	69	36	34
✅	15	**LG** LFCS31626S	$2000	80	Very Good	Excellent	Excellent	Very Good	70	20.8	69	36	34
✅	16	**Samsung** RF323TEDB[SR]	$2400	80	Excellent	Excellent	Very Good	Good	73	21.8	69	36	36
✅	17	**GE** Profile PFE28RSHSS	$3100	80	Very Good	Excellent	Excellent	Very Good	73	20.1	69	36	35
✅	18	**GE** Café CYE22USHSS	$3000	80	Excellent	Very Good	Very Good	Very Good	66	15.1	70	36	30

RATINGS KEY ⊘ POOR ⊖ FAIR ❶ GOOD ⌃ VERY GOOD ⌃⌃ EXCELLENT
💲 **CR BEST BUY** These models offer the best combination of performance and price. All are recommended.
✅ **RECOMMENDED** These are high-performing models that stand out.

Recommended	Rank	Brand & Model	Price	Score	Temperature Performance	Energy Efficiency	Noise	Ease of Use	Energy Cost/Yr. ($)	Total Usable Capacity (cu. ft.)	Exterior Height (in.)	Exterior Width (in.)	Exterior Depth (in.)
FOUR-DOOR (OR MORE) FRENCH-DOOR													
✓	1	**Samsung** Chef Collection RF34H9960S4	$5000	84	⌃	⌃	⌃	⌃	99	23.4	73	36	36
✓	2	**LG** LPCS34886C	$5300	84	⌃	⌃	⌃	!	73	24.4	73	36	37
✓	3	**Kenmore** Elite 72483	$3600	84	⌃	⌃	⌃	⌃	70	21.1	69	36	36
✓	4	**LG** LMXS30746S	$3130	84	⌃	⌃	⌃	⌃	70	21.1	69	36	36
$	5	**Samsung** RF30KMEDBSR	$2200	83	⌃	⌃	⌃	⌃	65	20.0	70	36	36
✓	6	**LG** LPXS30866D	$3440	82	⌃	⌃	⌃	!	74	21.7	69	36	37
✓	7	**LG** LMXS30786S	$3500	82	⌃	⌃	⌃	⌃	67	20.1	69	36	36
$	8	**Samsung** RF28JBEDBSR	$2665	82	⌃	⌃	⌃	⌃	70	16.8	70	36	34
$	9	**LG** LFXS24663S	$2100	80	⌃	⌃	⌃	!	60	16.7	70	36	32
✓	10	**Samsung** Family Hub RF28K9580SR	$4400	80	⌃	⌃	⌃	⌃	82	19.0	72	36	35
$	11	**Samsung** RF28HMEDBSR	$1900	80	⌃	⌃	⌃	⌃	73	18.8	69	36	34
✓	12	**Samsung** RF23J9011SR	$2890	80	⌃	⌃	⌃	⌃	64	16.1	72	36	29
✓	13	**Samsung** RF25HMEDBSR	$1900	80	⌃	⌃	⌃	⌃	66	16.6	69	33	34
✓	16	**Samsung** RF22KREDBSR	$2500	79	⌃	⌃	⌃	⌃	61	14.9	70	36	29
SIDE BY SIDE													
✓	1	**Samsung** RS25H5121SR	$1655	83	⌃	⌃	⌃	⌃	58	18.6	69	36	34
✓	2	**Samsung** RH25H5611SR	$1700	80	⌃	⌃	⌃	⌃	63	19.0	70	36	35
✓	3	**LG** LSXS26366S	$1500	78	⌃	⌃	⌃	⌃	63	20.7	69	36	34
✓	4	**Samsung** RH29H8000SR	$2250	77	⌃	⌃	⌃	⌃	71	22.9	69	36	36
✓	5	**LG** LSC22991ST	$1500	76	⌃	⌃	⌃	⌃	53	15.6	69	36	29
✓	6	**Samsung** RS22HDHPNSR	$1850	76	⌃	⌃	⌃	⌃	76	19.5	69	36	28
✓	7	**LG** LSXS26326S	$1300	76	⌃	⌃	⌃	⌃	64	20.6	69	36	34

Recommended	Rank	Brand & Model	Price	Score	Temperature Performance	Energy Efficiency	Noise	Ease of Use	Energy Cost/Yr. ($)	Total Usable Capacity (cu. ft.)	Exterior Height (in.)	Exterior Width (in.)	Exterior Depth (in.)
		SIDE BY SIDE (Continued)											
✓	8	**GE** Profile PSS28KSHSS	$1980	76	⌃	⌃	⊗	⊗	83	17.0	70	36	33
$	9	**GE** Profile PSE25KSHSS	$1845	75	⌃	⊗	❶	⊗	63	16.1	70	36	33
$	10	**GE** GSE25ESHSS	$1300	74	⊗	⊗	❶	❶	64	16.5	70	36	32
✓	11	**Whirlpool** WRS975SIDM	$1760	74	⌃	⊗	⌃	⌃	53	18.7	69	36	34
	12	**KitchenAid** KRSF505ESS	$2250	74	⌃	⌃	⌃	⌃	53	18.7	69	36	34
✓	13	**GE** GSE22ESHSS	$1275	74	⊗	⌃	❶	❶	54	14.4	68	34	33
✓	14	**Kenmore** 51813	$1100	72	⌃	⊗	⌃	❶	61	16.1	66	33	33
✓	15	**Whirlpool** WRS586FIEM	$1530	72	⌃	⊗	⌃	❶	66	18.9	69	36	33
✓	16	**GE** GSS20ESHSS	$1575	72	⊗	⌃	❶	❶	58	13.0	68	32	32
✓	17	**Samsung** RH29H9000SR	$2000	72	⌃	⊗	⊗	⌃	73	21.2	69	36	36

	Rank	Brand & Model	Price	Score	Temperature Performance	Energy Efficiency	Noise	Ease of Use	Exterior Height (in.)	Exterior Width (in.)	Exterior Depth (in.)	Bottom-Freezer	Side-by-Side	French-Door Style	Total Usable Capacity (cu. ft.)
		BUILT-INS													
✓	1	**Miele** Master-Cool KF1903SF	$8600	81	Excellent	Very Good	Excellent	Very Good	83	36	25	•			14.1
✓	2	**KitchenAid** KBFN502ESS	$9000	80	Excellent	Very Good	Excellent	Good	83	42	26	•		•	17.0
✓	3	**Jenn-Air** JF42NXFXDE	$8500	80	Excellent	Very Good	Excellent	Good	83	42	26	•		•	17.0
✓	4	**Thermador** Freedom Collection T36BB820SS	$7400	80	Excellent	Very Good	Excellent	Very Good	84	36	25	•			14.3
✓	5	**KitchenAid** KBBR306ESS	$8200	80	Excellent	Very Good	Excellent	Very Good	83	36	26	•			14.9
✓	6	**Jenn-Air** JB36NXFXRE	$7400	80	Excellent	Very Good	Excellent	Very Good	83	36	26	•			14.9
	7	**Bosch** Integra 800 Series B36BT830NS	$7500	78	Excellent	Good	Excellent	Very Good	84	36	25			○	13.8
	8	**Thermador** Freedom Collection T36BT810NS	$8000	78	Excellent	Good	Excellent	Very Good	84	36	25			•	13.8
	9	**Miele** Master-Cool KF1803SF	$8100	77	Excellent	Very Good	Excellent	Very Good	83	30	25	•			11.4
	10	**Samsung** RS27FDBTNSR	$6570	76	Very Good	Excellent	Very Good	Very Good	84	48	26		•		20.3
	11	**Miele** KF1901Vi	$7200	76	Excellent	Good	Excellent	Very Good	83	36	24	•			14.0
	12	**Liebherr** CS2060	$5000	75	Excellent	Very Good	Excellent	Good	80	36	25	•			13.9
	13	**LG** LSSB2791[ST]	$8500	73	Excellent	Very Good	Excellent	Very Good	84	42	26		•		17.0
	14	**Liebherr** CS2062	$5300	73	Very Good	Very Good	Excellent	Good	81	36	25	•		•	13.7
	15	**Thermador** Freedom Collection T30BB820SS	$7000	73	Very Good	Good	Excellent	Very Good	84	30	25	•			12.2
	16	**Bosch** Integra B30BB830SS	$6500	73	Very Good	Good	Excellent	Very Good	84	30	25	•			12.2
	17	**GE** Monogram ZIPP360NHSS	$8500	72	Excellent	Good	Good	Very Good	84	36	26	•		•	14.0

RATINGS KEY ⊘ POOR ⊙ FAIR ① GOOD ⌃ VERY GOOD ⌃⌃ EXCELLENT

$ CR BEST BUY These models offer the best combination of performance and price. All are recommended.
✓ RECOMMENDED These are high-performing models that stand out.

Recommended	Rank	Brand & Model	Price	Score	Temperature Performance	Energy Efficiency	Noise	Ease of Use	Exterior Height (in.)	Exterior Width (in.)	Exterior Depth (in.)	Bottom-Freezer	Side-by-Side	French-Door Style	Total Usable Capacity (cu. ft.)
		BUILT-INS (Continued)													
	18	**Viking** VCBB5363ERSS	$9050	72	⌃⌃	⌃	!	⌃	83	35	24	•			15.3
	19	**Sub-Zero** BI-42UFD/S	$9800	72	⌃	⌃⌃	⌃	⌃	83	42	26	•		•	17.4
	20	**Viking** VCSB5423SS	$10160	70	⌃	⌃	⌃	⌃	83	42	26		○		18.3
	21	**Dacor** Discovery DYF36BFTSR	$8000	69	⌃⌃	!	⌃	⌃	84	36	26	•			15.8
	22	**KitchenAid** KBFN406ESS	$8500	69	⌃	⌃	⌃⌃	!	83	36	26	○		•	14.5
	23	**Jenn-Air** JF36NXFXDE	$8000	69	⌃	⌃	⌃⌃	!	83	36	26	•		•	14.5
	24	**Sub-Zero** BI42SIDS/PH	$9800	69	⌃	⌃	⌃	⌃	84	42	26		○		16.4
	25	**GE** Monogram ZIC30GNZII	$7050	67	⌃	⌃	!	⌃	80	30	24	•			11.5
	26	**Sub-Zero** IT36CI	$7600	67	⌃	⌃	⌃⌃	⌣	83	36	25	•			15.1
	27	**Liebherr** HCB1560	$5600	67	⌃	!	⌃⌃	!	80	30	24	•			10.9

Guide to Ratings

Score is based primarily on temperature performance and energy efficiency. Noise and ease of use are also considered. The displayed score is out of a total of 100 points. **Temperature Performance** measures the accuracy of initial temperature settings along with performance at different room temperatures, including high heat, and how uniformly each maintained temperatures in the refrigerator and freezer. **Energy Efficiency** is energy consumption per cubic foot of measured usable storage space. Noise is with compressors running. **Ease of Use** assesses features and design including layout, controls, and lighting. **Energy Cost/Yr. ($)** is the estimated cost in dollars, based on the current year's average national electricity rate. Your cost will vary depending on the rate for electricity in your area. **Total Usable Capacity (cu. ft.)** is our measurement of total usable interior space. **Fridge/Freezer Usable Capacity (cu. ft.)** is our measurement of usable refrigerator/freezer space. **Exterior Height, Width, and Depth** are without handle, rounded up to the nearest inch (37-inch-wide freestanding models fit in 36-inch openings). Under Brand & Model, bracketed letters or numbers are color codes. **Price** is approximate retail.

Most & Least Reliable

Percentage likely to break by fifth year of ownership.

BOTTOM-FREEZERS
with icemaker

LG	23%
Kenmore	30%
GE	34%
Whirlpool	50%

TOP-FREEZERS
with icemaker

Maytag	14%
Frigidaire	14%
Whirlpool	20%
Kenmore	23%
GE	27%

TOP-FREEZERS
without icemaker

Frigidaire	13%
Kenmore	14%
GE	15%
Whirlpool	15%

SIDE-BY-SIDE
with icemaker

Frigidaire	32%
Kenmore	32%
Whirlpool	34%
Samsung	37%
GE	38%
KitchenAid	40%

FRENCH-DOOR
with icemaker

Kenmore	32%
GE	33%
LG	34%
Samsung	35%
Maytag	40%
KitchenAid	45%
Whirlpool	47%

The conclusions in this chart are based on our failure-rate estimates for refrigerators by the fifth year of ownership. Our data are gathered from 46,405 subscribers who purchased a new refrigerator between 2010 and 2016 not covered by a service contract. Differences of fewer than 8 percentage points aren't meaningful. Models within a brand may vary, and changes in design or manufacturer might affect future reliability.

Source 2016 Winter Product Reliability Survey, Consumer Reports National Research Center.

Smartphones

Smartphones are great for texting, email, and social networking, and they can play music, shoot photos and video, and direct you via GPS navigation. Many can access a host of apps, from multimedia to games and more.

What to Look For
■ The phone's operating system, which dictates its features and capabilities. That can vary by brand.
■ How many apps are available and what they cost.
■ A display large enough for viewing Web pages, maps, and videos but not so big that it makes the phone difficult to handle comfortably.

What to Skip
■ Phone insurance and extended warranties, which are not worth it when you weigh cost, high deductibles, and low chance of using them.

What You'll Pay
The two-year contract price with subsidy is largely a thing of the past. You can either pay full retail up front (often $500 or more) or make installment payments over time, generally about $25 per month for two years.

BUYING ADVICE
Make sure you can read the phone's display in bright sunlight, especially for texting and Web surfing.

For more buying advice, go to ConsumerReports.org/cellphones.

All tested models in performance order.

Recommended	Rank	Brand & Model	Price	Score	Ease of Use	Messaging	Web Browsing	Display Quality	Voice Quality	Phoning	Battery Life	Camera: Image Quality	Camera: Video Quality	Portability	Display Diagonal Size (in.)	Operating System
✓	1	**Samsung** Galaxy S7	$650	80	⌃⌃	⌃⌃	⌃⌃	⌃⌃	I	⌃⌃	⌃⌃	⌃⌃	⌃	⌃	5.1	A
✓	2	**Samsung** Galaxy S7 edge	$750	79	⌃⌃	⌃⌃	⌃⌃	⌃⌃	I	⌃	⌃⌃	⌃⌃	⌃	⌃	5.5	A
✓	3	**Samsung** Galaxy S 5	$520	79	⌃⌃	⌃⌃	⌃⌃	⌃⌃	I	⌃	⌃⌃	⌃⌃	⌃	⌃	5.1	A
✓	4	**LG** G5	$500	78	⌃⌃	⌃⌃	⌃⌃	⌃⌃	I	⌃	⌃⌃	⌃	I	⌃	5.3	A

Recommended	Rank	Brand & Model	Price	Score	Ease of Use	Messaging	Web Browsing	Display Quality	Voice Quality	Phoning	Battery Life	Camera: Image Quality	Camera: Video Quality	Portability	Display Diagonal Size (in.)	Operating System
✓	5	**LG** G4	$360	78	⌃⌃	⌃⌃	⌃⌃	⌃	❗	⌃	⌃	⌃	❗	⌃	5.5	A
✓	6	**Samsung** Galaxy S6 active	$695	78	⌃	⌃	⌃	⌃	❗	⌃	⌃⌃	❗	⌃	⌃	5.1	A
✓	7	**Apple** iPhone 6s	$650	77	⌃⌃	⌃	⌃	⌃⌃	❗	⌃	❗	⌃	⌃	⌃	4.7	iOS
✓	8	**Apple** iPhone 6	$550	77	⌃	⌃	⌃	⌃	❗	⌃	⌃	⌃	⌃	⌃	4.7	iOS
✓	9	**Samsung** Galaxy S6	$575	77	⌃	⌃	⌃	⌃	❗	⌃⌃	⌃	❗	⌃	⌃	5.1	A
✓	10	**Samsung** Galaxy S6 edge	$500	77	⌃	⌃	⌃	⌃	❗	⌃⌃	⌃	❗	⌃	⌃	5.1	A
✓	11	**HTC** 10	$625	77	⌃	⌃	⌃	⌃	❗	⌃	⌃	⌃	⌃	⌃	5.2	A
✓	12	**Nexus** 5X	$350	77	⌃	⌃	⌃	⌃	❗	⌃	⌃	⌃⌃	⌃	⌃	5.2	A
✓	13	**HTC** One A9	$410	76	⌃⌃	⌃	⌃	⌃	❗	⌃	⌃	⌃	❗	⌃	5.0	A
✓	14	**Samsung** Galaxy Note5	$700	75	⌃	⌃	⌃	⌃	❗	⌃	⌃	⌃	❗	❗	5.7	A
✓	15	**LG** V10	$600	75	⌃	⌃	⌃	⌃⌃	❗	❗	⌃	⌃⌃	⌃	⌄	5.7	A
✓	16	**Motorola** Moto X Pure Edition	$300	74	⌃	⌃⌃	⌃	⌃	❗	⌃	⌃	⌃	❗	❗	5.7	A
✓	17	**Motorola** Moto Z Droid Force	$720	74	⌃	⌃	⌃	⌃	❗	⌃	⌃	⌃⌃	❗	❗	5.5	A
✓	18	**Motorola** Droid Turbo 2	$530	74	⌃	⌃	⌃	⌃	❗	❗	⌃	⌃⌃	❗	❗	5.4	A
✓	19	**Apple** iPhone 6s Plus	$750	73	⌃	⌃	⌃	⌃	❗	❗	⌃	⌃	❗	⌄	5.5	iOS
✓	20	**Apple** iPhone 6 Plus	$650	73	⌃	⌃	⌃	⌃	❗	❗	⌃	⌃	❗	⌄	5.5	iOS
✓	21	**OnePlus** 3	$400	73	⌃	⌃⌃	⌃	⌃	❗	⌃	⌃	⌃	❗	⌃	5.5	A

Recommended	Rank	Brand & Model	Price	Score	Ease of Use	Messaging	Web Browsing	Display Quality	Voice Quality	Phoning	Battery Life	Camera: Image Quality	Camera: Video Quality	Portability	Display Diagonal Size (in.)	Operating System
✓	22	**Nexus** 6P	$500	73	Very Good	Excellent	Excellent	Excellent	Good	Good	Excellent	Excellent	Good	Fair	5.7	A
✓	23	**BlackBerry** Priv	$640	73	Very Good	Excellent	Excellent	Excellent	Good	Good	Excellent	Very Good	Good	Fair	5.4	A
✓	24	**Apple** iPhone SE	$400	72	Excellent	Excellent	Excellent	Excellent	Good	Good	Excellent	Excellent	Good	Excellent	4.0	iOS
✓	25	**Motorola** Droid Maxx 2	$385	72	Excellent	Very Good	Excellent	Excellent	Fair	Excellent	Excellent	Excellent	Excellent	Good	5.5	A
✓	26	**Sony** Xperia X Performance	$650	72	Excellent	Very Good	Very Good	Excellent	Very Good	Very Good	Very Good	Excellent	Excellent	Very Good	5.0	A
✓	27	**Microsoft** Lumia 950	$300	71	Very Good	Very Good	Very Good	Excellent	Good	Very Good	Good	Excellent	Excellent	Excellent	5.2	W10 Mobile
✓	28	**LG** Escape2	$200	71	Excellent	Very Good	Excellent	Excellent	Good	Excellent	Excellent	Good	Good	Excellent	4.7	A
✓	29	**Motorola** G4 Plus	$300	71	Very Good	Very Good	Excellent	Excellent	Good	Very Good	Very Good	Very Good	Very Good	Good	5.5	A
	30	**Samsung** Galaxy S7 active	$800	70	Very Good	Excellent	Excellent	Excellent	Good	Very Good	Excellent	Excellent	Excellent	Good	5.1	A
	31	**Sony** Xperia XA Ultra	$330	70	Very Good	Very Good	Excellent	Excellent	Good	Good	Very Good	Excellent	Very Good	Fair	6.0	A
	32	**LG** G Vista 2	$300	70	Very Good	Very Good	Excellent	Excellent	Good	Good	Excellent	Very Good	Good	Fair	5.7	A
	33	**OnePlus** X	$200	70	Excellent	Very Good	Excellent	Excellent	Very Good	Very Good	Very Good	Very Good	Fair	Very Good	5.0	A
	34	**Asus** ZenFone 2	$250	69	Excellent	Very Good	Very Good	Excellent	Good	Very Good	Good	Good	Good	Good	5.5	A
	35	**Blu** Vivo 5	$200	69	Very Good	Very Good	Excellent	Excellent	Good	Very Good	Very Good	Good	Good	Good	5.5	A
	36	**LG** G Stylo	$-3	69	Very Good	Excellent	Excellent	Very Good	Fair	Good	Very Good	Good	Good	Fair	5.7	A
	37	**Huawei** P8 Lite	$200	69	Very Good	Excellent	Excellent	Excellent	Good	Very Good	Very Good	Good	Good	Very Good	5.0	A
	38	**Samsung** Galaxy Grand Prime	$-3	68	Very Good	Very Good	Very Good	Excellent	Good	Excellent	Very Good	Good	Good	Very Good	5.0	A

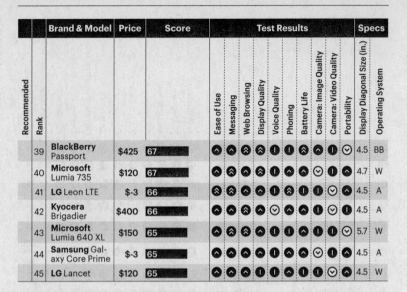

Recommended	Rank	Brand & Model	Price	Score	Ease of Use	Messaging	Web Browsing	Display Quality	Voice Quality	Phoning	Battery Life	Camera: Image Quality	Camera: Video Quality	Portability	Display Diagonal Size (in.)	Operating System
	39	**BlackBerry** Passport	$425	67	Very Good	Very Good	Excellent	Excellent	Good	Good	Excellent	Very Good	Good	Fair	4.5	BB
	40	**Microsoft** Lumia 735	$120	67	Very Good	Excellent	Very Good	Excellent	Good	Good	Good	Fair	Good	Very Good	4.7	W
	41	**LG** Leon LTE	$-3	66	Excellent	Excellent	Very Good	Very Good	Good	Excellent	Good	Good	Fair	Very Good	4.5	A
	42	**Kyocera** Brigadier	$400	66	Very Good	Very Good	Excellent	Very Good	Fair	Very Good	Good	Good	Fair	Good	4.5	A
	43	**Microsoft** Lumia 640 XL	$150	65	Very Good	Excellent	Excellent	Very Good	Good	Good	Very Good	Good	Good	Fair	5.7	W
	44	**Samsung** Galaxy Core Prime	$-3	65	Very Good	Very Good	Very Good	Good	Good	Very Good	Fair	Good	Good	Very Good	4.5	A
	45	**LG** Lancet	$120	65	Very Good	Very Good	Very Good	Good	Good	Very Good	Good	Good	Fair	Very Good	4.5	W

Guide to the Ratings

Score is based on test results. The displayed score is out of a total of 100 points. **Ease of Use** indicates how easy it is to access features and modes, such as phoning, messaging, Web browsing, the camera, the music player, applications, one-handed operation, and other multimedia content. **Messaging** assesses keyboard ergonomics, email readability, attachment capabilities, and text-messaging features. **Web Browsing** assesses browser capabilities. **Display Quality** represents overall picture quality, contrast in normal and bright lighting, and color accuracy. **Voice Quality** incorporates listening and talking in noisy and quiet settings using live phone calls. **Phoning** considers the step-saving functions for making and receiving calls, including hands-free capabilities such as voice command and Bluetooth, speed dialing, ringer controls, call timers, and more. We also evaluated keypad readability in different lighting. **Battery Life** was tested under nominal cell network signals and considers tasks that involve voice, data, standby, and other factors. **Camera: Image Quality** evaluates resolution, dynamic range, color accuracy, and visual noise. **Camera: Video Quality** judges recorded video images shot at the highest quality setting available. **Portability** represents our judgment based on the best combination of size and weight. **Display Diagonal Size (in.)** is to the nearest tenth of an inch. Under **Operating System:** And.=Android, BB=BlackBerry, iOS=iOS, WP=Windows Phone. In Price, **$-3** means discontinued with related/similar models on others providers, other than the major four (which is not shown on chart). **Price** is the lowest approximate retail cost for the smallest capacity available when purchased without a contract or agreement.

Snow Blowers

Bigger, better, and friendlier are the terms that best describe the latest snow blowers, also called snow throwers. The new models feature easier steering and more convenient chute controls.

What to Look For

■ A wide (28-inch-plus) two-stage gasoline snow blower, with driven wheels and a wider cut for heavier snow.
■ A compact two-stage or single-stage gas model for lighter-duty work.
■ A plug-in electric model solely for small areas and decks with very light snowfall.

What to Skip

■ Any single-stage model for gravel driveways; the auger that scoops snow and propels the machine will also pick up and hurl the gravel.

What You'll Pay

Figure on $900 to $1,600 for large two-stage models, $650 to $800 for smaller models; $500 to $700 for single-stage gas models.

BUYING ADVICE

Be sure you're comfortable with the height of the handle and with the chute adjustment controls.

For more buying advice, go to ConsumerReports.org/snowblowers.

All tested models in performance order.

Recommended	Rank	Brand & Model	Price	Score	Width (in.)	Removal speed	Plow pile removal	Throwing distance	Surface cleaning	Handling	Noise	Controls	Engine size	Electric start	Multiple speeds
								Test Results					Specs		
		TWO-STAGE GAS													
✔	1	**Cub** Cadet 3X 30HD 31AH57SZ710	$1650	92	30	⌃	⌃	⌃	⌃	⌃	⌄	⌃	420cc	•	•
$	2	**Troy-Bilt** Vortex 2890 31AH55Q	$1300	90	28	⌃	⌃	⌃	⌃	⌃	⌄	⌃	357cc	•	•
✔	3	**Craftsman** 88874	$1400	89	28	⌃	⌃	⌃	⌃	⌃	⌄	⌃	357cc	•	•
✔	4	**Cub** Cadet 930SWE 31AH95SU	$1600	89	30	⌃	⌃	⌃	⌃	⌃	⌄	⌃	357cc	•	•
✔	5	**Ariens** 921032	$1300	88	30	⌃	⌃	⌃	⌃	⌃	⌄	⌃	291cc	•	•
✔	6	**Craftsman** 88396	$1200	88	30	⌃	⌃	⌃	⌃	⌃	⌄	⌃	357cc	•	•

Recommended	Rank	Brand & Model	Price	Score	Width (in.)	Removal speed	Plow pile removal	Throwing distance	Surface cleaning	Handling	Noise	Controls	Engine size	Electric start	Multiple speeds
TWO-STAGE GAS (Continued)															
$	7	**Ariens** AX254 921030	$1000	87	28	⇑	⇑	⇑	↑	⇑	↓	⇑	254cc	•	•
✓	8	**Troy-Bilt** Storm 3090XP 31AH55Q	$1100	87	30	⇑	⇑	↑	↑	↑	↓	⇑	357cc	•	•
$	9	**Troy-Bilt** Storm 2840 31AH64Q	$900	81	28	⇑	⇑	↑	↑	↑	↓	⇑	277cc	•	•
✓	10	**Craftsman** 88694	$900	80	26	⇑	↑	↑	↑	⇑	●	↑	208cc	•	•
COMPACT TWO-STAGE GAS															
$	1	**Troy-Bilt** Vortex 2490 31AH54Q	$1100	82	24	↑	⇑	↑	↑	⇑	↓	⇑	277cc	•	•
✓	2	**Craftsman** 88870	$1200	79	24	↑	⇑	↑	↑	⇑	↓	⇑	277cc	•	•
✓	3	**Cub** Cadet 2X 24HP 31AM53SR710	$900	78	24	↑	⇑	↑	⇑	⇑	↓	⇑	208cc	•	•
$	4	**Craftsman** 88173	$680	73	24	↑	⇑	●	●	↑	●	↑	208cc	•	•
✓	5	**Toro** Power Max 724 OE 37779	$800	69	24	↑	⇑	↑	●	●	●	↑	205cc	•	•
✓	6	**Ariens** 920021	$800	68	24	●	⇑	↑	↑	↑	↓	↑	208cc	•	•
$	7	**Sno-Tek** 920402	$600	66	24	●	↑	↑	↑	↑	↓	↑	208cc	•	•
SINGLE-STAGE GAS															
$	1	**Toro** Power Clear 721E	$570	71	21	↑	⇑	●	↑	⇑	↓	●	212cc	•	
✓	2	**Toro** Power Clear 621 38458	$650	70	21	↑	↑	●	↑	⇑	↓	↑	163cc		
✓	3	**Cub** Cadet 221 LHP 31AM2T6D	$550	67	21	●	↑	–	↑	⇑	↓	⇑	208cc	•	
✓	4	**Honda** HS 720AS	$700	64	20	↑	↑	●	⇑	↑	↓	●	187cc		

Guide to the Ratings

Score is based mainly on removal speed, throwing distance, surface cleaning, controls, and handling. Width (in.) is the clearing width, or swath, in inches. **Removal Speed** indicates how quickly models could remove snow without laboring. **Plow Pile Removal** is how fast the snow thrower can remove a simulated pile of snow left by a plow at the end of a driveway. **Throwing Distance** is how far snow was dispersed straight ahead, left, and right with the discharge chute set for maximum distance. **Surface Cleaning** indicates how much snow was left on our blacktop surface after clearing with the skid shoes and/or scraper set for best clearing. **Handling** denotes ease of pushing, pulling, and steering. **Noise** measures sound pressure at the operator's ear. Hearing protection is strongly advised for a rating of less than good. **Controls** include ease of discharge chute adjustment, handle height and comfort, engine controls, and speed selection. **Price** is approximate retail.

Soundbars

A soundbar speaker system is an easy way to improve your TV's sound. Most are 2.1-channel systems that consist of a bar-shaped enclosure housing an array of speakers, plus a separate wireless subwoofer.

What to Look For
■ Enough audio and video inputs of the right type if you want to connect components to the sound bar rather than the TV.
■ A powered sound bar with amplification if you won't use a receiver or an amplifier.
■ Bluetooth for streaming music from a phone or tablet.

■ A bar that's an appropriate width for your TV.

What to Skip
■ 3D pass-through if you don't have a 3D set or plan to use that feature.

What You'll Pay
Sound bar prices vary widely, from about $100 to $750. Some can cost as much as $2,000.

BUYING ADVICE

Because TVs sit on the sound bars, be sure the bases are rated to support the weight of your TV set.

For more buying advice, go to ConsumerReports.org/theater.

All tested models in performance order.

Recommended	Rank	Brand & Model	Price	Score	Sound Quality	Ease of Use	Versatility	Number of Channels	Number of Speakers Supplied	Active Subwoofer	Wireless Subwoofer
✓	1	**Sonos** Playbar	$700	61	⌃	⌃	⌄	5.1	1	NA	Opt.
✓	2	**Denon** HEOS HomeCinema	$600	58	❶	⌃	⌄	2.1	1.1	•	•
✓	3	**Sony** HT-ST7	$1,000	57	⌃	⌃	⌄	7.1	1.1	•	•
✓	4	**Yamaha** YSP-2500	$1,000	56	❶	⌃	❶	7.1	1.1	•	•
✓	5	**Samsung** HW-J6500	$480	56	❶	❶	❶	6.1	1.1	•	•
✓	6	**Samsung** HW-J7500	$550	56	❶	❶	❶	8.1	1.1	•	•

Test Results columns: Sound Quality, Ease of Use, Versatility, Number of Channels, Number of Speakers Supplied. *Specs* columns: Active Subwoofer, Wireless Subwoofer.

RATINGS KEY ⊗ POOR ⌄ FAIR ❶ GOOD ⌃ VERY GOOD ⊛ EXCELLENT
Ⓢ **CR BEST BUY** These models offer the best combination of performance and price. All are recommended.
✓ **RECOMMENDED** These are high-performing models that stand out.

Recommended	Rank	Brand & Model	Price	Score	Sound Quality	Ease of Use	Versatility	Number of Channels	Number of Speakers Supplied	Active Subwoofer	Wireless Subwoofer
✓	7	**Yamaha** SRT-1500	$600	56	●	●	⌄	8.1	1		
	8	**LG** SH7B	$350	53	●	●	⌄	4.1	1.1	•	•
	9	**Samsung** HW-K650	$420	53	●	●	●	5.1	1.1	•	•
	10	**Klipsch** Reference R-4B	$400	52	●	●	⌄	2.1	1.1	•	
	11	**Klipsch** Reference R-10	$500	52	●	●	⌄	2.1	1.1	•	•
	12	**Sony** HT-XT1	$200	51	●	⌃	⌄	2	1	NA	
	13	**LG** LAS751M	$300	50	●	●	⌄	4.1	1.1	•	•
	14	**JBL** Cinema Base	$150	50	●	●	⌄	2	1	NA	
	15	**Vizio** SB4051	$350	50	●	⌄	●	5.1	3.1	•	•
	16	**Bose** Solo 15 Series II	$450	50	●	●	⌄	3	1	NA	
	17	**Yamaha** YSP-1600	$500	50	●	●	⌄	8.1	1	NA	
	18	**Vizio** SB3821-C6	$160	49	●	⌄	⌄	2.1	1.1	•	•
	19	**Sony** HT-CT780	$400	49	●	⌃	⌄	2.1	1.1	•	•
	20	**Philips** HTL3150B/37	$200	49	●	●	⌄	3.1	1.1	•	•
	21	**Sony** HT-CT380	$265	49	●	⌃	⌄	2.1	1.1	•	•
	22	**Yamaha** YAS-105	$250	48	●	⌃	⌄	2.1	1	NA	
	23	**ZVOX** SoundBase 570	$300	48	●	●	⌄	2	1	NA	
	24	**ZVOX** SoundBase 670	$370	48	●	●	⌄	2	1	NA	
	25	**Vizio** SB3851-D0	$300	47	●	⌄	●	5.1	3.1	•	•
	26	**Sony** HT-ST5	$800	47	●	⌃	⌄	7.1	1.1	•	•
	27	**JBL** Cinema SB 400	$500	47	●	●	⌄	2.1	1.1	•	•
	28	**Bose** Solo 5 TV Sound System	$250	47	●	●	⌄	2	1	NA	
	29	**Bose** CineMate 15	$600	46	●	⌄	⌄	2.1	1.1	•	

Guide to the Ratings

Score is based mainly on sound quality; ease of use and versatility are also factored in. The displayed score is out of a total of 100 points. **Sound Quality** represents tonal accuracy and ability to reproduce fine sonic detail. **Ease of Use** refers to setup and use of controls. **Versatility** is based on useful features. **Number of Channels** refers to audio signal channels supplied by the system. **Number of Speakers Supplied** are those that come with the system. **Price** is approximate retail.

Recommended	Rank	Brand & Model	Price	Score	Sound Quality	Ease of Use	Versatility	Number of Channels	Number of Speakers Supplied	Active Subwoofer	Wireless Subwoofer
	30	**Samsung** HW-K360	$150	45	Good	Good	Fair	4.1	1.1	•	•
	31	**Vizio** SS2521	$170	45	Good	Fair	Fair	2	1	NA	
	32	**LG** SH4	$200	45	Good	Good	Fair	2.1	1.1	•	•
	33	**JBL** Boost TV	$200	44	Good	Good	Excellent	2	1	NA	
	34	**LG** LAP250H	$230	44	Good	Good	Fair	2	1	NA	
	35	**Definitive** Technology W Studio Micro Sound Bar	$800	42	Good	Good	Excellent	3.1	1.1	•	•
	36	**Cambridge** Audio TV5	$400	42	Good	Fair	Excellent	2	1	NA	
	37	**LG** LAS950M	$800	41	Good	Good	Fair	7.1	1.1	•	•
	38	**Polk** Audio Omni SB1 Plus	$700	41	Good	Fair	Excellent	5.1	1.1	•	•
	39	**Harman** Kardon SB26	$600	40	Good	Fair	Fair	2.1	1.1	•	•
	40	**Sony** HT-NT5	$800	40	Fair	Very Good	Fair	4.1	1.1	•	•
	41	**Sony** HT-NT3	$800	40	Fair	Very Good	Fair	2.1	1.1	•	•
	42	**Polk** Audio MagniFi	$300	38	Fair	Very Good	Excellent	3.1	1.1	•	•
	43	**Yamaha** YAS-203	$400	37	Fair	Good	Excellent	2.1	1.1	•	•
	44	**JBL** Cinema SB350	$400	37	Fair	Good	Fair	2.1	1.1	•	•
	45	**Definitive** Technology W Studio Sound Bar	$1,000	37	Fair	Fair	Fair	5.1	1.1	•	•
	46	**Pyle** Wave Base (PSBV600BT)	$100	36	Fair	Fair	Excellent	2	1	NA	
	47	**ZVOX** SoundBar SB400	$500	20	Poor	Good	Excellent	3	1	NA	

RATINGS KEY ⊝ POOR ⊙ FAIR ❶ GOOD ⌃ VERY GOOD ✷ EXCELLENT

$ CR BEST BUY These models offer the best combination of performance and price. All are recommended.

⊘ **RECOMMENDED** These are high-performing models that stand out.

Streaming Media Players

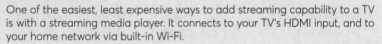

One of the easiest, least expensive ways to add streaming capability to a TV is with a streaming media player. It connects to your TV's HDMI input, and to your home network via built-in Wi-Fi.

What to Look For

- A player that has all of the streaming services you want right out of the box. More services may be added later, but don't assume that they will—or that the one you want will be among them.
- A stick-style player that plugs directly into a TV's HDMI port if you don't want to deal with another set-top box.
- A Roku if you want the widest selection of content channels. An Apple TV if you have a lot of content stored in iTunes, on a Mac computer, or on Apple's iCloud. An Amazon Fire TV player if you want to use Amazon's Alexa voice service and if you have an Amazon Prime membership.

What to Skip

- A pricier model with tons of content if all you really want is Netflix.

What You'll Pay

From $35 to $100 for most models.

BUYING ADVICE

With some models, you can mirror the screen of a smartphone or tablet on your TV so that you can enjoy the content on a big screen.

For more buying advice, go to ConsumerReports.org/streamingmediaplayers.

All tested models in performance order.

Rec.	Rank	Brand & Model	Price	Score	Picture Quality	Features	Everyday Use	Connectivity	First Time Setup	App or Channel Store	Streaming Services
✅	1	**Roku** 4	$130	81	Excellent	Excellent	Very Good	Excellent	Good	Channel Store	N, A, V, H, C, M-Go, HBO, GP and TV, SHO, CBS All Access, ST
✅	2	**Roku** 3 (2nd gen)	$100	76	Excellent	Excellent	Very Good	Very Good	Fair	Channel Store	N, A, V, H, B, C, M-Go, HBO, HBO Now, SHO, CBS All Access, ST
💲	3	**Roku** 2 (2nd gen)	$70	72	Excellent	Excellent	Very Good	Very Good	Fair	Channel Store	N, A, V, H, B, C, M-Go, HBO, SHO, CBS All Access, ST
✅	4	**Amazon** Fire TV (2nd Gen)	$100	71	Excellent	Excellent	Very Good	Good	Good	Amazon Apps	N, A, H, HBO Go, SHO, ST
✅	5	**Amazon** Fire TV Gaming Edition	$140	71	Excellent	Excellent	Very Good	Very Good	Good	Amazon Apps	N, A, H, HBO
💲	6	**Roku** 1	$50	69	Excellent	Excellent	Very Good	Good	Fair	Channel Store	N, A, V, H, B, C, M-Go, HBO, SHO, CBS All Access, ST
💲	7	**Google** Chromecast (2nd Gen)	$35	69	Excellent	Very Good	Very Good	Fair	Very Good	None	N, V, H, M-Go, HBO, SHO, CBS, ST
💲	8	**Roku** Streaming Stick (HDMI Version)	$40	68	Excellent	Excellent	Good	Good	Good	Channel Store	N, A, V, H, B, C, M-Go, HBO, SHO, CBS All Access, ST
✅	9	**NVIDIA** Shield	$175	68	Excellent	Excellent	Good	Very Good	Good	Google Play Store	N, H, C, HBO, CBS All Access, SHO, ST (and any app that supports Google Cast like Vudu, M-Go, etc.)
✅	10	**Apple** TV (64 GB) (4th Gen)	$200	67	Excellent	Very Good	Very Good	Good	Good	App Store	N, H, HBO, SHO, CBS, iTunes
💲	11	**Amazon** Fire TV Stick w/ Voice Remote	$50	66	Excellent	Very Good	Very Good	Fair	Very Good	Amazon Apps	N, A, H, HBO, SHO, ST
💲	12	**Amazon** Fire TV Stick	$40	65	Excellent	Very Good	Good	Fair	Very Good	Amazon Apps	HBO, SHO, ST

RATINGS KEY ⊗ POOR ⊙ FAIR ❶ GOOD ⌃ VERY GOOD ⌃⌃ EXCELLENT
💲 CR BEST BUY These models offer the best combination of performance and price. All are recommended.
✅ RECOMMENDED These are high-performing models that stand out.

Rec.	Rank	Brand & Model	Price	Score	Picture Quality	Features	Everyday Use	Connectivity	First Time Setup	App or Channel Store	Streaming Services
$	13	**Google** Nexus Player	$50	63	⊗	∧	∧	⊙	❶	Google Play Store	N, H, HBO, MLB. TV, CBS All Access, SHO, ST (and any app that supports Google Cast like Vudu, C, M-Go, etc.)
$	14	**Apple** TV (3rd gen)	$70	61	⊗	∧	❶	❶	❶	None	N, H, HBO SHO, CBS, iTunes
	15	**Mohu** Channels	$100	60	⊗	❶	❶	❶	⊗	Google Play Store	N, V, H, B, C, M-Go, HBO, Google Play, SHO, ST, CBS All Access, Fox Now
	16	**Vudu** Spark	$25	36	⊗	⊗	❶	⊙	❶	None	V

Guide to the Ratings

Score is based mainly on the number of features and how easy the player is to use but also includes its picture quality performance. The displayed score is out of a total of 100 points. **Picture Quality** includes image clarity, color accuracy, and contrast of streaming video. **Features** reflects the presence or absence of features, including the number of streaming video services, other Internet services, and the ability to play media files. **Everyday Use** evaluates how easy it is to use on a normal basis. **Connectivity** is the amount and type of connections that will make the player more versatile. **First-Time Setup** evaluates how easy it is to set up the product out of the box. In features, under **Streaming Services,** A=Amazon Instant Video, B=Blockbuster, C=CinemaNow, GP=Google Play, H=Hulu, HBO=HBO Go, iTunes=iTunes Store, M-Go=M-Go, N=Netflix, SHO=Showtime Anytime, ST=Sling Television, V=Vudu. **Price** is approximate retail.

QUICK GUIDE

String trimmers

If you're environmentally conscious you might consider an electric string trimmer. But today's gas-powered string trimmers emit fewer pollutants than they used to. And cordless, battery-powered trimmers are now more powerful.

What to Look For

■ Handle a string trimmer in the store to check its balance. Its weight should feel evenly distributed from top to bottom or slightly heavier at the top. Be sure the controls work smoothly and are easy to reach.

■ Look for models with two cutting strings; they cut more quickly.

What to Skip

■ A feature we don't recommend is the split shaft.

With these models, the shaft comes apart to accept a leaf blower, hedge trimmer, edging blade, or other yard tools. But most add-on tools haven't been very effective in our tests.

What You'll Pay

Electric corded models cost the least, starting at $40 and up to about $90. Battery models start at $65, but the top-rated EGO ST1505-S retails for $180. Gas models start at $75, and the higher end models top out at $290.

BUYING ADVICE

Purchase a can of pre-mixed ethanol-free fuel where you purchase your gas trimmer rather than mixing it yourself.

For more buying advice, go to ConsumerReports.org/ string-trimmers

All tested models in performance, within types.

Rec.	Rank	Brand & Model	Price	Score	Trimming	Edging	Tall Grass and Weeds	Handling	Ease of Use	Weight (lb.)	Engine Size
		Test Results								**Specs**	
		ELECTRIC CORDED									
✓	1	**Black+Decker** GH3000	$70	72	⌃	⌃	⌃	⌃	⌃	6.9	7.5-amp
✓	2	**GreenWorks** 21142	$90	71	⌃⌃	⌃	⌃⌃	⌃	⌃	9.7	10-amp
✓	3	**Stihl** FSE 60	$110	70	⌃	⌃	⌃	⌃⌃	⌃	8.7	5.3-amp

[1] Fixed-line head; other models have automatic or bump-feed.

Rec.	Rank	Brand & Model	Price	Score	Trimming	Edging	Tall Grass and Weeds	Handling	Ease of Use	Weight (lb.)	Engine Size
BATTERY											
CR Best Buy	1	**EGO** ST1501-S	$180	80	Excellent	Excellent	Very Good	Excellent	Excellent	9.0	56-volt
Recommended	2	**Troy-Bilt** TB4200	$280	76	Excellent	Excellent	Very Good	Fair	Excellent	12.0	40-volt
CR Best Buy	3	**Ryobi** RY40220	$180	75	Excellent	Excellent	Very Good	Excellent	Very Good	11.5	40-volt
Recommended	4	**Stihl** FSA 65	$510	72	Excellent	Very Good	Very Good	Very Good	Very Good	8.1	36-volt
Recommended	5	**Toro** 51488	$190	70	Very Good	Excellent	Very Good	Very Good	Good	9.4	48-volt
GAS CURVED SHAFT											
CR Best Buy	1	**Stihl** FS 38	$130	83	Excellent	Excellent	Excellent	Excellent	Very Good	10.5	27-cc
Recommended	2	**Stihl** FS 40 C-E	$190	81	Excellent	Excellent	Excellent	Very Good	Very Good	11.0	27.2-cc
CR Best Buy	3	**Ryobi** RY252CS	$100	80	Excellent	Excellent	Excellent	Very Good	Very Good	11.4	25-cc
Recommended	4	**Echo** GT-225r	$160	79	Excellent	Very Good	Excellent	Very Good	Excellent	10.1	21.2-cc
Recommended	5	**Poulan** Pro PP25CFA	$110	78	Excellent	Very Good	Excellent	Very Good	Very Good	12.5	25-cc
Recommended	6	**Echo** GT-225	$160	77	Excellent	Very Good	Excellent	Very Good	Very Good	10.0	21.2-cc
CR Best Buy	7	**Bolens** BL110	$70	76	Excellent	Very Good	Excellent	Very Good	Good	10.2	25-cc
CR Best Buy	8	**Craftsman** 71102	$100	76	Excellent	Very Good	Very Good	Very Good	Very Good	11.2	25-cc
Recommended	9	**Hitachi** CG22EABSLP	$180	76	Very Good	Very Good	Very Good	Very Good	Very Good	9.7	22-cc
CR Best Buy	10	**Troy-Bilt** TB22 EC [1]	$100	75	Excellent	Excellent	Very Good	Very Good	Very Good	11.2	25-cc
GAS STRAIGHT SHAFT											
Recommended	1	**Echo** SRM-230	$290	82	Excellent	Excellent	Excellent	Very Good	Very Good	12.5	23-cc
CR Best Buy	2	**Troy-Bilt** TB2044 XP	$170	80	Excellent	Excellent	Very Good	Very Good	Very Good	13.0	27cc
Recommended	3	**Echo** SRM-225	$220	80	Excellent	Excellent	Excellent	Very Good	Very Good	12.0	21.2-cc
Recommended	4	**Snapper** S28BC	$170	79	Excellent	Excellent	Very Good	Very Good	Very Good	14.2	28-cc
Recommended	5	**Stihl** FS 56 RC-E	$240	78	Excellent	Excellent	Excellent	Very Good	Excellent	12.5	27.2-cc

[1] Fixed-line head; other models have automatic or bump-feed.

Rec.	Rank	Brand & Model	Price	Score	Test Results					Specs	
					Trimming	Edging	Tall Grass and Weeds	Handling	Ease of Use	Weight (lb.)	Engine Size
		GAS STRAIGHT SHAFT (Continued)									
✓	6	**Husqvarna** 322L	$240	77	●	●	●	●	●	10.6	22.5cc
✓	7	**Ryobi** RY34447	$200	77	●	●	●	●	●	13.2	30cc
✓	8	**Husqvarna** 128LD	$200	76	●	●	●	●	➊	13.6	28-cc
$	9	**Troy-Bilt** TB35 EC	$130	76	●	●	●	●	●	12.8	25cc
✓	10	**Craftsman** 71120	$170	75	●	●	●	●	●	13.0	27-cc
$	11	**Ryobi** RY253SS	$130	75	●	●	●	●	●	12.2	25-cc
$	12	**Troy-Bilt** TB32 EC	$130	75	●	●	●	●	●	12.5	25-cc

➊ Fixed-line head; other models have automatic or bump-feed.

Guide to the Ratings

Score is based mainly on trimming neatness, edging speed, how well the model cuts through tall grass and weeds, handling response and balance and ease of use. **Trimming** indicates how quickly and neatly models cut grass. **Edging** is how neatly and quickly models trimmed a vertical line along a walkway. **Tall Grass and Weeds** indicates cutting power in tall grass and weeds. **Handling** denotes responsiveness and balance. **Ease of Use** denotes ease of starting, feeding out more line, and accessing controls, along with handle comfort. **Price** is approximate retail.

Tablets

Lightweight and highly portable, tablets are made to be carried wherever you go. Most have 7- to 10-inch screens, but larger models are available as well.

What to Look For

■ A 10-inch screen for Web surfing, video, and gaming; a 7-inch screen for portability; or an 11- or 12-inch screen and detachable keyboard for work (but watch the weight!).
■ Excellent performance if you want to play more than simpler games.
■ The same operating system as your other devices if you want to sync across hardware.
■ A rich variety of apps authorized by the OS maker.

What to Skip

■ A 4G model, unless you need "everywhere access" and will pay extra for it.

What You'll Pay

At least $350 for a good 10-inch Android tablet with 16 gigabytes of memory and Wi-Fi-only access. An equivalent iPad costs $500. Smaller Android tablets that we recommend start at $200 or less.

BUYING ADVICE

Look for a compatible keyboard if you're planning to do a lot of typing.

For more buying advice, go to ConsumerReports.org/tablets.

All tested models in performance order.

Rec.	Rank	Brand & Model	Price	Score	Portability	Ease of Use	Display	Versatility	Battery Life (hr.)	Weight (lb.)	Operating System
		9-INCH-SCREEN AND LARGER TABLETS, WiFi-ONLY									
✓	1	**Apple** iPad Pro 9.7 (32GB)	$600	85	⌃⌃	⌃	⌃⌃	⌃	15.6	1	iOS 9.3
✓	2	**Samsung** Galaxy Tab S2 9.7 (32GB)	$500	82	⌃	⌃	⌃⌃	⌃⌃	9.6	0.8	And. 6
✓	3	**Apple** iPad Air 2 (64GB)	$450	81	⌃⌃	⌃	⌃⌃	⌃	13.3	1	iOS 8.3
✓	4	**Google** Pixel C 10.1 (32GB)	$500	81	⌃⌃	⌃	⌃⌃	⌃	15.2	1.1	And. 6
✓	5	**Apple** iPad Pro 12.9 (32GB)	$800	79	⌃	⌃⌃	⌃⌃	⌃	12.5	1.6	iOS 9.2

Rec.	Rank	Brand & Model	Price	Score	Portability	Ease of Use	Display	Versatility	Battery Life (hr.)	Weight (lb.)	Operating System
		9-INCH-SCREEN AND LARGER TABLETS, WiFi-ONLY (Continued)									
✓	6	**Lenovo** Yoga Tab 3 Pro (32GB)	$470	79	Very Good	Very Good	Excellent	Very Good	13.8	1.5	And. 5.1
✓	7	**Samsung** Galaxy Tab A 10.1 SM-T580 (16GB)	$300	78	Excellent	Very Good	Excellent	Very Good	15.8	1.1	And. 6
✓	8	**Microsoft** Surface 3 (64GB)	$500	76	Very Good	Very Good	Excellent	Very Good	10.2	1.4	Wind. 10
✓	9	**Huawei** MateBook (128GB)	$700	75	Very Good	Very Good	Very Good	Very Good	9.6	1.4	Wind. 10
✓	10	**Asus** Transformer Book T100CHI-C1-BK (64GB)	$350	74	Very Good	Very Good	Very Good	Very Good	10.8	1.3	Wind. 10
✓	11	**Microsoft** Surface Pro 4 (128GB, m3)	$900	74	Good	Very Good	Excellent	Very Good	9.1	1.7	Wind. 10
✓	12	**Microsoft** Surface Pro 3 (128GB, i5)	$900	74	Good	Very Good	Excellent	Very Good	10.1	1.8	Wind. 10
$	13	**Lenovo** Tab 2 A10-70 (16GB)	$180	74	Excellent	Very Good	Very Good	Very Good	14.5	1.2	And. 4.4
✓	14	**Samsung** Galaxy Tab A 9.7 SM-T550 (16GB)	$200	73	Excellent	Very Good	Very Good	Very Good	18.5	1	And. 5
	15	**Asus** Transformer Book T300CHI-F1-DB (128GB)	$700	71	Good	Very Good	Very Good	Very Good	7.2	1.6	Wind. 10
	16	**Samsung** Galaxy Tab E 9.6 (16GB)	$230	71	Excellent	Very Good	Very Good	Very Good	16.8	1.2	And. 5.1
	17	**Toshiba** DynaPad WT12PE-A64 (64GB)	$500	71	Good	Very Good	Very Good	Very Good	6.8	1.2	Wind. 10
	18	**Samsung** Galaxy Tab E Nook 9.6 (16GB)	$230	70	Excellent	Very Good	Very Good	Very Good	16.1	1.2	And. 5.1
	19	**Asus** ZenPad 10.0 Z300M (16GB)	$170	70	Very Good	Very Good	Very Good	Very Good	12.1	1	And. 6
	20	**Lenovo** Yoga Tab 3 10 (16GB)	$190	69	Excellent	Very Good	Very Good	Very Good	20.7	1.5	And. 5.1
	21	**Asus** ZenPad 10 Z300C-A1 (16GB)	$180	68	Very Good	Very Good	Very Good	Very Good	9.2	1.1	And. 5
	22	**Amazon** Fire HD 10 (16GB)	$230	67	Very Good	Very Good	Very Good	Good	9.4	1	Fire OS 5.1
	23	**Acer** Iconia Tab 10 A3-A30-18P1 (16GB)	$240	66	Good	Very Good	Very Good	Very Good	6.7	1.2	And. 5

RATINGS KEY ⊗ POOR ⊖ FAIR ❶ GOOD ⌃ VERY GOOD ⊛ EXCELLENT
$ **CR BEST BUY** These models offer the best combination of performance and price. All are recommended.
✓ **RECOMMENDED** These are high-performing models that stand out.

Rec.	Rank	Brand & Model	Price	Score	Portability	Ease of Use	Display	Versatility	Battery Life (hr.)	Weight (lb.)	Operating System
		9-INCH-SCREEN AND LARGER TABLETS, WiFi-ONLY (Continued)									
	24	**Acer** Iconia One 10 B3-A20-K8UH (16GB)	$150	66	⌃	⌃	⊝	⌃	13.2	1.2	And. 5.1
	25	**Acer** Aspire Switch 12 SW5-271-62X3 (128GB)	$470	66	⌄	⌃	⌃	⌃	8.2	2.4	Wind. 10
	26	**Acer** Iconia One 10 B3-A10-K3BF (16GB)	$160	65	⌃	⌃	⌃	⊝	10.1	1.1	And. 5.1
	27	**Nextbook** Flexx 9 (32GB)	$100	62	⌃	⌃	⊝	⊝	8.3	1.1	Wind. 10
	28	**RCA** Viking II (16GB)	$110	55	⊝	⌃	⊝	⊝	7.1	1.7	And. 6
		8-INCH-SCREEN AND SMALLER TABLETS, WiFi-ONLY										
✓	1	**Samsung** Galaxy Tab S2 8 (32GB)	$350	83	⌃	⌃	⌃⌃	⌃⌃	11.1	0.6	And. 6
✓	2	**Apple** iPad Mini 4 (16GB)	$350	79	⌃	⌃⌃	⌃⌃	⌃	11.9	0.7	iOS 9.1
✓	3	**Apple** iPad Mini 2 (16GB)	$220	78	⌃	⌃⌃	⌃⌃	⊝	12.8	0.7	iOS 8.3
✓	4	**Asus** ZenPad S 8.0 Z580CA-C1-BK (64GB)	$270	75	⌃	⌃	⌃	⌃	9.1	0.7	And. 5
$	5	**NVIDIA** Shield K1 (16GB)	$200	75	⌃	⌃	⌃⌃	⌃	9.6	0.8	And. 6
$	6	**Asus** ZenPad S 8.0 Z580C-B1 (32GB)	$170	74	⌃	⌃	⌃⌃	⌃	9.1	0.7	And. 5
✓	7	**Dell** Venue 8 Pro 5000 HD (64GB)	$400	72	⊝	⌃	⌃	⌃	10	0.9	Wind. Pro 10
	8	**Acer** Iconia One 8 B1-810-11TV (16GB)	$160	71	⌃	⌃	⌃	⊝	11	0.7	And. 4.4
	9	**LG** G Pad II 8.0 (16GB)	$180	71	⌃⌃	⌃	⌃	⌃	15.7	0.8	And. 5
	10	**Dell** Venue 8 Pro 5000 FHD (64GB)	$450	71	⊝	⌃	⌃	⌃	8.7	0.9	Wind. Pro 10
	11	**Samsung** Galaxy Tab A 8.0 SM-T350 (16GB)	$200	70	⌃⌃	⌃	⌃	⌃	14.2	0.7	And. 5
	12	**Lenovo** Yoga Tablet 3 8 (16GB)	$170	69	⌃	⌃	⌃	⌃	21.2	1	And. 5.1
	13	**Asus** ZenPad 8.0 Z380M (16GB)	$130	69	⌃	⌃	⌃	⌃	11.3	0.8	And. 6
	14	**Acer** Iconia One 8 B1-820-16FX (16GB)	$100	69	⌃	⌃	⌃	⊝	11.5	0.8	And. 5
	15	**Samsung** Galaxy Tab 4 7.0 (8GB)	$150	68	⌃	⌃⌃	⌃	⌃	12.2	0.6	And. 4.4

8-INCH-SCREEN AND SMALLER TABLETS, WiFi-ONLY (Continued)

Rec.	Rank	Brand & Model	Price	Score	Portability	Ease of Use	Display	Versatility	Battery Life (hr.)	Weight (lb.)	Operating System
	16	**Samsung** Galaxy Tab A 7.0 (8GB)	$120	68	Excellent	Very Good	Very Good	Good	14.1	0.6	And. 5.1
	17	**Amazon** Fire HD 6 (16GB)	$90	67	Very Good	Very Good	Excellent	Good	10.1	0.6	Fire OS 5.1
	18	**Acer** Iconia One 7 B1-750-103A (16GB)	$100	67	Very Good	Very Good	Very Good	Good	7.4	0.6	And. 4.4
	19	**Amazon** Fire HD 8 (16GB)	$170	66	Very Good	Very Good	Excellent	Good	8.2	0.7	Fire OS 5.1
	20	**Lenovo** TAB 3 8 (16GB)	$110	66	Excellent	Excellent	Very Good	Good	15.7	0.8	And. 6
	21	**Lenovo** TAB 3 7 (16GB)	$100	66	Excellent	Very Good	Very Good	Very Good	12	0.6	And. 6
	22	**Acer** Iconia One 8 B1-850-K3SX (16GB)	$90	66	Very Good	Very Good	Very Good	Very Good	10.6	0.8	And. 5.1
	23	**Asus** ZenPad C 7.0 Z170C-A1-BK (16GB)	$100	65	Very Good	Very Good	Very Good	Good	9.9	0.6	And. 5
	24	**Asus** ZenPad 8.0 Z380CX-A2 (16GB)	$130	65	Good	Very Good	Very Good	Good	9	0.8	And. 5
	25	**Lenovo** TAB 3 7 Essential (8GB)	$70	62	Very Good	Very Good	Very Good	Good	10	0.7	And. 5
	26	**Toshiba** Encore 2 WT8-B32CN (32GB)	$110	62	Good	Very Good	Very Good	Good	7.2	0.8	Wind. 10
	27	**Amazon** Fire 7 (8GB)	$50	57	Good	Very Good	Good	Good	8.4	0.7	Fire OS 5.1
	28	**Samsung** Galaxy Tab 3 Lite (8GB)	$120	56	Very Good	Very Good	Good	Good	11.5	0.7	And. 4.4
	29	**Samsung** Galaxy Tab E Lite 7.0 (8GB)	$120	54	Very Good	Very Good	Fair	Good	12	0.7	And. 4.4
	30	**Nextbook** Flexx 8 (32GB)	$100	54	Good	Very Good	Fair	Good	7	0.8	Wind. 10

8-INCH-SCREEN AND SMALLER TABLETS, MOBILE DATA+WiFi

Rec.	Rank	Brand & Model	Price	Score	Portability	Ease of Use	Display	Versatility	Battery Life (hr.)	Weight (lb.)	Operating System
✓	1	**Apple** iPad Mini 4 (4G, 16GB)	$480	82	Very Good	Excellent	Excellent	Very Good	11.9	0.7	iOS 9.1
✓	2	**Apple** iPad Mini 2 (4G, 16GB)	$400	80	Very Good	Excellent	Excellent	Very Good	12.7	0.8	iOS 8.3
$	3	**Asus** ZenPad Z8 (4G, 16GB)	$250	78	Very Good	Very Good	Excellent	Very Good	11.3	0.7	And. 6

Rec.	Rank	Brand & Model	Price	Score	Portability	Ease of Use	Display	Versatility	Battery Life (hr.)	Weight (lb.)	Operating System
8-INCH-SCREEN AND SMALLER TABLETS, MOBILE DATA+WiFi (Continued)											
$	4	**Asus** MeMO Pad 7 LTE ME375CL (4G, 16GB)	$90	75	Excellent	Very Good	Very Good	Very Good	12.5	0.7	And. 4.4
	5	**Dell** Venue 8 Pro 5000 FHD (4G, 64GB)	$580	71	Good	Very Good	Very Good	Very Good	8.7	0.9	Wind. Pro 10
	6	**Samsung** Galaxy Tab E 8.0 (4G, 16GB)	$250	71	Excellent	Very Good	Very Good	Very Good	17.4	0.8	And. 6
	7	**LG** G Pad F 8.0 (4G, 16GB)	$150	71	Excellent	Very Good	Very Good	Very Good	14.3	0.8	And. 5
	8	**HP** Envy 8 Note (4G, 32GB)	$280	67	Good	Very Good	Excellent	Very Good	5.7	0.8	Wind. 10
	9	**Verizon** Ellipsis 8 (4G, 16GB)	$250	66	Very Good	Very Good	Very Good	Very Good	10.4	0.8	And. 4.4
	10	**AT&T** Trek HD (4G, 16GB)	$90	66	Very Good	Very Good	Very Good	Very Good	11.8	0.8	And. 5
	11	**Alcatel** OneTouch POP 7 LTE (4G, 8GB)	$130	56	Very Good	Very Good	Fair	Very Good	9.1	0.7	And. 6
9-INCH-SCREEN AND LARGER TABLETS, MOBILE DATA+WiFi											
✓	1	**Apple** iPad Pro 9.7 (4G, 32GB)	$730	88	Excellent	Very Good	Excellent	Very Good	15.6	1	iOS 9.3
✓	2	**Apple** iPad Air 2 (4G, 64GB)	$600	84	Excellent	Very Good	Excellent	Very Good	13.3	1	iOS 8.3
✓	3	**Amazon** Fire HDX 8.9 (4G, 32GB)	$430	84	Excellent	Very Good	Excellent	Excellent	15.3	0.8	Fire OS 4.5
$	4	**LG** G Pad X 10.1 (4G, 32GB)	$300	82	Excellent	Very Good	Excellent	Very Good	15.2	1.1	And. 5.1
✓	5	**Apple** iPad Pro 12.9 (4G, 128GB)	$1030	82	Very Good	Excellent	Excellent	Very Good	12.5	1.6	iOS 9.2
✓	6	**Microsoft** Surface 3 (4G, 64GB)	$600	77	Very Good	Very Good	Excellent	Excellent	10.2	1.4	Wind. 10
✓	7	**Samsung** Galaxy Tab E 9.6 (4G, 16GB)	$350	72	Excellent	Very Good	Very Good	Very Good	16.8	1.2	And. 5.1

RATINGS KEY ⊘ POOR ⊙ FAIR ❶ GOOD ⌃ VERY GOOD ⌃⌃ EXCELLENT

$ CR BEST BUY These models offer the best combination of performance and price. All are recommended.

✓ RECOMMENDED These are high-performing models that stand out.

Guide to the Ratings

Score is based on portability, ease of use, display, versatility, performance, touch response, and camera quality. **Portability** is based on size, weight, and battery life. **Ease of Use** considers tasks such as reading books, playing media, and using e-mail and the Web. **Display** score reflects color, clarity, viewing angle, brightness, and outdoor readability. **Versatility** reflects the presence of useful features. **Battery Life (hr.)** indicates the time it takes to deplete a fully charged battery while the tablet loads a sequence of Web pages over Wi-Fi. **Weight (lb.)** is without a case or cover. Under **Operating System:** And.=Android, iOS=iOS, and Wind.=Windows. **Price** is approximate retail.

Most & Least Reliable

Percentage likely to break by second year of ownership.

Apple	2%
Amazon	4%
Samsung	4%
LG	4%
Sony	7%
Toshiba	8%
Microsoft	8%
HP	8%
Google	8%
Acer	10%
Lenovo	10%
Dell	11%
Asus	13%

The graph shows our failure-rate estimates for tablets by the second year of ownership, gathered from 35,527 subscribers who purchased 48,518 devices new between 2012 and 2015. We estimate failure rates for tablets not covered by a service contract, accounting for the number of hours they're used per week. Differences of fewer than 8 points aren't meaningful. Models within a brand may vary, and changes in design or manufacturer may affect future reliability. Still, choosing a brand with a good reliability estimate can improve your odds of getting a dependable model.

Source 2015 Spring Product Reliability Survey, Consumer Reports National Research Center.

TVs

More sets are now smart TVs with access to streaming video services, but 1080p sets are still going strong. New Internet TVs have Wi-Fi .

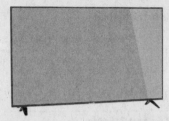

What to Look For

■ Top-rated 1080p full HD set if you want great picture quality and the best value.
■ A 4K Ultra HD set if you're willing to pay for the latest technology and you're buying a 60-inch or larger set

What to Skip

■ Pricey HDMI or UHD/4K cables; high-speed cables costing a few dollars are fine.
■ An extended warranty; TVs from major brands have been very reliable.
■ Internet connectivity if your Blu-ray player, game system, or streaming device has the services you want.

What You'll Pay

To start, about $300 for 40- to 42-inch sets, about $500 for 47- to 50-inch sets, and about $900 for 60-inch sets. make installment payments over time, generally about $25 per month for two years.

BUYING ADVICE

Check the viewing angle of an LCD or "LED" TV in the store to see whether the picture looks washed out when viewed from the side.

For more buying advice, go to ConsumerReports.org/tvs.

All tested models in performance order.

Rec.	Rank	Brand & Model	Price	Score	HD Picture Quality	Ultra HD Performance	Viewing Angle	Sound Quality	TV Resolution Type	Internet-Enabled	Screen Size (in.)
		60-INCH AND LARGER									
✓	1	**LG** OLED65C6P	$4000	82	⊗	⊗	⊗	❶	Ultra HD	•	65
✓	2	**LG** 65EF9500	$3000	81	⊗	⊗	⊗	❶	Ultra HD	•	65
$	3	**Samsung** UN65JS9500	$3000	81	⊗	⊗	❶	⊗	Ultra HD	•	65

60-INCH AND LARGER (Continued)

Rec.	Rank	Brand & Model	Price	Score	HD Picture Quality	Ultra HD Performance	Viewing Angle	Sound Quality	TV Resolution Type	Internet-Enabled	Screen Size (in.)
✓	4	**Sony** Bravia XBR-65X930C	$4750	79	Excellent	Excellent	Good	Excellent	Ultra HD	•	65
✓	5	**Samsung** UN65KS9800	$4500	78	Excellent	Excellent	Good	Very Good	Ultra HD	•	65
✓	6	**Samsung** UN65KS8500	$2200	77	Excellent	Excellent	Good	Very Good	Ultra HD	•	65
✓	7	**Samsung** UN65KS800D	$1980	77	Excellent	Excellent	Good	Very Good	Ultra HD	•	65
✓	8	**Samsung** UN65KS8000	$2000	77	Excellent	Excellent	Good	Very Good	Ultra HD	•	65
✓	9	**Samsung** UN65KS850D	$2180	76	Excellent	Excellent	Good	Very Good	Ultra HD	•	65
$	10	**Samsung** UN65JS9000	$5000	76	Excellent	Excellent	Good	Very Good	Ultra HD	•	65
$	11	**LG** 60UH8500	$1600	75	Excellent	Excellent	Very Good	Good	Ultra HD	•	60
✓	12	**LG** 65UH9500	$2500	75	Excellent	Excellent	Very Good	Very Good	Ultra HD	•	65
✓	13	**LG** 65UF9500	$4500	75	Excellent	Excellent	Very Good	Very Good	Ultra HD	•	65
✓	14	**Samsung** UN65KS9000	$2800	75	Excellent	Excellent	Good	Very Good	Ultra HD	•	65
$	15	**Samsung** UN65JS850D	$1450	75	Excellent	Excellent	Good	Very Good	Ultra HD	•	65
$	16	**Samsung** UN65JS8500	$3000	75	Excellent	Excellent	Good	Very Good	Ultra HD	•	65
✓	17	**LG** 65UH7700	$1600	74	Excellent	Excellent	Very Good	Good	Ultra HD	•	65
$	18	**LG** 60UH6550	$1500	74	Excellent	Excellent	Very Good	Good	Ultra HD	•	60
✓	19	**Samsung** UN65KU7500	$1600	73	Excellent	Excellent	Good	Good	Ultra HD	•	65
✓	20	**Samsung** UN60JU7100	$1395	72	Excellent	Excellent	Good	Good	Ultra HD	•	60
$	21	**LG** 65UH615A	$1000	72	Very Good	Excellent	Very Good	Good	Ultra HD	•	65
✓	22	**Sony** XBR-65Z9D	$6000	72	Excellent	Excellent	Good	Good	Ultra HD	•	65
$	23	**Samsung** UN60JU6500	$950	71	Excellent	Excellent	Good	Good	Ultra HD	•	60
✓	24	**Sony** XBR-65X930D	$2800	71	Excellent	Excellent	Good	Fair	Ultra HD	•	65
✓	25	**Samsung** UN60KS8000	$1900	71	Excellent	Excellent	Good	Good	Ultra HD	•	60

RATINGS KEY ⊘ POOR ⊙ FAIR ❶ GOOD ⌃ VERY GOOD ⌃⌃ EXCELLENT

$ **CR BEST BUY** These models offer the best combination of performance and price. All are recommended.

✓ **RECOMMENDED** These are high-performing models that stand out.

Rec.	Rank	Brand & Model	Price	Score	HD Picture Quality	Ultra HD Performance	Viewing Angle	Sound Quality	TV Resolution Type	Internet-Enabled	Screen Size (in.)
		60-INCH AND LARGER (Continued)									
✓	26	**Sony** Bravia XBR-65X850C	$2000	71	⬆⬆	⬆	●	●	Ultra HD	•	65
✓	27	**LG** 65UF8500	$2810	70	⬆	⬆	⬆	●	Ultra HD	•	65
✓	28	**LG** 60UF7700	$2100	70	⬆	⬆	⬆	●	Ultra HD	•	60
$	29	**Sony** Bravia KDL-65W850C	$1000	69	⬆⬆	NA	●	●	HDTV	•	65
✓	30	**Samsung** UN65J6300	$1300	68	⬆	NA	●	●	HDTV	•	65
$	31	**LG** 60UH6150	$1000	68	⬆	⬆⬆	⬆	●	Ultra HD	•	60
✓	32	**LG** 65UH6150	$1300	66	⬆	⬆⬆	⬆	●	Ultra HD	•	65
✓	33	**Samsung** UN65JU670D	$2080	65	⬆⬆	⬆⬆	⬇	●	Ultra HD	•	65
✓	34	**Sony** Bravia XBR-65X900C	$1600	65	⬆	⬆⬆	⬆	●	Ultra HD	•	65
✓	35	**Sharp** Aquos LC-65UB30U	$1410	65	⬆	●	●	●	Ultra HD	•	65
	36	**LG** 70UF7700	$4000	64	⬆	⬆	●	⬇	Ultra HD	•	70
	37	**Vizio** E60-C3	$700	63	⬆⬆	NA	●	⬇	HDTV	•	60
	38	**Samsung** UN60J6200	$700	63	⬆	NA	●	⬇	HDTV	•	60
	39	**Vizio** P65-C1	$2000	63	⬆⬆	⬆	●	⬇	Ultra HD	•	65
$	40	**Sharp** Aquos LC-65LE654U	$995	63	⬆⬆	NA	●	⬇	HDTV	•	65
	41	**Vizio** E65-C3	$600	62	⬆⬆	NA	●	⬇	HDTV	•	65
	42	**Sony** XBR-65X850D	$1800	62	⬆	⬆⬆	⬆	⬇	Ultra HD	•	65
	43	**Vizio** E65u-D3	$930	62	⬆⬆	●	●	⬇	Ultra HD	•	65
	44	**Vizio** E60u-D3	$800	61	⬆⬆	●	●	⬇	Ultra HD	•	60
	45	**Vizio** M60-C3	$1000	60	⬆	●	⬆	⬇	Ultra HD	•	60
	46	**Vizio** D60-D3	$650	60	⬆⬆	NA	●	⬇	HD	•	60
	47	**Sharp** LC-60N7000U	$900	59	●	⬆	⬆	●	Ultra HD	•	60
	48	**Vizio** M70-C3	$1900	59	⬆	●	●	⬇	Ultra HD	•	70
	49	**Sharp** LC-60N5100U	$600	58	⬆	NA	⬆	⬇	HD	•	60
	50	**Kenmore** Elite 71398	$1200	58	⬆⬆	●	●	⬇	Ultra HD	•	65
	51	**Vizio** D65u-D2	$1000	58	⬆	●	⬇	●	Ultra HD	•	65

Rec.	Rank	Brand & Model	Price	Score	HD Picture Quality	Ultra HD Performance	Viewing Angle	Sound Quality	TV Resolution Type	Internet-Enabled	Screen Size (in.)
60-INCH AND LARGER (Continued)											
	52	**Sharp** Aquos LC-60UE30U	$1335	57	Good	Very Good	Good	Good	Ultra HD	•	60
	53	**Sharp** Aquos LC-70UE30U	$1755	56	Good	Very Good	Fair	Good	Ultra HD	•	70
	54	**Philips** 65PFL7900	$950	55	Good	Very Good	Good	Good	Ultra HD	•	65
55- TO 59-INCH											
✅	1	**LG** OLED55E6P	$3500	84	Very Good	Excellent	Excellent	Very Good	Ultra HD	•	55
✅	2	**LG** OLED55B6P	$2500	83	Very Good	Excellent	Excellent	Good	Ultra HD	•	55
✅	3	**LG** 55EG9100	$1295	80	Excellent	NA	Excellent	Good	HDTV	•	55
✅	4	**LG** 55EF9500	$2840	78	Very Good	Excellent	Excellent	Good	Ultra HD	•	55
✅	5	**LG** 55EG9600	$1795	78	Very Good	Excellent	Excellent	Good	Ultra HD	•	55
✅	6	**Samsung** UN55KS8000	$1400	78	Very Good	Excellent	Good	Very Good	Ultra HD	•	55
✅	7	**Samsung** UN55KS800D	$1380	78	Very Good	Excellent	Good	Very Good	Ultra HD	•	55
✅	8	**Samsung** UN55KS9500	$2000	74	Very Good	Excellent	Good	Good	Ultra HD	•	55
✅	9	**Samsung** UN55JS8500	$1800	74	Very Good	Excellent	Good	Good	Ultra HD	•	55
$	10	**Samsung** UN55KU6500	$1000	74	Very Good	Excellent	Good	Very Good	Ultra HD	•	55
✅	11	**LG** 55UH6550	$900	73	Very Good	Excellent	Very Good	Good	Ultra HD	•	55
$	12	**Samsung** UN55JU7500	$1095	73	Very Good	Excellent	Good	Good	Ultra HD	•	55
✅	13	**LG** 55UH7700	$1000	73	Very Good	Very Good	Good	Good	Ultra HD	•	55
$	14	**Samsung** UN55KU630D	$730	72	Very Good	Excellent	Good	Good	Ultra HD	•	55
$	15	**Samsung** UN55KU6300	$800	72	Very Good	Excellent	Very Good	Good	Ultra HD	•	55
✅	16	**Sony** XBR-55X930D	$1800	71	Very Good	Excellent	Very Good	Fair	Ultra HD	•	55
✅	17	**Samsung** UN55J620D	$600	70	Excellent	NA	Good	Good	HDTV	•	55
✅	18	**Sony** XBR-55X850D	$1200	69	Very Good	Excellent	Very Good	Good	Ultra HD	•	55

RATINGS KEY ⊖ POOR ⊘ FAIR ● GOOD ⌃ VERY GOOD ⌃⌃ EXCELLENT

$ **CR BEST BUY** These models offer the best combination of performance and price. All are recommended.
✅ **RECOMMENDED** These are high-performing models that stand out.

Rec.	Rank	Brand & Model	Price	Score	HD Picture Quality	Ultra HD Performance	Viewing Angle	Sound Quality	TV Resolution Type	Internet-Enabled	Screen Size (in.)
		55- TO 59-INCH (Continued)									
$	19	**Samsung** UN55JU6700	$650	68	⌃⌃	⌃⌃	◑	◑	Ultra HD	•	55
✓	20	**Samsung** UN55JU670D	$1280	68	⌃⌃	⌃⌃	◔	◑	HDTV	•	55
✓	21	**Sony** Bravia KDL-55W800C	$1175	68	⌃⌃	NA	◑	◑	HDTV	•	55
$	22	**LG** 55UH6150	$700	68	⌃	⌃⌃	⌃	◑	Ultra HD	•	55
✓	23	**LG** 55UF7600	$2000	68	⌃⌃	⌃	⌃	◔	Ultra HD	•	55
✓	24	**LG** 55LF6000	$450	67	⌃	NA	⌃	◑	HDTV	•	55
✓	25	**Sony** Bravia XBR-55X850C	$1500	67	⌃⌃	⌃⌃	◑	◑	Ultra HD	•	55
	26	**Vizio** M55-C2	$650	64	⌃⌃	◑	◑	◑	Ultra HD	•	55
	27	**Sony** Bravia XBR-55X900C	$980	63	⌃	⌃⌃	◑	◔	Ultra HD	•	55
	28	**Vizio** E55-C2	$550	63	⌃	NA	⌃	◔	HDTV	•	55
$	29	**Sharp** Aquos LC-55LE653U	$495	63	⌃⌃	NA	◑	◔	HDTV	•	55
	30	**LG** 55UH615A	$680	62	⌃	⌃⌃	⌃	◔	Ultra HD	•	55
	31	**TCL** 55UP120	$490	62	⌃	⌃	◑	◑	Ultra HD	•	55
	32	**Vizio** D55u-D1	$650	62	⌃	◑	⌃	◔	Ultra HD	•	55
	33	**Sharp** Aquos LC-55UB30U	$500	61	⌃	◑	◔	◑	Ultra HD	•	55
	34	**LG** 55LH5750	$500	61	⌃	NA	⌃	◑	HD	•	55
	35	**Philips** 55PFL6900	$1000	61	⌃	⌃⌃	⌃	◑	Ultra HD	•	55
	36	**Samsung** UN55JU6500	$900	59	◑	⌃⌃	⌃	◑	Ultra HD	•	55
	37	**Vizio** E55-C1	$600	59	⌃	NA	◑	◔	HDTV	•	55
	38	**Insignia** NS-55DR710NA17	$540	59	⌃	◑	◑	◔	Ultra HD	•	55
	39	**Vizio** E55-D0	$470	59	⌃⌃	NA	◑	◔	HD	•	55
	40	**Samsung** UN55K6250	$700	57	⌃	NA	◑	◑	HD	•	55
	41	**TCL** 55US5800	$550	57	⌃	⌃	◔	◔	Ultra HD	•	55
	42	**Hisense** 55H5C	$450	52	⌃	NA	◔	◑	HD	•	55

46- TO 52-INCH

Rec.	Rank	Brand & Model	Price	Score	HD Picture Quality	Ultra HD Performance	Viewing Angle	Sound Quality	TV Resolution Type	Internet-Enabled	Screen Size (in.)
✓	1	Samsung UN49KS8000	$1200	73	Excellent	Excellent	Good	Good	Ultra HD	•	49
✓	2	Samsung UN49KU7500	$1300	72	Excellent	Excellent	Good	Good	Ultra HD	•	49
✓	3	Samsung UN49KS8500	$1200	72	Excellent	Excellent	Good	Good	Ultra HD	•	49
✓	4	Samsung UN50JU7500	$1365	71	Excellent	Excellent	Good	Good	Ultra HD	•	50
$	5	Samsung UN48J5500	$450	70	Excellent	NA	Good	Good	HDTV	•	48
✓	6	Samsung UN49KU7000	$900	70	Excellent	Excellent	Good	Good	Ultra HD	•	49
✓	7	Samsung UN50JU7100	$600	69	Excellent	Excellent	Good	Good	Ultra HD	•	50
✓	8	Samsung UN50J6200	$580	69	Excellent	NA	Good	Good	HDTV	•	50
$	9	Samsung UN50JU6500	$800	68	Excellent	Excellent	Good	Good	Ultra HD	•	50
$	10	Samsung UN48JU6700	$1150	68	Excellent	Excellent	Good	Good	Ultra HD	•	48
✓	11	Sony Bravia KDL-50W800C	$775	67	Excellent	NA	Fair	Good	HDTV	•	50
✓	12	Sharp LC-50N7000U	$575	66	Excellent	Excellent	Fair	Good	Ultra HD	•	50
✓	13	LG 49UH6100	$550	66	Very Good	Excellent	Very Good	Good	Ultra HD	•	49
✓	14	Samsung UN50J520D	$450	65	Excellent	NA	Good	Fair	HDTV	•	50
✓	15	Vizio E48-C2	$400	65	Excellent	NA	Very Good	Fair	HDTV	•	48
✓	16	LG 50LF6100	$800	65	Excellent	NA	Good	Fair	HDTV	•	50
	17	Sony Bravia XBR-49X830C	$850	64	Very Good	Very Good	Very Good	Fair	Ultra HD	•	49
	18	Hisense 50H8C	$500	64	Very Good	Very Good	Fair	Good	Ultra HD	•	50
	19	Samsung UN50J5200	$500	64	Excellent	NA	Good	Fair	HDTV	•	50
	20	Samsung UN48JU6400	$750	63	Excellent	Excellent	Fair	Good	Ultra HD	•	48
	21	Vizio D50u-D1	$530	63	Excellent	Good	Fair	Fair	Ultra HD	•	50

RATINGS KEY ⊝ POOR ⊙ FAIR ❶ GOOD ⌃ VERY GOOD ⊗ EXCELLENT
$ **CR BEST BUY** These models offer the best combination of performance and price. All are recommended.
✓ **RECOMMENDED** These are high-performing models that stand out.

Rec.	Rank	Brand & Model	Price	Score	Test Results				Features		
					HD Picture Quality	Ultra HD Performance	Viewing Angle	Sound Quality	TV Resolution Type	Internet-Enabled	Screen Size (in.)
		46- TO 52-INCH (Continued)									
	22	**LG** 49UH6090	$600	63	⌃	⌃⌃	⌃	◑	Ultra HD	•	49
	23	**Vizio** M50-C1	$600	61	⌃⌃	◑	◑	⌄	Ultra HD	•	50
	24	**Vizio** P50-C1	$1000	61	⌃⌃	⌃	⌄	⌄	Ultra HD	•	50
	25	**Sharp** LC-50N6000U	$500	60	⌃	⌃⌃	⌄	⌄	Ultra HD	•	50
	26	**Vizio** E50-C1	$420	59	⌃	NA	◑	⌄	HDTV	•	50
	27	**Sony** KDL-48W650D	$480	59	⌃⌃	NA	⌄	⌄	HD	•	48
	28	**Vizio** E48u-D0	$400	58	⌃	◑	◑	◑	Ultra HD	•	48
	29	**LG** 49LH5700	$400	58	⌃	NA	⌃	⌄	HD	•	49
	30	**Vizio** D48-D0	$380	58	⌃	NA	◑	◑	HD	•	48
	31	**Hitachi** LE49A509	$320	57	⌃	NA	⌃	⌄	HDTV		49
	32	**Insignia** NS-48DR510NA17	$350	56	⌃	NA	◑	◑	HD	•	48
	33	**Hisense** 50H5C	$380	55	⌃	NA	⌄	⌄	HD	•	50
	34	**TCL** 48FS3750	$330	53	⌃	NA	⌄	⌄	HD	•	48
	35	**Insignia** NS-50D510NA17	$300	38	⌄	NA	◑	⌄	HD		50

Rec.	Rank	Brand & Model	Price	Score	HD Picture Quality	Ultra HD Performance	Viewing Angle	Sound Quality	TV Resolution Type	Internet-Enabled	Screen Size (in.)
		39- TO 43-INCH									
$	1	**Samsung** UN40JU7100	$1025	72	⊗	⊗	❶	❶	Ultra HD	•	40
✓	2	**Samsung** UN40KU6300	$500	71	⊗	⊗	❶	❶	Ultra HD	•	40
✓	3	**Samsung** UN43KU6300	$600	69	⊗	⊗	⊙	❶	Ultra HD	•	43
✓	4	**Samsung** UN40J6200	$400	68	⊗	NA	❶	❶	HDTV	•	40
✓	5	**Samsung** UN43J5200	$380	67	⊗	NA	❶	❶	HDTV	•	43
✓	6	**Samsung** UN40JU6500	$550	66	⊗	⊗	⊙	❶	Ultra HD	•	40
✓	7	**LG** 43UH6500	$550	66	⊗	⊗	⊙	❶	Ultra HD	•	43
$	8	**Sony** Bravia KDL-40R510C	$300	65	⊗	NA	❶	⊙	HDTV	•	40
	9	**Vizio** E40-C2	$350	64	⊙	NA	⊙	⊙	HDTV	•	40
	10	**Samsung** UN40J520D	$300	63	⊗	NA	⊙	❶	HDTV	•	40
	11	**Vizio** D40u-D1	$400	63	⊙	❶	⊙	⊙	Ultra HD	•	40
$	12	**Sharp** Aquos LC-43LE653U	$300	63	⊙	NA	❶	❶	HDTV	•	43
	13	**Vizio** E43-C2	$345	62	⊙	NA	⊙	⊙	HDTV	•	43
	14	**Sony** Bravia XBR-43X830C	$660	62	⊙	⊗	⊙	⊙	Ultra HD	•	43
	15	**Insignia** NS-43DR710NA17	$365	61	⊙	⊙	❶	❶	Ultra HD	•	43
	16	**Vizio** D43-D2	$330	61	⊙	NA	⊙	❶	HD	•	43
	17	**Hisense** 43H7C	$370	61	⊙	⊗	⊙	⊙	Ultra HD	•	43
	18	**Philips** 43PFL4609	$280	61	⊙	NA	⊙	⊙	HD	•	43
	19	**Sharp** LC-43N6100U	$380	60	⊙	⊙	⊙	⊙	Ultra HD	•	43
$	20	**JVC** EM40NF5	$300	59	⊗	NA	⊙	⊙	HDTV		40

RATINGS KEY ⊙ POOR ⊙ FAIR ❶ GOOD ⊙ VERY GOOD ⊗ EXCELLENT
$ **CR BEST BUY** These models offer the best combination of performance and price. All are recommended.
✓ **RECOMMENDED** These are high-performing models that stand out.

Rec.	Rank	Brand & Model	Price	Score	HD Picture Quality	Ultra HD Performance	Viewing Angle	Sound Quality	TV Resolution Type	Internet-Enabled	Screen Size (in.)
		39- TO 43-INCH (Continued)									
	21	**Sony** KDL-40W650D	$380	59	⊗	NA	⊘	⊘	HD	•	40
$	22	**Westinghouse** DWM42F2G1	$290	59	⌃	NA	⌃	⊘	HDTV		42
	23	**Insignia** NS-39D220NA16	$180	59	⌃	NA	⊘	⊘	HDTV		39
	24	**Sharp** Aquos LC-43LB371U	$310	59	⌃	NA	❶	❶	HDTV	•	43
	25	**Sharp** Aquos LC-43UB30U	$610	58	⌃	❶	⊘	⊘	Ultra HD	•	43
	26	**LG** 43LH5700	$330	58	⌃	NA	⌃	⊘	HD	•	43
	27	**Hisense** 40H4C1	$255	58	⌃	NA	❶	⊘	HD	•	40
	28	**Vizio** M43-C1	$350	57	⌃	❶	❶	⊘	Ultra HD	•	43
	29	**Vizio** E40-D0	$280	57	⊗	NA	❶	⊘	HD	•	40
	30	**Hitachi** LE43A509	$260	57	⌃	NA	⌃	⊘	HDTV		43
	31	**Vizio** D40-D1	$280	56	⌃	NA	❶	⊘	HD	•	40
	32	**TCL** 40FS3750	$270	56	⌃	NA	❶	⊘	HD	•	40
	33	**Hisense** 40H5B	$250	56	⌃	NA	⌃	⊘	HD	•	40
	34	**Vizio** E43u-D2	$380	55	⌃	❶	⊘	⊘	Ultra HD	•	43
	35	**Sharp** LC-43N4000U	$290	55	⌃	NA	❶	⊘	HD	•	43
	36	**LG** 43LH5000	$300	55	⌃	NA	⌃	⊘	HD		43
	37	**Sceptre** X405BV-FHDR	$180	54	⌃	NA	❶	⊘	HDTV		40
	38	**Vizio** D43-C1	$450	54	⌃	NA	⌃	⊘	HDTV		43
	39	**Insignia** NS-40D510NA17	$220	54	⌃	NA	⌃	⊘	HD		40
	40	**Vizio** D39hn-D0	$210	51	⌃	NA	⊘	⊘	HD		39
	41	**Vizio** D43-D1	$330	51	❶	NA	⌃	⊘	HD	•	43
	42	**Haier** 40E3500	$185	46	❶	NA	⊘	⊘	HDTV		40

Rec.	Rank	Brand & Model	Price	Score	Test Results: HD Picture Quality	Test Results: Ultra HD Performance	Test Results: Viewing Angle	Test Results: Sound Quality	Features: TV Resolution Type	Features: Internet-Enabled	Features: Screen Size (in.)
		32-INCH									
✓	1	**LG** 32LF5600	$380	68	Excellent	NA	Very Good	Good	HDTV		32
✓	2	**Samsung** UN32J5500	$280	66	Excellent	NA	Good	Fair	HDTV	•	32
	3	**Samsung** UN32J4000	$180	63	Very Good	NA	Very Good	Fair	HDTV		32
	4	**LG** 32LF595B	$200	62	Very Good	NA	Fair	Fair	HDTV	•	32
	5	**Vizio** E32-C1	$230	61	Very Good	NA	Very Good	Fair	HDTV	•	32
	6	**Vizio** D32x-D1	$200	59	Very Good	NA	Very Good	Fair	HD	•	32
	7	**Philips** 32PFL4609	$200	58	Very Good	NA	Very Good	Fair	HD	•	32
	8	**LG** 32LF500B	$170	58	Very Good	NA	Very Good	Fair	HDTV		32
	9	**Vizio** D32h-C0	$150	57	Very Good	NA	Good	Fair	HDTV		32
	10	**LG** 32LH570B	$190	57	Very Good	NA	Very Good	Fair	HD	•	32
	11	**LG** 32LH500B	$150	56	Very Good	NA	Very Good	Fair	HD		32
	12	**Insignia** NS-32D310NA17	$120	56	Very Good	NA	Very Good	Fair	HD		32
	13	**TCL** 32S3800	$195	55	Very Good	NA	Fair	Fair	HDTV	•	32
	14	**Hitachi** LE32E6R9	$230	54	Very Good	NA	Very Good	Fair	HDTV	•	32
	15	**RCA** LED32G30RQ	$170	53	Very Good	NA	Fair	Fair	HDTV		32
	16	**TCL** 32S3700	$185	53	Very Good	NA	Fair	Fair	HDTV	•	32
	17	**Sanyo** FW32D06F	$140	53	Very Good	NA	Very Good	Fair	HD		32
	18	**Vizio** E32-D1	$220	53	Very Good	NA	Very Good	Fair	HD	•	32
	19	**Vizio** D32hn-D0	$150	52	Very Good	NA	Very Good	Fair	HD		32
	20	**TCL** 32S3750	$160	52	Very Good	NA	Fair	Fair	HD	•	32
	21	**Magnavox** 32ME306V	$200	51	Very Good	NA	Very Good	Fair	HD		32
	22	**Vizio** D32h-D1	$210	51	Good	NA	Very Good	Fair	HD	•	32
	23	**Sharp** LC-32LB480U	$180	49	Very Good	NA	Fair	Fair	HD		32
	24	**Insignia** NS-32DR310NA17	$150	49	Very Good	NA	Fair	Fair	HD	•	32
	25	**Vizio** E32h-C1	$200	42	Fair	NA	Fair	Fair	HDTV	•	32

Rec.	Rank	Brand & Model	Price	Score	HD Picture Quality	Ultra HD Performance	Viewing Angle	Sound Quality	TV Resolution Type	Internet-Enabled	Screen Size (in.)
		29-INCH AND SMALLER									
$	1	**Samsung** UN28H4000	$180	63	⌃	NA	⌃	⌄	HDTV		28
✓	2	**LG** 28LF4520	$150	62	⌃⌃	NA	⌄	⌄	HDTV		28
✓	3	**LG** 24LF4520	$150	61	⌃⌃	NA	⌄	⌄	HDTV		24
✓	4	**LG** 28LH4530	$190	59	⌃	NA	⌃	⌄	HD	•	28
✓	5	**Vizio** E28h-C1	$145	58	⌃	NA	⌄	⌄	HDTV	•	28
✓	6	**Vizio** D28h-C1	$160	58	⌃⌃	NA	⌄	⌄	HDTV		28
✓	7	**Vizio** D28h-D1	$150	58	⌃	NA	⌃	⌄	HD		28
✓	8	**Vizio** E24-C1	$160	58	⌃	NA	◯	⌄	HDTV	•	24
✓	9	**LG** 22LH4530	$150	56	⌃	NA	⌃	⌄	HD		22
	10	**Element** ELEFW248	$130	54	⌃	NA	⌃	⌄	HD		24
	11	**Vizio** D24-D1	$150	54	⌃	NA	◯	⌄	HD	•	24
	12	**Insignia** NS-28D220NA16	$140	52	◯	NA	⌄	⌄	HDTV		28
	13	**LG** 24LH4530	$150	52	⌃	NA	⌄	⌄	HD		24
	14	**Insignia** NS-24ER310NA17	$130	50	⌃	NA	⌄	⌄	HD	•	24
	15	**Seiki** SE23HEB2	$120	49	⌃	NA	⌄	⌄	HD		23
	16	**Westinghouse** WD28HC1160	$100	48	◯	NA	⌄	⌄⌄	HDTV		28

Guide to the Ratings

Score is based on HD picture quality, sound quality, 3D performance, viewing angle, motion blur performance, ease of use, versatility, and power consumption. **HD Picture Quality** assesses detail, color accuracy, and contrast, using signals from a Blu-ray player, cable box, and professional broadcast equipment and meters. All signals are routed through an HDMI input. **Ultra HD Performance** evaluates a model's ability to deliver the best UHD experience from various 4K sources. **Viewing Angle** evaluates picture quality for clarity and color accuracy at various horizontal and vertical viewing angles. **Sound Quality** is measured from the set's built-in speakers using test equipment, with additional subjective testing by a listening panel. **TV Resolution Type** indicates whether the set is an HDTV or Ultra HD set; all sets are LCD models with LED backlighting except for two OLED models, as noted. **Screen Size (in.)** is the size of the television's screen, measured diagonally in inches. **Price** is approximate retail.

Most & Least Reliable
Percentage likely to break by third year of ownership.

LCDS

Samsung	2%
Hitachi	2%
Panasonic	3%
Sanyo	3%
Dynex (Best Buy)	3%
Hisense	4%
Sony	4%
Magnavox	4%
Insignia	4%
Emerson	4%
Element	4%
Samsung	5%
JVC	5%
LG	5%
Toshiba	5%
Seiki	5%
Philips	5%
Sharp	5%
RCA	6%
Haier	6%
TCL	7%
Vizio	7%
Westinghouse	7%
Sceptre	10%

The graph shows what we found based on the feedback from 105,411 owners of 165,614 LCD (LED) televisions who reported on their experiences when purchased new between 2011 and 2016. The chart shows the estimated failure rates for three-year-old TVs by brand. Differences of fewer than 4 percentage points are not meaningful. Models within a brand may vary, and changes in design or manufacturer may affect reliability. Still, choosing a brand with a good repair history can improve your odds of getting a reliable model.

Source 2016 Spring Product Reliability Survey, Consumer Reports National Research Center.

Vacuums

The best upright models, especially with a bag, deliver the most power for deep-cleaning carpets. But you might want to give up a little oomph and opt for a canister, which is easier to maneuver, better for stairs, and quieter to run.

What to Look For

- Easy pushing, pulling, lifting, and carrying; try before you buy, if possible.
- An upright, if carpet deep-cleaning is important.
- A canister for cleaning drapes and upholstery, on stairs, and under furniture, because you move mostly the hose and wand instead of the entire machine.
- Consider models with a manual carpet pile-height adjustment control, along with suction control for cleaning draperies and other delicate fabrics.

What to Skip

- Splurging on extra cleaning tools, when the basic tools that come standard should suffice for most cleaning jobs.
- Bagless models if you have asthma or allergies, because emptying their bin is usually a dusty, messy chore.

What You'll Pay

Capable bagless uprights start at about $120; figure on $200-plus for most canisters and bagged uprights.

BUYING ADVICE

Even if you order online, go to a store first. Push, pull, turn, and lift the vacuum cleaners you're considering.

For more buying advice, go to ConsumerReports. org/vacuums.

All tested models in performance order.

Recommended	Rank	Brand & Model	Price	Score	Carpet	Bare Floors	Tool Airflow	Noise	Emissions	Handling	Pet Hair	Brush On/Off	Manual-Pile Adjust
		BAGLESS UPRIGHT											
✅	1	**Shark** Navigator Powered Lift-Away NV581	$300	70	⌃	⌃	⌃	⊙	⌃	⌃	⌃	•	
$	2	**Hoover** WindTunnel T-Series Rewind Bagless UH70120	$130	69	⌃	⌃	⌃	⊙	⌃	⌃	⌃		•

[1] Does not accept tools.

BAGLESS UPRIGHT (Continued)

Recommended	Rank	Brand & Model	Price	Score	Carpet	Bare Floors	Tool Airflow	Noise	Emissions	Handling	Pet Hair	Brush On/Off	Manual-Pile Adjust
✓	3	**Dyson** Ball Animal	$500	69	⌃	⌃⌃	—	—	⌃⌃	⌃	⌃⌃	•	
✓	4	**Shark** Rotator Powered Lift-Away XL Capacity NV755	$400	67	⌃	⌃⌃	⌃	—	⌃⌃	⌃	⌃⌃	•	
✓	5	**Dyson** Ball Multi Floor	$400	65	⌃	⌃⌃	—	—	⌃⌃	⌃	⌃	•	
✓	6	**Dyson** Cinetic Big Ball Animal	$600	65	⌃	⌃⌃	—	—	⌃⌃	—	⌄	•	
✓	7	**Shark** Rotator Powered Lift-Away Speed NV680	$260	65	⌃	⌃⌃	—	⌃	⌃⌃	⌃	⌃⌃	•	
✓	8	**Shark** Rotator Professional Lift-Away NV501	$260	65	⌃	⌃⌃	—	⌃	⌃⌃	⌃	⌄	•	
✓	9	**Dyson** Cinetic Big Ball Animal + Allergy	$700	64	⌃	⌃⌃	—	—	⌃⌃	⌃	—	•	
✓	10	**Shark** Rotator Powered Lift-Away NV650	$300	63	—	⌃⌃	⌃	⌃	⌃⌃	⌃	⌃⌃	•	
✓	11	**Shark** Navigator Lift-Away NV352	$200	63	⌃	⌃⌃	—	—	⌃⌃	⌃	⌄	•	
	12	**Panasonic** MC-UL815	$200	62	⌃	⌃	—	—	⌃	—	⌃⌃		
	13	**Shark** Navigator Professional Lift-Away NV356E	$200	62	⌃	⌃⌃	—	⌃	⌃⌃	⌃	⌄	•	
	14	**Hoover** WindTunnel Pet Rewind UH70210	$160	61	—	⌃⌃	⌃	⌃	⌃⌃	—	⌃⌃	•	•
	15	**Kenmore** Elite CrossOver Ultra 10335	$300	61	⌃	⌃⌃	⌃	—	⌄	—	⌃⌃	•	
	16	**Samsung** VU3000 VU10H3021PY	$200	60	—	⌃⌃	—	⌃	⌃⌃	⌃	⌃⌃	•	
	17	**Samsung** VU4000 Motion Sync VU12F40SBBT/AA	$350	60	—	⌃⌃	—	⌃	⌃⌃	⌃	⌄	•	
	18	**Hoover** WindTunnel Rewind Plus UH70205	$150	59	—	⌃⌃	—	—	⌃⌃	—	⌃⌃	•	•
	19	**Panasonic** MC-UL915	$230	59	—	⌃⌃	—	—	⌃	—	⌃⌃	•	
	20	**Hoover** WindTunnel MAX Pet Plus Multi-Cyclonic UH70605	$220	59	⌃	⌃⌃	—	—	—	⌄	⌃⌃	•	•
	21	**Panasonic** MC-UL810	$170	58	⌃	⌃	⌃	—	—	—	⌃⌃		
	22	**Shark** Navigator NV22L	$150	58	—	⌃⌃	—	⌃	⌃	⌃	⌃⌃	•	
	23	**Hoover** WindTunnel Max UH70600	$220	57	⌃	⌃	—	⌄	⌃⌃	—	—	•	•

① Does not accept tools.

Recommended	Rank	Brand & Model	Price	Score	Carpet	Bare Floors	Tool Airflow	Noise	Emissions	Handling	Pet Hair	Brush On/Off	Manual-Pile Adjust
		BAGLESS UPRIGHT (Continued)											
	24	**Hoover** WindTunnel 2 Rewind UH70825	$130	57	⌃	⌃⌃	•	•	⌃	•	⌃		•
	25	**Panasonic** JetForce MC-UL427	$170	57	•	⌃⌃	⌃	•	•	⌃	⌃	•	
	26	**Hoover** Air Steerable UH72400	$190	57	•	⌃⌃	⌄	•	⌃	⌃	⌃	•	
	27	**Bissell** PowerClean 16N5-9	$200	56	•	⌃	•	⌄	⌃	•	•	•	
	28	**Shark** Rocket Professional NV480	$200	55	⌃	•	⌄	⌃	⌃	⌃	⌄	•	
	29	**Hoover** Air Pro UH72450	$230	55	•	⌃⌃	•	•	•	•	⌃	•	
	30	**Bissell** CleanView Plus with OnePass 9595	$80	53	•	⌃	•	•	•	⌃	⌃⌃		•
	31	**Dyson** Small Ball Multi Floor	$400	53	•	⌃	⌄	⌃	⌃	⌃	⌄	•	
	32	**Samsung** VU7000 Motion Sync	$450	51	•	⌃⌃	⌄	•	⌃	•	⌃	•	
	33	**Kenmore** Agility 10325	$200	50	⌃	⌃⌃	⌃	•	⌄⌄	•	⌃	•	
	34	**Hoover** WindTunnel Air UH70400	$180	50	•	⌃⌃	•	•	⌃	⌃	•		
	35	**Hoover** WindTunnel 3 High Performance Pet UH72630PC	$190	49	⌃	⌃⌃	•	⌄	⌄⌄	⌄	⌃⌃	•	•
	36	**Eureka** AirSpeed All Floors AS3011A	$100	47	⌃	⌃⌃	⌃	⌄	⌄⌄	•	⌃	•	•
	37	**Gtech** AirRam ⓘ	$350	47	•	⌃⌃	NA	•	⌃	⌃	⌄		
	38	**Dirt Devil** Total Power Cyclonic UD70212	$80	47	•	⌃	•	•	•	⌃	⌃		
	39	**Eureka** AirSpeed Unlimited Rewind AS3030A	$130	47	⌃	⌃⌃	•	•	⌄⌄	•	⌃	•	•
	40	**Fuller Brush** Jiffy Maid FB-JFM.PET	$210	47	•	⌃⌃	•	•	•	•	⌃		•
	41	**Kenmore** Progressive 10135	$170	47	•	⌃	•	•	•	⌃	•	•	•
	42	**Eureka** Brushroll Clean AS3401A	$200	46	⌃	⌃⌃	•	•	⌄⌄	•	⌃	•	•
	43	**Dirt Devil** Lift & Go UD70300B	$120	44	•	⌃	•	•	⌄⌄	⌄	⌄		
	44	**Hoover** WindTunnel 3 UH72600	$175	43	⌃	⌃⌃	•	⌄	⌄⌄	•	⌃	•	•
	45	**Eureka** SuctionSeal 2.0 Pet AS3104A	$150	43	⌃	⌃⌃	•	•	⌄⌄	⌃	⌃	•	•

ⓘ Does not accept tools.

Recommended	Rank	Brand & Model	Price	Score	Carpet	Bare Floors	Tool Airflow	Noise	Emissions	Handling	Pet Hair	Brush On/Off	Manual-Pile Adjust
		BAGLESS UPRIGHT (Continued)											
	46	**Bissell** PowerGlide Pet 1646	$150	43	Good	Excellent	Good	Good	Poor	Very Good	Excellent	•	
	47	**Hoover** Air Lift UH72511	$200	43	Very Good	Very Good	Poor	Good	Excellent	Good	Fair	•	
	48	**Dyson** Ball Compact Animal	$450	43	Good	Excellent	Poor	Good	Excellent	Very Good	Excellent	•	
	49	**Black+Decker** AirSwivel BDASV102	$80	42	Good	Good	Poor	Good	Fair	Good	Excellent	•	
	50	**Bissell** Powerlifter Pet 1309	$100	41	Good	Good	Good	Good	Good	Very Good	Excellent		•
	51	**Bissell** CleanView Plus 1334	$90	38	Good	Excellent	Good	Good	Good	Very Good	Excellent		•
	52	**Bissell** PowerGlide Deluxe Pet 2763	$180	37	Very Good	Excellent	Fair	Fair	Poor	Good	Excellent	•	
	53	**Bissell** PowerGlide Cordless 1534	$200	37	Fair	Excellent	Poor	Very Good	Excellent	Very Good	Excellent	•	
	54	**Bissell** Pet Hair Eraser 1650	$250	36	Fair	Good	Good	Good	Poor	Good	Excellent	•	•
	55	**Hoover** Air Cordless BH50140	$300	34	Fair	Excellent	Poor	Good	Poor	Excellent	Fair	•	
	56	**Hoover** Air Cordless Lift BH51120PC	$400	33	Fair	Excellent	Poor	Fair	Poor	Very Good	Good	•	
	57	**Eureka** AirSpeed Ultra AS4008A	$100	33	Fair	Excellent	Poor	Fair	Poor	Very Good	Excellent		•
		BAGGED UPRIGHT											
✓	1	**Kenmore** Elite 31150	$350	74	Very Good	Excellent	Excellent	Good	Excellent	Good	Excellent	•	•
✓	2	**Miele** Dynamic U1 Twist	$450	72	Excellent	Very Good	Very Good	Excellent	Good	Excellent		•	
✓	3	**Miele** Dynamic U1 Cat & Dog	$650	72	Very Good	Excellent	Very Good	Excellent	Good	Excellent		•	
$	4	**Kenmore** 31140	$200	71	Very Good	Excellent	Excellent	Good	Excellent	Good	Excellent	•	•
$	5	**Kenmore** Progressive 31069	$200	71	Very Good	Excellent	Excellent	Good	Very Good	Good	Excellent	•	•
$	6	**Hoover** WindTunnel Max UH30600	$180	70	Very Good	Excellent	Very Good	Good	Very Good	Good	Excellent	•	•

⊞ Does not accept tools.

RATINGS KEY ⊗ POOR ⊘ FAIR ● GOOD ◗ VERY GOOD ◉ EXCELLENT
$ **CR BEST BUY** These models offer the best combination of performance and price. All are recommended.
✓ **RECOMMENDED** These are high-performing models that stand out.

BAGGED UPRIGHT (Continued)

Recommended	Rank	Brand & Model	Price	Score	Carpet	Bare Floors	Tool Airflow	Noise	Emissions	Handling	Pet Hair	Brush On/Off	Manual-Pile Adjust
✓	7	**Kirby** Avalir	$1600	69	●	●	●	●	●	●	●	•	•
$	8	**Eureka** Boss Smart Vac 4870[ ]	$160	69	●	●	●	●	●	●	●	•	•
✓	9	**Miele** Dynamic U1 Jazz	$550	69	●	●	●	●	●	●	●	•	
✓	10	**Hoover** WindTunnel Anniversary U6485-900	$230	67	●	●	●	●	●	●	●	•	•
✓	11	**Sebo** Felix Premium	$600	66	●	●	●	●	●	●	●	•	
✓	12	**Hoover** WindTunnel T-Series Pet UH30310	$150	65	●	●	●	●	●	●	●	•	•
✓	13	**Hoover** WindTunnel T-Series UH30300	$140	65	●	●	●	●	●	●	●	•	•
✓	14	**Miele** Dynamic U1 AutoEco	$750	65	●	●	●	●	●	●	●	•	
	15	**Maytag** M1200	$900	64	●	●	●	●	●	●	●	•	•
	16	**Panasonic** MC-UG471	$150	63	●	●	●	●	●	●	●		
	17	**Hoover** Platinum Bagged UH30010COM	$300	61	●	●	NA	●	●	●	●		
	18	**Fuller Brush** Mighty Maid FBMM-PWCF	$400	58	●	●	●	●	●	●	●		
	19	**Oreck** Elevate Command	$450	58	●	●	●	●	●	●	●		
	20	**Oreck** Elevate Conquer	$600	58	●	●	●	●	●	●	●		
	21	**Oreck** Magnesium [ ]	$500	57	●	●	NA	●	●	●	●		
	22	**Riccar** Brilliance Premium	$900	57	●	●	●	●	●	●	●	•	•
	23	**Riccar** Supralite RSL4 [ ]	$470	55	●	●	NA	●	●	●	●		
	24	**Fuller Brush** Speedy Maid FB-SM [ ]	$300	54	●	●	NA	●	●	●	●		
	25	**Maytag** M700	$630	54	●	●	●	●	●	●	●	•	
	26	**Soniclean** VTPlus S-200 [ ]	$200	52	●	●	NA	●	●	●	●		
	27	**Maytag** M500 [ ]	$380	49	●	●	NA	●	●	●	●		
	28	**Oreck** Elevate Control	$300	49	●	●	●	●	●	●	●		
	29	**Sebo** automatic X5	$700	48	●	●	●	●	●	●	●		
	30	**Oreck** Graphite [ ]	$350	47	●	●	NA	●	●	●	●		

[ ] Does not accept tools.

BAGGED CANISTER

Recommended	Rank	Brand & Model	Price	Score	Carpet	Bare Floors	Tool Airflow	Noise	Emissions	Handling	Pet Hair	Brush On/Off	Manual-Pile Adjust
✓	1	**Miele** Complete C3 Marin	$1100	75	Very Good	Excellent	Excellent	Very Good	Excellent	Good	Excellent	•	•
✓	2	**Kenmore** Elite 21814	$500	74	Very Good	Excellent	Excellent	Good	Excellent	Fair	Very Good	•	•
✓	3	**Kenmore** Elite 81714	$400	73	Very Good	Excellent	Very Good	Good	Excellent	Good	Excellent	•	•
✓	4	**Kenmore** Progressive 21714	$400	72	Very Good	Excellent	Very Good	Good	Excellent	Good	Excellent	•	•
$	5	**Panasonic** MC-CG937	$330	71	Very Good	Excellent	Very Good	Good	Excellent	Good	Excellent	•	•
$	6	**Kenmore** Progressive 21614	$300	70	Very Good	Excellent	Very Good	Good	Excellent	Good	Excellent	•	•
$	7	**Kenmore** Progressive 21514	$250	68	Very Good	Excellent	Good	Good	Excellent	Good	Good	•	•
$	8	**Panasonic** MC-CG902	$250	65	Very Good	Excellent	Very Good	Good	Excellent	Good	Good	•	•
	9	**Hoover** WindTunnel S3670	$250	64	Very Good	Excellent	Good	Very Good	Excellent	Good	Fair	•	
	10	**Miele** Classic C1 Titan	$600	63	Good	Excellent	Excellent	Very Good	Excellent	Good	Excellent	•	
	11	**Panasonic** MC-CG983	$500	63	Very Good	Excellent	Very Good	Good	Excellent	Good	Good	•	•
	12	**Panasonic** MC-CG917	$300	63	Very Good	Good	Excellent	Good	Excellent	Good	Excellent	•	•
	13	**Riccar** Immaculate Premier	$1400	63	Good	Excellent	Very Good	Fair	Excellent	Good	Excellent	•	
	14	**Miele** Complete C3 Alize	$650	63	Good	Excellent	Excellent	Excellent	Excellent	Good	Very Good	NA	
	15	**Miele** Classic C1 Olympus	$330	58	Good	Excellent	Very Good	Good	Excellent	Good	Very Good	NA	NA
	16	**Miele** Classic C1 Delphi	$500	56	Good	Excellent	Very Good	Good	Excellent	Good	Fair	•	
	17	**Miele** Compact C2 Topaz	$750	55	Good	Excellent	Very Good	Good	Excellent	Good	Very Good	•	
	18	**Aerus** Lux Legacy	$1300	55	Good	Excellent	Very Good	Good	Excellent	Good	Excellent	•	
	19	**Aerus** Lux Guardian Ultra	$1500	52	Good	Excellent	Good	Good	Excellent	Good	Excellent	•	
	20	**Hoover** QuietForce SH30050	$300	51	Good	Excellent	Good	Good	Excellent	Good	Fair	•	
	21	**Sebo** Air Belt K3	$880	51	Good	Excellent	Good	Very Good	Excellent	Good	Excellent		

⊡ Does not accept tools.

RATINGS KEY ⊘ POOR ⊙ FAIR ❶ GOOD ⌃ VERY GOOD ⌃⌃ EXCELLENT

$ CR BEST BUY These models offer the best combination of performance and price. All are recommended.

✓ RECOMMENDED These are high-performing models that stand out.

Recommended	Rank	Brand & Model	Price	Score	Test Results							Brush On/Off	Manual-Pile Adjust
					Carpet	Bare Floors	Tool Airflow	Noise	Emissions	Handling	Pet Hair		
		BAGLESS CANISTER											
$	1	**Kenmore** 22614	$350	68								•	•
$	2	**Panasonic** MC-CL935	$330	68								•	•
✓	3	**Hoover** Platinum S3865	$400	65								•	•
	4	**Samsung** VC5000 SC12F50PJ	$600	61								•	
	5	**Rainbow** e-series E2	$1350	54								•	•
	6	**Samsung** VC-F700G with Power Brush VC12F70PRJ	$450	53								•	
	7	**Dyson** Ball Multi Floor	$400	51								•	
	8	**Hoover** Multi-Cyclonic SH40060	$150	49								Yes	No
	9	**Hoover** WindTunnel Air SH40070	$180	48								Yes	No
	10	**Hoover** Elite Cyclonic S3825	$200	45								Yes	Yes
	11	**Hoover** Zen Whisper SH40080	$250	44								Yes	No
	12	**Samsung** Electric Blue VCC88P0H1B	$350	43								Yes	Yes
	13	**Samsung** Champagne VCC96P0H1G	$450	42								Yes	Yes
	14	**Hoover** Air Pro SH40075	$230	41								Yes	No
	15	**Dyson** Cinetic Animal	$550	41								No	No
	16	**Dyson** Ball Compact Animal	$450	34								Yes	No

1 Does not accept tools.

Guide to the Ratings

Score is based mainly on cleaning performance and ease of use. The displayed score is out of a total of 100 points. **Carpet** indicates how much embedded talc and sand a vacuum lifted from a medium-pile carpet. **Bare Floors** shows how well a vacuum picked up sand without dispersing it on bare floors. **Tool Airflow** indicates the strength of airflow through the hose. **Noise** is based on measurements in decibels. **Emissions** indicates our measurement of the quantity of wood-flour particles a vacuum released under two conditions: when only the motor was turned on and while vacuuming. **Handling** reflects how easy it is to push, pull, and carry a vacuum. **Pet Hair** reflects how well a vacuum picks up pet hair from medium-pile carpet. **Price** is approximate retail.

Most & Least Reliable
Percentage likely to break by third year of ownership.

CANISTERS
Panasonic	7%
Miele	10%
Kenmore	11%
Electrolux	14%
Hoover	15%
Dyson	16%

UPRIGHTS
Kirby	4%
Shark	6%
Dirt Devil	8%
Kenmore	8%
Bissell	9%
Hoover	11%
Eureka	11%
Riccar	12%
Oreck	12%
Simplicity	13%
Dyson	13%
Miele	15%
Electrolux	16%

The graph shows the estimated failure rates for vacuums by the third year of ownership for each brand. Differences of fewer than 6 percentage points aren't meaningful. Results are based on the responses of 19,562 owners of full-sized upright vacuums and full-sized canister vacuums. The statistical model estimates failure rates for vacuums purchased new and not covered by a service contract. Note that models within a brand may vary.

Source 2015 Summer Product Reliability Survey, Consumer Reports National Research Center.

Wall ovens

Flexibility is one of the biggest attractions of wall ovens, which can go where you want them, even under a counter or in an island base. And lower prices have made wall oven and cooktop combinations more affordable.

What to Look For

■ Large oven capacity and a very good or excellent baking score, if you like to bake.

■ Five or more oven rack positions for more flexibility in arranging racks and bakeware.

■ A covered heating element that's below the oven floor, making spill cleanup easier and faster.

■ Easy-to-reach and -read controls. Consider side-swing and French-door styles for easy accessibility, if your budget allows.

What to Skip

■ A small oven window, which won't allow a full view of the interior.

■ Menu databases and other perks if you want to save money.

What You'll Pay

You can get an electric cooktop and wall oven starting at $2,000, though capable ranges can cost far less.

BUYING ADVICE

Measure your cutout space, then check the manual of the wall oven you're considering for its cutout dimensions.

For more buying advice, go to ConsumerReports.org/ovens.

All tested models in performance order.

Recommended	Rank	Brand & Model	Price	Score	Baking	Broiling	Oven Capacity	Self-Cleaning	Width (in.)	Covered Element	Convection Mode	Temperature Probe
		SINGLE ELECTRIC										
$	1	**Whirlpool** WOS92ECOAH	$1500	80	⌃	⌃⌃	⌃⌃	⌃⌃	30	•	•	
✓	2	**GE** Café CT9070SHSS	$3600	76	⌃	⌃	⌃	⌃⌃	30	•	•	•
✓	3	**KitchenAid** KOSE500ESS	$2300	74	⌃	⌃⌃	⌃⌃	❶	30	•	•	•
✓	4	**GE** Profile PT9050SFSS	$2430	73	⌃	⌃	⌃	⌃	30	•	•	•

Recommended	Rank	Brand & Model	Price	Score	Baking	Broiling	Oven Capacity	Self-Cleaning	Width (in.)	Covered Element	Convection Mode	Temperature Probe
		SINGLE ELECTRIC (Continued)										
$	5	**Whirlpool** WOS51ECOAS	$1300	72	Very Good	Excellent	Excellent	Excellent	30	•		
✓	6	**Maytag** MEW9530DS	$1800	72	Very Good	Very Good	Excellent	Very Good	30	•	•	
	7	**GE** JT5000SFSS	$1800	70	Very Good	Very Good	Excellent	Very Good	30	•	•	
	8	**Frigidaire** Gallery FGEW3065PW	$1260	70	Excellent	Good	Good	Very Good	30	•	•	
	9	**Kenmore** 49513	$1350	68	Very Good	Good	Good	Excellent	30	•	•	
	10	**Electrolux** EW30EW55PS	$2100	66	Very Good	Very Good	Good	Excellent	30	•	•	
	11	**Viking** VESO5302SS	$4300	66	Very Good	Very Good	Good	Very Good	30	•	•	•
	12	**Thermador** ME301JS	$2700	63	Very Good	Very Good	Good	Very Good	30	•	•	•
	13	**LG** LWS3063	$1800	60	Good	Excellent	Very Good	Excellent	30	•	•	
	14	**GE** JT3000SFSS	$1400	58	Good	Very Good	Excellent	Very Good	30	•		
	15	**Viking** Professional VSOF730SS	$5250	56	Very Good	Fair	Very Good	NA	30	•	•	•
	16	**Bosch** HBLP451RUC	$2900	55	Good	Very Good	Very Good	Excellent	30	•	•	
	17	**Kenmore** 48363	$2430	52	Good	Very Good	Very Good	Very Good	30	•	•	
	18	**Bosch** HBL5351UC	$1500	51	Good	Very Good	Very Good	Excellent	30			
	19	**Frigidaire** Professional FPEW3077RF	$2300	48	Fair	Excellent	Very Good	Very Good	30	•	•	•
		DOUBLE ELECTRIC										
✓	1	**Whirlpool** WOD93ECOAS ⊞	$2350	80	Very Good	Excellent	Excellent	Excellent	30	•	•	
✓	2	**GE** PT9550SFSS ⊞	$3350	73	Very Good	Very Good	Very Good	Very Good	30	•	•	
✓	3	**Whirlpool** WOD51ECOA ⊞	$1850	72	Very Good	Excellent	Very Good	Excellent	30	•	•	
	4	**GE** JT5500SFSS ⊞	$2550	70	Very Good	Very Good	Excellent	Very Good	30	•	•	
	5	**LG** LWD3010ST ⊞	$2500	65	Good	Excellent	Very Good	Good	30	•	•	
	6	**Thermador** ME302JS ⊞	$4000	63	Very Good	Very Good	Good	Very Good	30	•	•	•
	7	**GE** JT3500SFSS ⊞	$1900	58	Good	Very Good	Excellent	Very Good	30	•		

⊞ The performance of this model is based on the tested oven in the single electric wall oven category.

RATINGS KEY ⊖ POOR ⊘ FAIR ❶ GOOD ⌃ VERY GOOD ⌃⌃ EXCELLENT
$ **CR BEST BUY** These models offer the best combination of performance and price. All are recommended.
✓ **RECOMMENDED** These are high-performing models that stand out.

Guide to the Ratings

Score reflects oven capacity and baking, broiling, and self-cleaning ability. The displayed score is out of a total of 100 points. **Baking** reflects whether cakes and cookies baked on two racks were evenly browned. **Broiling** is based on even browning of a pan of burgers, and high-heat searing ability. **Oven Capacity** measures usable space. **Self-Cleaning** gauges the self-cleaning cycle's effectiveness. **Price** is approximate retail. The performance of double wall-oven models is based on the tested single electric oven.

Most & Least Reliable

Percentage likely to break by third year of ownership.

ELECTRIC

Kenmore	7%
GE	8%
Whirlpool	11%
Frigidaire	11%
Bosch	11%
Electrolux	12%
KitchenAid	14%

The chart shows what we found when we surveyed 4,703 subscribers who reported on their experiences with wall ovens purchased new between 2010 and 2015. The statistical model estimates failure rates for wall ovens that were purchased new and not covered by a service contract, by the third year of ownership. Differences of fewer than 6 percentage points are not meaningful. Models within a brand may vary, and design or manufacture changes may affect future reliability. Still, choosing a brand with a good repair history can improve your odds of getting a reliable model.

Source 2015 Summer Product Reliability Survey, Consumer Reports National Research Center.

QUICK GUIDE

Washers

Larger capacities let you wash more things at once so that you can do laundry less often. You'll also find options that cut wash time without affecting cleaning and Wi-Fi-enabled washers that provide remote control via your smart device.

What to Look For
- Capacity that matches your needs.
- A stainless-steel tub, which can withstand higher spin speeds, extracting more water and cutting dryer time.
- An automatic dispenser that releases detergent at the right time in the cycle.
- An extra rinse cycle, if you or others in your home are sensitive to detergent residue or need that extra water to get rid of pet hair.

What to Skip
- The steam option did boost cleaning slightly in our tests, but washers with it cleaned well without using that feature.

What You'll Pay
Capable machines that combine performance and value start at less than $500.

Compact Washers
These washers and dryers are an appealing option when space is tight. Despite their reduced size, their price isn't—you'll spend $900 to $2,000 on each appliance. All of the models we tested are stackable.

BUYING ADVICE
Look at washers that score very good or better for noise and vibration if your laundry room is near bedrooms or the family room.

For more buying advice, go to ConsumerReports.org/washers.

Recommended	Rank	Brand & Model	Price	Score	Washing Performance	Energy Efficiency	Water Efficiency	Gentleness	Noise	Vibration	Claimed Capacity (cu. ft.)	Cycle Time (min.)
		FRONT LOADERS										
✓	1	**Maytag** Maxima MHW8200FW	$1150	86							4.5	70
✓	2	**Samsung** WF56H9110CW	$1450	84							5.6	90
$	3	**LG** WM3170CW	$720	84							4.3	110
✓	4	**LG** WM9000HVA ⓘ	$1350	83							5.2	105
✓	5	**LG** WM8500HVA ⓘ	$1450	83							5.2	90
✓	6	**Samsung** WF45K6500AW	$1000	83							4.5	100
✓	7	**Samsung** WF50K7500AW	$1100	82							5	100
✓	8	**Maytag** Maxima MHW8100DC	$1400	82							4.5	75
✓	9	**LG** WM5000HWA	$1000	82							4.5	105
$	10	**Maytag** Maxima MHW5100DW	$900	81							4.5	75
✓	11	**Whirlpool** Duet WFL98HEBU	$1440	81							4.3	75
✓	12	**Whirlpool** Duet WFW87HEDW	$650	81							4.3	70
		TOP LOAD HIGH-EFFICIENCY WASHERS										
✓	1	**LG** WT5680HVA	$1000	72							5.2	75
✓	2	**Samsung** WA52J8700AP	$1080	72							5.2	75
✓	3	**LG** WT1701CV	$700	71							5.0	75
✓	4	**Samsung** WA52J8060AW	$900	71							5.2	75
$	5	**Samsung** WA45H7000AW	$530	71							4.5	80
	6	**Samsung** WA56H9000AP	$1200	70							5.6	75
	7	**Whirlpool** Cabrio WTW8500DW	$750	70							5.3	80
	8	**LG** WT1101CW	$670	69							4.3	75

ⓘ This washer is several inches wider and deeper than most other washers.

Recommended	Rank	Brand & Model	Price	Score	Washing Performance	Energy Efficiency	Water Efficiency	Gentleness	Noise	Vibration	Claimed Capacity (cu. ft.)	Cycle Time (min.)
		TOP LOAD HIGH-EFFICIENCY WASHERS (Continued)										
	9	**Kenmore** 28132	$640	69	Very Good	Very Good	Very Good	Good	Very Good	Excellent	5.3	60
	10	**Maytag** Bravos MVWB855DW	$1000	69	Very Good	Very Good	Excellent	Good	Very Good	Excellent	5.3	80
	11	**GE** GTW860SSJWS	$1000	69	Very Good	Excellent	Excellent	Good	Good	Excellent	5.1	70
	12	**Kenmore** 26132	$500	69	Very Good	Very Good	Very Good	Good	Very Good	Excellent	4.8	60
	13	**Kenmore** 27132	$580	69	Very Good	Very Good	Very Good	Good	Very Good	Excellent	4.8	60
		COMPACT FRONT LOADERS										
	1	**Bosch** 800 Series WAT28402UC	$1250	78	Very Good	Excellent	Excellent	Excellent	Excellent	Good	2.2	60
	2	**Electrolux** EIFLS20QSW	$900	75	Excellent	Very Good	Very Good	Good	Very Good	Good	2.4	110
	3	**Kenmore** 41912	$880	75	Excellent	Very Good	Very Good	Good	Very Good	Good	2.4	110
	4	**Miele** W3048	$2000	73	Very Good	Very Good	Excellent	Excellent	Excellent	Good	2.0	85
	5	**Samsung** WW22K6800AW	$900	69	Very Good	Excellent	Excellent	Very Good	Very Good	Fair	2.2	100
	6	**GE** WCVH4800KWW	$900	64	Good	Excellent	Excellent	Excellent	Very Good	Good	2.2	65
	7	**Asko** XL Series W8844XLW	$2300	56	Very Good	Very Good	Good	Good	Very Good	Fair	2.7	145
	8	**LG** WM1377HW	$900	53	Good	Excellent	Excellent	Excellent	Good	Good	2.3	75
	9	**Asko** W6424W	$900	50	Good	Very Good	Very Good	Very Good	Very Good	Fair	2.0	75
	10	**Blomberg** WM98400SX	$1200	45	Good	Very Good	Very Good	Very Good	Very Good	Fair	2.5	95

RATINGS KEY ⊘ POOR ⌄ FAIR ❶ GOOD ⌃ VERY GOOD ⌃⌃ EXCELLENT
🅢 **CR BEST BUY** These models offer the best combination of performance and price. All are recommended.
✅ **RECOMMENDED** These are high-performing models that stand out.

Guide to Ratings

Score is based mainly on washing ability, efficiency, capacity, and noise. The displayed score is out of a total of 100 points. **Washing Performance** reflects the degree of color change to swatches of fabric using the most aggressive normal cycle. **Energy Efficiency** is based on the energy needed to heat the water using a warm wash and cold rinse, to run the washer, and to dry the remaining moisture in the clothes at the end of a cycle. **Water Efficiency** is based on total water used when washing our 8-pound load. **Capacity** is based on claimed tub volume. Models that earned lower scores for **Gentleness** are more likely to treat your clothes roughly, causing wear and tear. **Noise** reflects panelists' judgments during the fill, agitate, and spin cycles. **Vibration** reflects usage on a suspended wooden floor. Cycle Time (min.) is rounded to the nearest 5 minutes. **Price** is approximate retail.

Most & Least Reliable

Percentage likely to break by fifth year of ownership.

FRONT-LOADERS

LG	18%
Samsung	19%
Kenmore	23%
Electrolux	23%
Whirlpool	25%
Maytag	26%
GE	27%
Frigidaire	29%

HIGH-EFFICENCY TOP-LOADERS

Maytag	19%
LG	19%
GE	20%
Whirlpool	22%
Kenmore	23%
Samsung	24%

These conclusions are based on our failure-rate estimates for washing machines by the fifth year of ownership, gathered from 69,277 subscribers who purchased a new washer between 2008 and 2016. Our statistical model estimates failure rates for washers not covered by a service contract and accounts for the number of loads of laundry run through the machines per week. Differences of less than 5 points aren't meaningful. Models within a brand may vary, and changes in design or manufacturer may affect future reliability.

Source 2016 Winter Product Reliability Survey, Consumer Reports National Research Center.

Autos

⚠ What You Need to Know About Semi-Autonomous Technology

Consumer Reports believes that autonomous vehicle technology has the potential to improve driver safety. But we also have serious concerns about the way certain semi-autonomous systems, some of which allow a car to steer for itself, are currently being designed, deployed, and marketed. We think automakers need to clearly communicate the capabilities—and the limitations—of these systems.

Because this is a new and rapidly evolving technology, little data exists on the safety or benefits of these systems, so we currently don't factor them into our ratings criteria. Our ratings and recommendations are based on a performance assessment from Consumer Reports track evaluations of how well a car drives (i.e., braking, handling, fuel economy) and reliability scores from our Annual Auto Survey, as well as safety evaluations and external crash tests.

But we do monitor these types of emerging technologies closely. Many automakers have promoted semi-autonomous systems as a safety feature to help with driver distraction and fatigue, but drivers are supposed to remain engaged with the driving process at all times. Some companies, such as Tesla and Mercedes-Benz, have used names such as Autopilot and Drive Pilot, which can give the false and dangerous impression that these cars are more capable than they really are. Several of these systems also allow you to take your hands off the wheel. Consumer Reports believes that as long as these systems require driver engagement, they should also require the driver to keep his or her hands on the wheel.

Several of the vehicles in these reliability charts offer semi-autonomous features. They include Tesla's Model S, whose reliability improved enough to qualify for recommended status under our criteria, as well as certain vehicles from BMW, Mercedes-Benz, and Volvo.

We will continue to monitor the evolution of self-driving technology and evaluate whether to make future adjustments to our ratings.

To learn more about self-driving technology and see our expert evaluations, go to consumerreports.org/selfdriving.

The Highs and Lows of the 2017 Models

This overview of the highs and lows of all the major 2017 models can start you on your search for a new car, minivan, SUV, or pickup. Each listing includes the positive and negative attributes for the model.

The majority of the highs and lows are based on our experiences with tested vehicles, and the findings are applicable to the 2017 model-year vehicles.

In some cases there are models that we have not put through our formal testing. However, we have spent time with them, either by renting a version from the manufacturer and evaluating it at our Auto Test Center, or by participating in a media event. We have indicated those tested models whose powertrain has changed since we last tested with asterisks (**) following the vehicle name.

After reading the overviews, turn to our Vehicle Ratings (page 169) to see how individual models ranked according to their overall score, which accounts for a vehicle's performance in our road tests, results from our reliability and owner satisfaction surveys, the availability of a frontal crash-prevention system, and, if applicable, safety tests done by the government and insurance industry.

The Ratings include Consumer Reports' predicted reliability rating, an indication of how problematic we expect a model to be. It is based on our 2016 Annual Auto Survey, where we asked owners about any serious problems they've had with their vehicles in the previous 12 months. Turn to page 192 for more information on reliability.

Recommended models (✓) must perform well in our road tests; have average or better reliability; and perform adequately if included in safety tests conducted by the Insurance Institute for Highway Safety (IIHS) and the National Highway Traffic Safety Administration (NHTSA).

Make & Model	Highs	Lows
Acura ILX Premium	Fuel economy.	Stiff ride, loud cabin, access, controls, overpriced for what you get.
Acura MDX Tech	Fuel economy, fit and finish, easy third-row access, rear seat, standard electronic safety features, headlights.	Controls, transmission and shifter, agility, suspension noise, rear visibility.
Acura RDX	Acceleration, access, front-seat comfort.	Ride, at-the-limit handling, rear visibility.
Acura RLX Tech	Spacious and plush interior, seat comfort, braking.	Ride, agility, complicated controls, suspension noise.
Acura TLX 2.4L	Powertrain, fuel economy, braking.	Reliability, annoying audio controls, lacks panache.
Acura TLX SH-AWD	Acceleration, fuel economy, braking.	Reliability, transmission and shifter, annoying audio controls, lacks panache.
Alfa Romeo Giulia	Have not evaluated yet.	
Audi A3 Premium	Handling, feels solid, braking, standard frontal collision avoidance.	Rear seat, some controls, pricey, tepid power off the line, headlights, reliability.
Audi A4	Ride, handling, quietness, transmission, fit and finish, front seat comfort, fuel economy, high-tech features, standard forward collision avoidance.	Controls take getting used to, unintuitive shifter, tight rear seat.
Audi A6 3.0 Premium Plus Quattro	Powertrain, handling, ride, quietness, fuel economy, front-seat comfort, fit and finish, high-tech features.	Controls take getting used to, turning circle.
Audi A8 L**	Handling, acceleration, transmission, braking, seat comfort, quietness, fit and finish, fuel economy, high-tech features.	Controls take getting used to, small trunk.
Audi Allroad	Have not evaluated redesign.	
Audi Q3 Premium Plus	Ride, handling, quietness, fit and finish, reliability.	Tight quarters, narrow driving position.

Make & Model	Highs	Lows
Audi Q5 Premium Plus (2.0T)	Handling, transmission, braking, fit and finish.	Controls take getting used to.
Audi Q7 Premium Plus	Powertrain, quietness, handling, braking, high-tech features, luxury interior, towing capacity, standard forward-collision avoidance.	Controls take getting used to, rear visibility, shifter.
Audi TT Coupe 2.0T (AT)	Agility, braking, front-seat comfort, fit and finish, fuel economy, versatility, hatch-back, high-tech features.	Controls take getting used to, ride, access, tiny rear seat.
BMW 328d xDrive	Handling, ride, fuel economy, transmission, front-seat comfort, fit and finish, visibility.	Tight rear seat, some controls, diesel-engine noise, pricey options.
BMW 328i**	Handling, ride, acceleration, transmission, front-seat comfort, fit and finish, fuel economy, visibility.	Engine clatter, some controls, tight rear seat, pricey options.
BMW 535i	Powertrain, acceleration, ride, quietness, fit and finish, front-seat comfort.	Disappointing handling, controls.
BMW 750i xDrive ⚠	Ride, quietness, powertrain, seat comfort, room, fit and finish, lots of high-tech features, fuel economy.	Narrow trunk, steep learning curve for controls.
BMW i3 Giga	Energy efficiency, acceleration, agility, reduced range anxiety with optional gasoline engine.	Long trips require frequent fill-ups, seats only four, rear-seat access, cargo space, stingy instrumentation.
BMW M235i**	Acceleration, handling, braking, front-seat comfort, quietness, reliability.	Rear seat room, some controls.
BMW X1 xDrive28i	Fuel economy, braking, transmission.	Road noise, narrow front seats, stiff ride, no blind-spot monitoring.
BMW X3 xDrive28i (2.0T)	Agility, powertrain, braking, fuel economy, fit and finish.	Controls, low rear seat.
BMW X5 xDrive35i	Drivetrain, fuel economy, quietness, seat comfort, fit and finish, visibility.	Reliability, some controls.

⚠ **Alert:** This vehicle can be outfitted with a semi-autonomous driving package. Consumer Reports believes automakers should take stronger steps to ensure that vehicles with those systems are designed, deployed, and marketed safely. Please heed all warnings, and keep your hands on the wheel.

Make & Model	Highs	Lows
BMW Z4 sDrive28i	Acceleration, fuel economy, braking.	Steering feel, ride, noise, tight quarters, access.
Buick Enclave CXL	Ride, handling, interior room and flexibility, quietness, fit and finish, easy access to usable third seat.	Fuel economy, rear visibility.
Buick Encore Leather	Ride, quietness, braking, maneuverability, fuel economy, reliability.	Acceleration, driving position, narrow cabin, rear visibility, value.
Buick Envision	Have not evaluated redesign.	
Buick LaCrosse	Have not evaluated redesign.	
Buick Regal Premium I	Acceleration, ride, handling, braking, controls.	Rear seat, rear visibility.
Buick Verano Leather (2.4)	Quietness, transmission, braking.	Front-seat comfort, tight rear-seat, narrow driving position.
Cadillac ATS Luxury (turbo)	Handling, fun to drive, acceleration, braking, fit and finish, front-seat comfort.	Reliability, CUE, tight interior, small trunk, turbo lacks refinement, access.
Cadillac CT6	Have not evaluated redesign.	
Cadillac CTS Luxury (V6, AWD)	Agility, fun to drive, front seats, plush interior, braking.	Complicated CUE controls, rear seat, trunk.
Cadillac Escalade Premium	Quietness, fit and finish, front-seat comfort, towing capacity, headlights.	Reliability, stiff ride, handling, braking, unintuitive CUE infotainment system, tiny third-row seat.
Cadillac XT5	Have not evaluated redesign.	
Cadillac XTS Premium	Roomy interior and trunk, seat comfort, fit and finish, quietness, braking, transmission.	Frustrating CUE control interface, ride not plush enough, visibility, small trunk opening.
Chevrolet Bolt	Have not evaluated yet.	
Chevrolet Camaro 2SS (V8)	Acceleration, handling, braking, styling.	Visibility, tight interior, low dash vents.

Make & Model	Highs	Lows
Chevrolet Colorado LT (V6)	Maneuverability, towing and payload capacities, fuel economy standard rear camera, damped tail gate.	Reliability, ride, uncomfortable seats and driving position, gets pricey.
Chevrolet Corvette Stingray 3LT	Acceleration, handling, braking, engine sound, controls, fit and finish, performance for the price.	Ride, noise, access, visibility, shifter.
Chevrolet Cruze LT	Ride, quietness, among roomiest in class, reliability.	Front seat support, rear visibility.
Chevrolet Equinox 1LT (4-cyl.)	Rear seat, ride, handling, fuel economy.	Acceleration, transmission, visibility, turning circle.
Chevrolet Equinox LTZ (V6)	Acceleration, ride, roomy rear seat, access.	Visibility, sluggish feel.
Chevrolet Impala 2LTZ (3.6)	Ride, handling, braking, quietness, spacious cabin and trunk, advanced electronic safety features.	Rear visibility.
Chevrolet Malibu 1LT (1.5T)	Ride, quietness, controls, fuel economy.	Raspy 1.5-liter turbo, front seat comfort, so-so visibility.
Chevrolet Silverado 1500 LT (5.3L V8)	Fuel economy, quietness, relatively good agility and access, payload and towing capacity, low-effort tailgate.	Reliability, ride, long wet stopping distances, seat comfort.
Chevrolet Sonic LT (1.8L)	Braking, trunk, quick and quiet for class.	Fuel economy, darty steering, narrow driving position, seat comfort.
Chevrolet Sonic LTZ (hatchback, 1.4T, MT)	Braking, quick and quiet for class.	So-so fuel economy, manual gear ratios and shifter, narrow driving position, seat comfort, rear visibility.
Chevrolet Spark 1LT	Easy to park, braking, fuel economy.	Acceleration, ride, noise, seat comfort, driving position.
Chevrolet SS	Acceleration, handling, braking, interior room, controls, feature content.	Fuel-thirsty, no exterior trunk release, summer tires are unusable in snow.
Chevrolet Suburban LTZ	Utility, quietness, fit and finish, easy to use infotainment system, cargo and towing capacity.	Reliability, step-in height, long length to park, feels underpowered, price.

Make & Model	Highs	Lows
Chevrolet Tahoe LT	Quietness, fit and finish, easy to use infotainment system, cargo and towing capacity.	Reliability, handling, stiff ride, feels underpowered, step-in height, price.
Chevrolet Traverse LT	Ride, handling, quietness, interior room and flexibility, usable third-row seat, blind-spot mirrors.	Rear visibility, fuel economy, wet braking.
Chevrolet Trax LT	Fuel economy, easy to park, decent room within a small footprint, crash-test results.	Acceleration, ride, engine noise, rear visibility, front seats, touch-screen radio.
Chevrolet Volt LT	Can be electric without range anxiety, ride, quietness, controls.	Visibility, tight rear-seat, front-seat comfort, driving position, access, reliability.
Chrysler 200 C (V6)	Powerful V6, controls.	Reliability, agility, access, rear-seat head room, visibility.
Chrysler 200 Limited (4-cyl.)	Fuel economy, controls.	Reliability, transmission, ride, touchy brakes, agility, access, rear-seat head room, visibility.
Chrysler 300 C (V8)	Acceleration, transmission, ride, quietness, seat comfort, fit and finish.	None.
Chrysler 300 Limited (V6)	Acceleration, transmission, ride, quietness, seat comfort, fit and finish.	Headlights.
Chrysler Pacifica Touring L	Interior space and flexibility, ride, quietness, Uconnect 8.4 infotainment system, access, fuel economy, lots of optional features.	Expensive to get advanced safety gear, coarse-sounding engine, Chrysler reliability.
Dodge Challenger R/T Plus (V8)	Braking, exhaust note, infotainment system, habitable rear seat, brawn.	Reliability, ride, noise, visibility, wide-hipped around town.
Dodge Charger R/T Plus (V8)	V8 sound and power, transmission, easy-to-use infotainment system.	Reliability, visibility, access.
Dodge Charger SXT (V6)	Transmission, quietness, ride, interior room, feature content.	Reliability, visibility, access.
Dodge Dart SXT (2.4L)	Handling, braking, easy to use Uconnect screen.	Engine clatter at idle, seat comfort, fit and finish.

Make & Model	Highs	Lows
Dodge Durango Limited (V6)	Ride, quietness, transmission, interior space, access, front-seat comfort, usable third-row seat, towing capacity.	Rear visibility, maneuverability, reliability.
Dodge Grand Caravan R/T	Ride, quietness, foldaway second-row seats, cargo flexibility.	Poor IIHS small overlap crash-test results, fuel economy, cornering limits, unrefined transmission, radio controls.
Dodge Journey Limited (V6)	Ride, quietness, cabin storage.	Poor IIHS small overlap crash-test results, reliability, handling, unresponsive transmission, fuel economy, rear visibility, tiny third-row.
Fiat 500 Abarth	Invigorating exhaust note, agility, braking, fuel economy.	Reliability, noise, ride, steering feel, driving position, controls, tiny rear seat and cargo area, rear visibility, turning circle.
Fiat 500 Sport (MT)	Handling, shifter, fuel economy, front access.	Reliability, poor IIHS small overlap crash-test results, acceleration, ride, noise, seats, driving position, controls.
Fiat 500C Pop (MT)	Fuel economy, agility, shifter, front access, clever top design.	Reliability, acceleration, ride, driving position, front-seat comfort, rear visibility, trunk.
Fiat 500L Easy**	Roomy interior, handy size, access.	Reliability, poor IIHS small overlap crash-test results, stiff ride, touchy brake pedal, front seats, driving position.
Fiat 500X Easy	Maneuverability, upscale features.	Ride, transmission, noise, idle vibration, touchy brake pedal, visibility, front-seat comfort.
Ford C-Max Energi	Fuel economy, ride, handling, quietness, access, maximizes electric mode.	Grabby brakes, battery robs cargo area, expensive to get rear camera.
Ford C-Max Hybrid SE	Fuel economy, ride, handling, quietness, access, utility.	Some controls, grabby brakes, small cargo area, expensive to get rear camera.
Ford Edge SEL (2.0 EcoBoost)	Ride, quietness, handling, rear seat and cargo, access, luxury amenities in high-end versions.	Visibility, acceleration.

Make & Model	Highs	Lows
Ford Escape SE (1.6T)**	Agility, ride, quietness, solid feel, access.	Narrow driving position, some controls.
Ford Escape Titanium (2.0T)	Agility, ride, quietness, solid feel, access.	Narrow driving position, some controls.
Ford Expedition EL Limited	Huge interior, plenty of power, comfortable third-row seat, towing capacity, reliability.	Fuel economy, noise, clumsy handling, cheap cabin finish, lacks advanced safety gear, feels outdated.
Ford Explorer XLT (V6)	Interior room and flexibility, usable third-row, cabin storage.	Agility, driving position, some controls, unrefined transmission, reliability.
Ford F-150 XLT (2.7 V6 EcoBoost)	Quiet cabin, acceleration, fuel economy, towing and payload capacities, lots of clever features.	Jittery ride, lackluster handling, braking, reliability.
Ford F-150 XLT (3.5 V6 EcoBoost)	Quiet cabin, acceleration, fuel economy, towing and payload capacities, lots of clever features.	Jittery ride, lackluster handling, braking.
Ford Fiesta SE	Handling, ride, noise, fuel economy, turning circle.	Reliability, acceleration, rear seat, some controls, braking.
Ford Fiesta SE (3-cyl., MT)	Handling, braking, ride, noise, fuel economy, turning circle.	Reliability, some controls, rear seat, rear visibility, narrow power band, relatively expensive.
Ford Fiesta SE (hatchback, MT)	Handling, ride, noise, fuel economy, turning circle.	Reliability, acceleration, rear seat, some controls, rear visibility.
Ford Fiesta ST	Handling agility, effortless power delivery, sound, braking, fuel economy, fun-to-drive.	Reliability, ride, snug optional Recaro seats.
Ford Flex SEL	Ride, quietness, interior room and flexibility.	Lackluster handling, turning circle, rear visibility.
Ford Focus Electric	Fun to drive, handling, ride, instant power delivery, quietness.	Reliability, touchy throttle and brake pedal, battery takes up trunk space, rear seat, limited range.
Ford Focus SE (1.0T)	Agility, ride, quietness.	Reliability, Snug interior, slow acceleration without any fuel-economy benefit.

Make & Model	Highs	Lows
Ford Focus SE (2.0L)	Agility, ride, quietness.	Reliability, Snug interior, transmission causes low-speed vibration.
Ford Focus ST	Handling, fun to drive, acceleration, braking, relatively civilized as a daily driver.	Reliability, driving position, snug Recaro seats, some torque steer, turning circle.
Ford Fusion SE (1.5T)	Agility, ride, quietness, fun to drive, braking.	Fuel economy, visibility, slightly snug cabin, small trunk opening.
Ford Fusion SE Hybrid	Fuel economy, agility, ride, quietness, fun to drive, powertrain.	Visibility, touchy brakes, slightly snug cabin, small trunk opening.
Ford Fusion Titanium (2.0T)	Agility, ride, quietness, fun to drive, braking.	Fuel economy, visibility, slightly snug cabin, small trunk opening.
Ford Mustang GT Premium (V8)	Handling, acceleration, braking, interior details, exhaust note.	Reliability, rear seat, ride.
Ford Mustang Premium (4-cyl., AT)	Handling, braking, fuel economy, interior details.	Reliability, rear seat, noise, raspy engine sound.
Ford Taurus Limited (3.5, V6)	Quietness, trunk space.	Visibility, driving position.
Ford Transit Connect XLT (2.5L)	Interior space, access, front visibility, handling, ride.	Acceleration, difficult to fold seats, wind noise, some controls, fit and finish, sparse on features.
Genesis G80 3.8 (AWD)	Ride, braking, quietness, slick powertrain, plush interior, long warranty, standard frontal collision avoidance.	Overzealous lane-keeping assist.
Genesis G90	Have not evaluated yet.	
GMC Acadia	Have not evaluated redesign.	
GMC Canyon SLE (V6)	Maneuverability, towing and payload capacities, fuel economy, standard rear camera, damped tailgate.	Reliability, ride, uncomfortable seats and driving position, gets pricey.

Make & Model	Highs	Lows
GMC Sierra 1500 SLT (5.3L V8)	Fuel economy, quietness, relatively good agility and access, payload and towing capacity, low-effort tailgate.	Reliability, ride, long wet stopping distances, seat comfort.
GMC Terrain SLE1 (4-cyl.)	Rear seat, ride, handling, fuel economy.	Acceleration, transmission, visibility, turning circle.
GMC Terrain SLT2 (V6)	Acceleration, ride, roomy rear seat, access.	Visibility, sluggish feel.
GMC Yukon SLT	Quietness, fit and finish, easy to use infotainment system, cargo and towing capacity.	Reliability, handling, stiff ride, feels underpowered, step-in height, price.
GMC Yukon XL SLT	Utility, quietness, fit and finish, easy to use infotainment system, cargo and towing capacity.	Reliability, handling, stiff ride, step-in height, long length to park, feels underpowered, price.
Honda Accord EX-L (V6)	Fuel economy, powertrain, handling, roomy interior, visibility, driving position.	Complicated optional radio, ride a bit choppy.
Honda Accord LX (4-cyl.)	Fuel economy, powertrain, handling, roomy interior, visibility, driving position, controls.	Complicated optional radio, ride a bit choppy.
Honda Civic EX-T	Fuel economy, ride, handling, interior storage.	Awkward access, front-seat comfort, complicated infotainment for EX and higher trims, reliability.
Honda Civic LX	Fuel economy, ride, handling, interior storage.	Awkward access, front seat comfort, reliability.
Honda CR-V EX	Rear seat, roomy and functional, fuel economy, active safety features on higher trims.	Ride, noise, unintuitive infotainment system.
Honda Fit EX	Fuel economy, interior room, versatility, handling, access, standard rear camera.	Ride, noise, confusing uplevel audio system.
Honda HR-V LX	Fuel economy, roomy interior, storage, secure handling.	Ride, noise, acceleration, front-seat comfort, rear door handles.

Make & Model	Highs	Lows
Honda Odyssey EX-L	Ride, powertrain, fuel economy, spacious and flexible interior, comfortable seats.	Confusing uplevel radio, fit and finish.
Honda Pilot EX-L	Roomy interior, visibility, access, smooth powertrain, fuel economy, crash-test results, available safety gear.	Clumsy handling, touch-screen radio, blind-spot monitor only on Elite trim, annoying nine-speed automatic with push button shifter on high-end versions.
Honda Ridgeline RTL	Ride, quietness, clever in-bed storage, and dual-mode tailgate.	Complex optional radio, low towing capacity, shallow bed, rear access.
Hyundai Accent SE	Fuel economy, transmission, secure handling, controls, long warranty.	Poor IIHS small overlap crash-test results, ride, noise.
Hyundai Accent Sport (hatchback, MT)	Fuel economy, secure handling, controls, long warranty.	Poor IIHS small overlap crash-test results, ride, noise, rear visibility.
Hyundai Elantra SE	Relatively roomy, easy controls, fuel economy.	Engine noise, ride, front-seat comfort.
Hyundai Ioniq	Have not evaluated yet	
Hyundai Santa Fe SE (V6)	Powertrain, fuel economy, roomy and versatile cabin, access, controls, long warranty.	Tight third-row with difficult access.
Hyundai Santa Fe Sport (4-cyl.)	Roomy interior, fuel economy, transmission, controls, feature content, long warranty.	Rear three-quarters visibility.
Hyundai Sonata Hybrid SE	Fuel economy, spacious interior, ride, rear seat, controls, long warranty.	Low tire grip hurts cornering and braking, too easy to turn off daytime running lights.
Hyundai Sonata SE (2.4L)	Spacious rear seat, ride, transmission, controls, fuel economy, long warranty.	Low tire grip hurts cornering and braking, too easy to turn off daytime running lights.
Hyundai Tucson SE (2.0L)	Room, ride, agility, braking, upscale features, long warranty.	Acceleration, engine noise, rear visibility, expensive with options.
Hyundai Tucson Sport (1.6T)	Room, quietness, ride, agility, braking, fuel economy, upscale features, long warranty.	Vibration at low speeds, rear visibility, expensive with options.

Make & Model	Highs	Lows
Hyundai Veloster (base, MT)	Handling, fuel economy, extra door, turning circle, long warranty.	Ride, noise, lacks low-end torque, rear visibility, rear seat.
Infiniti Q50 Premium (AWD)**	Acceleration, braking, visibility	Reliability, ride, road noise, fuel economy, some controls, restrictive options packages, small trunk.
Infiniti Q70 (V6)	Acceleration, transmission, agility, braking, fit and finish.	Busy dashboard, overbearing electronic safety aids.
Infiniti Q70 Hybrid	Fuel economy, acceleration, fit and finish.	Abrupt transition between electric and gas modes, touchy brake pedal, trunk.
Infiniti QX60 (3.5L)	Plush interior, roomy cabin, quietness, fit and finish, access, front-seat comfort, controls, surround-view camera.	Reliability, agility, rear visibility.
Infiniti QX70	Acceleration, transmission, handling, fit and finish, front seat.	Ride, rear visibility, cargo area.
Infiniti QX80	Powertrain, quietness, rear seat, fit and finish, cargo capacity, towing, off-road, headlights.	Handling, access.
Jaguar XF	Have not evaluated redesign.	
Jaguar XJL Portfolio**	Acceleration, transmission, handling, ride, quietness, seat comfort, fit and finish.	Trunk, some controls, access, rear visibility.
Jaguar F-Pace	Have not evaluated yet.	
Jeep Cherokee Latitude (4-cyl.)	Access, rear seat, high-end options.	Reliability, transmission, choppy ride, agility, visibility, front-seat comfort, confusing price structure.
Jeep Cherokee Limited (V6)	Quietness, access, rear seat, high-end options.	Reliability, transmission, choppy ride, agility, visibility, confusing pricing structure.
Jeep Compass Latitude**	Simple controls.	Engine noise, acceleration, braking, driving position, front-seat comfort, rear visibility, cornering limits.

Make & Model	Highs	Lows
Jeep Grand Cherokee Limited (diesel)	Quietness, ride, fuel economy, off-road and towing capabilities, seat comfort, fit and finish, easy-to-use Uconnect infotainment system.	Reliability.
Jeep Grand Cherokee Limited (V6)	Quietness, ride, off-road and towing capability, seat comfort, fit and finish, easy to use Uconnect system.	Reliability.
Jeep Patriot Latitude**	Compliant ride.	Poor IIHS small overlap crash-test results, engine noise, acceleration, complicated optional radio controls, driving position, front-seat comfort.
Jeep Renegade Latitude	Styling, upscale features.	Transmission, ride, visibility, front-seat comfort, grabby brakes, idle vibration, reliability, gets pricey.
Jeep Wrangler Unlimited Sahara	Powertrain, off-road capability.	Ride, handling, braking, wind noise, access, driving position, seat comfort, visibility, fit and finish.
Kia Cadenza	Have not evaluated redesign.	
Kia Forte LX**	Ride, braking, controls, relatively roomy rear seat.	Agility, low rear seat.
Kia Niro	Have not evaluated yet.	
Kia Optima EX (2.4L)	Roomy interior, seat comfort, controls, braking, fuel economy, lots of equipment for price.	Expensive to get active safety equipment, too easy to turn off DRL, low dash vents.
Kia Rio EX	Transmission, controls, equipment levels.	Ride, noise.
Kia Rio EX (hatchback)	Transmission, controls, equipment levels.	Ride, rear visibility, noise, fuel economy for class.
Kia Sedona EX	Powertrain, second-row comfort, fit and finish.	Clumsy handling, stiff ride, lacks expected minivan flexibility.
Kia Sportage LX	Handling, powertrain, room, easy controls.	So-so fuel economy, rear visibility.

Make & Model	Highs	Lows
Kia Sorento EX (V6)	Ride, quietness, smooth V6, fuel economy, three-row seating, easy to maneuver yet roomy, reliability.	Rear visibility, tight third-row seat, small infotainment system screen on EX trim.
Kia Soul Plus	Handy size, inexpensive upscale features, access, controls, braking.	Stiff ride, limited cargo room with rear seat up.
Land Rover Discovery Sport HSE	Access, rear seat, some off-road ability.	Transmission, uneven power delivery, ride, handling, controls, rear visibility, price.
Land Rover Range Rover (base, 3.0L)	Ride, quietness, acceleration, interior room, fit and finish, visibility, seat comfort, off-road and towing capabilities.	Agility, controls.
Land Rover Range Rover Sport HSE (3.0L)	Handling, acceleration, fit and finish, front visibility, towing and off-road capability.	Stiff ride, poor snow traction, controls, fussy shifter.
Lexus CT 200h Premium	Fuel economy, secure handling, reliability.	Ride, noise, acceleration, snug interior, rear visibility, cargo space.
Lexus ES 300h	Fuel economy, hybrid drive-train, quietness, front-seat comfort, reliability, standard frontal collision avoidance.	Lackluster handling, controls, touchy brake pedal.
Lexus ES 350	Acceleration, fuel economy, drivetrain, quietness, front-seat comfort, reliability, standard frontal collision avoidance.	Lackluster handling, controls.
Lexus GS 350**	Quietness, ride, powertrain, front-seat comfort, fit and finish, visibility, reliability, standard frontal collision avoidance.	Fussy controls.
Lexus GX 460	Powertrain, quietness, ride, fit and finish, front-seat comfort, off-road ability, towing, reliability.	Agility, tight third-row seat, side-hinged tailgate.
Lexus IS300 (AWD)	Powertrain refinement, reliability, standard frontal collision avoidance.	Cramped interior and driving position, ride, road noise, lackluster handling, fuel economy, controls, access.

Make & Model	Highs	Lows
Lexus LS 460L	Acceleration, ride, powertrain, fuel economy, quietness, interior room, fit and finish, seat comfort, reliability.	Agility, fussy controls.
Lexus NX 200t	Fuel economy, handling, maneuverability, reliability.	Tight quarters, visibility, fussy touchpad controller, in-cabin storage.
Lexus NX 300h	Fuel economy, handling, maneuverability, reliability.	Tight quarters, visibility, fussy touchpad controller, in-cabin storage.
Lexus RX 350	Quietness, ride, fuel economy, fit and finish, standard frontal collision avoidance.	Agility, wet stopping distances, frustrating mouse-like controller, rear visibility.
Lexus RX 450h	Quietness, ride, fuel economy, fit and finish, standard frontal collision avoidance.	Agility, wet stopping distances, frustrating mouse-like controller, rear visibility.
Lincoln Continental	Have not evaluated yet.	
Lincoln MKC Reserve	Quietness, braking, nicely trimmed interior.	Reliability, unsettled ride, agility, short cruising range, driving position, rear visibility.
Lincoln MKT	Have not evaluated.	
Lincoln MKX (2.7 EcoBoost)	Ride, handling, quietness, acceleration, fit and finish.	Fuel economy, shifter, small fonts in instrument cluster, reliability.
Lincoln MKZ 2.0 EcoBoost**	Handling, ride, quietness.	Visibility, snug interior, hidden exterior trunk release.
Lincoln MKZ Hybrid	Handling, ride, quietness, fuel economy.	Visibility, snug interior, hidden exterior trunk release.
Lincoln Navigator Base	Ride, effortless power, spacious interior and third row, towing capacity.	Wind noise, interior fit and finish, agility.
Maserati Ghibli S Q4	Exhaust sound, steering feedback, braking, acceleration, transmission, fit and finish.	Ride, initial turbo lag, wind noise, rear seat, access, touchy brake pedal, fussy shifter.
Maserati Levante	Have not evaluated yet.	

Make & Model	Highs	Lows
Mazda CX-3 Touring	Handling, fuel economy, upscale features.	Noise, tight rear seat and cargo room, cumbersome infotainment system, visibility.
Mazda CX-5 Touring (2.5L)	Fuel economy, agility, rear-seat, blind-spot detection.	Ride, noise, cumbersome infotainment system, low dash vents.
Mazda CX-9 Touring	Ride, handling, quietness, fuel economy, high-end versions feel upscale	Cumbersome infotainment system, rear visibility, limited seat adjustments, tight driving position.
Mazda MX-5 Miata Club	Agility, shifter, fuel economy, easy manual top.	Ride, noise, tight quarters, cumbersome infotainment system, access.
Mazda3 i Grand Touring (hatch-back, 2.0L, MT)	Handling, fuel economy, transmission, high-end options.	Ride, noise, rear seat, rear visibility, cumbersome infotainment system, relatively pricey.
Mazda3 i Touring (2.0L)	Handling, fuel economy, transmission, high-end options.	Ride, noise, rear seat.
Mazda6 Sport	Fuel economy, agility, transmission.	Noise, ride, snug interior, low dash vents, cumbersome infotainment system, Sport trim lacks power seat.
Mercedes-Benz C300 (4MATIC) ⚠	Ride, quietness, handling, acceleration, fuel economy, front-seat comfort, fit and finish, standard frontal collision avoidance.	Reliability, controls, price.
Mercedes-Benz CLA250	Braking, fuel economy, fit and finish, standard frontal collision avoidance.	Ride, noise, cramped interior, uneven power delivery, visibility, access, small trunk opening.
Mercedes-Benz E300 ⚠	Have not evaluated redesign.	
Mercedes-Benz GLA250	Acceleration, braking, fuel economy, fit and finish, standard frontal collision avoidance.	Ride, noise, uneven power delivery, rear seat, visibility, some controls.

⚠ **Alert:** This vehicle can be outfitted with a semi-autonomous driving package. Consumer Reports believes automakers should take stronger steps to ensure that vehicles with those systems are designed, deployed, and marketed safely. Please heed all warnings, and keep your hands on the wheel.

Make & Model	Highs	Lows
Mercedes-Benz GLC300 ⚠	Ride, agility, fuel economy, fit and finish, front seat comfort, reliability, standard frontal collision avoidance.	Controls, engine noise.
Mercedes-Benz GLE350 (ML) ⚠	Quietness, transmission, front-seat comfort, fit and finish, towing capacity, standard frontal collision avoidance.	Some controls, backup camera only works with radio on.
Mercedes-Benz GLS350d** ⚠	Fuel economy, quietness, ride, plush interior, front-seat comfort, roomy rear and third-row seats, towing capacity, standard frontal collision avoidance.	Reliability, clumsy emergency handling, some controls, backup camera only works with radio on.
Mercedes-Benz S550 (4MATIC) ⚠	Most comfortable riding car, quietness, acceleration, braking, interior room, seat comfort, fit and finish, standard frontal collision avoidance.	Reliability, complicated and distracting controls, price.
Mercedes-Benz SLC	Have not evaluated redesign.	
Mini Cooper Clubman Base (1.5T)	Handling, roomier than any other Mini, thick option list allows personalization.	Ride, noise, visibility, controls have a learning curve.
Mini Cooper Countryman S	Handling, transmission, acceleration, fuel economy, thick option list allows personalization.	Ride, noise, controls, cargo space, premium fuel, flimsy interior details, pricey.
Mini Cooper (base, AT)	Handling, fuel economy, thick option list allows personalization.	Rear seat, some controls, expensive rear camera, gets pricey, reliability, three-cylinder engine a bit gruff, premium fuel.
Mini Cooper S	Handling, fuel economy, manual shifter, thick option list allows personalization.	Rear seat, some controls, expensive rear camera, reliability, gets pricey.
Mitsubishi i-MiEV SE	Low energy consumption, parking ease, turning circle.	Short range, weak heat, acceleration, ride, agility, driving position, Spartan interior, complicated radio.
Mitsubishi Lancer ES	Agility, steering, controls.	Noise, fit and finish, braking, fuel economy.

Make & Model	Highs	Lows
Mitsubishi Mirage ES	Fuel economy, turning circle, relatively roomy rear seat, hatchback versatility, feature content.	Handling, noise, vibration, acceleration, feels cheap and insubstantial.
Mitsubishi Outlander SEL (4-cyl.)	Standard third-row seat, access, visibility.	Agility, acceleration, engine noise, unsettled ride, no A/C vents for rear passengers.
Nissan 370Z Touring (coupe)	Acceleration, handling, braking, fit and finish.	Ride, noise, visibility, access.
Nissan Altima 2.5 SV	Rear seat, controls, fuel economy.	Unsettled ride, overly light steering.
Nissan Altima 3.5 SL	Acceleration, rear seat, controls.	Agility, ride.
Nissan Armada	Have not evaluated redesign.	
Nissan Leaf S	Running costs, ride, instant power delivery, quietness, access, turning circle.	Poor IIHS small overlap crash-test results, limited range, high-pitched whine, no telescoping wheel, agility.
Nissan Maxima Platinum	Acceleration, fuel economy, controls, fit and finish.	Ride, steering, engine noise, access, snug driving position, visibility, rear-seat room.
Nissan Murano SL	Fuel economy, plush interior, access, easy infotainment system, readily available advanced safety features.	Visibility, overly light steering, agility, towing capacity.
Nissan Pathfinder SL	Roominess, controls, access.	Reliability, handling, rear visibility, second-row thigh support.
Nissan Quest SL	Ride, quietness, powertrain, plush interior, fold-flat seats.	Poor IIHS small overlap crash-test results, agility.
Nissan Rogue SV	Ride, access, spacious interior, fuel economy, optional surround-view camera, available third-row seat.	Engine noise, cloth front-seat lacks support, gets pricey.
Nissan Sentra SV	Braking, fuel economy, spacious rear seat, access, lots of features for the money.	Ride, noise, fit and finish, front-seat comfort.

⚠ **Alert:** This vehicle can be outfitted with a semi-autonomous driving package. Consumer Reports believes automakers should take stronger steps to ensure that vehicles with those systems are designed, deployed, and marketed safely. Please heed all warnings, and keep your hands on the wheel.

Make & Model	Highs	Lows
Nissan Titan xD	Kinder and gentler than other HD trucks, towing capacity, light gate, simple controls.	Clumsy handling, stiff ride, high step-in, short rear seat, so-so payload capacity.
Nissan Versa Note SV	Space, access, versatility, fuel economy, controls, reliability.	Driving position, unsupportive front seats, acceleration.
Nissan Versa SV (sedan)	Fuel economy, rear seat, trunk.	Handling, engine noise, front-seat comfort, fit and finish.
Porsche 718 Boxster	Have not evaluated redesign.	
Porsche 911 Carrera S	Acceleration, handling, braking, engine sound, visibility, fit and finish, handy small rear seat.	Ride, noise, access, controls.
Porsche Cayenne (V6)	Handling, transmission, fit and finish, towing capacity, headlights.	Controls, slow start-stop feature, low-speed ride, pricey options.
Porsche Macan S	Handling, powertrain, ride, quietness, braking, front-seat comfort, fit and finish, towing capacity.	Rear visibility, modest cargo area, stingy standard in-car electronics, lots of buttons, price.
Porsche Panamera	Have not evaluated redesign.	
Ram 1500 Big Horn (5.7L V8)	Powertrain, ride, quietness, cabin space, Uconnect system.	Reliability, access, heavy rear tailgate.
Ram 1500 Big Horn (V6, diesel)	Fuel economy, ride, transmission, quietness, roomy cabin, Uconnect system.	Reliability, access, heavy tailgate, diesel gets expensive.
Smart ForTwo Passion	Easy parking, access, turning circle, fuel economy.	Ride, noise, acceleration, requires premium fuel.
Subaru BRZ Premium	Driving fun, handling, braking, fuel economy.	Ride, noise, access, vestigial rear seating.
Subaru Crosstrek Premium	Fuel economy, controls, rear seat, visibility, reliability.	Noise, ride, unrefined CVT.
Subaru Crosstrek Hybrid	Visibility, fuel economy, reduced engine noise, ride and handling better than regular Crosstrek, reliability.	Modest fuel-economy gain for a hybrid.

Make & Model	Highs	Lows
Subaru Forester 2.5i Premium	Fuel economy, visibility, braking, roomy interior, access, controls.	Noise, touchy throttle.
Subaru Impreza	Have not evaluated redesign.	
Subaru Legacy 2.5i Premium	Ride, handling, braking, transmission, fuel economy, visibility, controls, standard AWD.	Hard to read clock and temperature, acceleration, touchy throttle.
Subaru Outback 2.5 Premium	Ride, fuel economy, visibility, controls, access, practicality, standard AWD.	Hard-to-read clock and temperature, acceleration, touchy throttle.
Subaru Outback 3.6R Limited	Ride, fuel economy, visibility, controls, access, practicality, standard AWD.	Hard-to-read clock and temperature.
Subaru WRX Premium	Acceleration, cornering grip, braking, four-door practicality, visibility.	Hard ride, constant engine drone, stiff clutch, clunky shifter, turbo lag, reliability.
Tesla Model S P85D** ⚠	Energy efficiency, handling, acceleration, big touch-screen, luggage capacity, optional third-seat.	Limited range, access, visibility, controls, reduced ride comfort and quietness with 21-inch tires.
Tesla Model X ⚠	Have not evaluated yet.	
Toyota 4Runner SR5 (V6)	Off-road ability, power-retractable rear window, reliability.	Handling, ride, driving position, fit and finish, access, turning circle.
Toyota 86 (Scion FR-S)	Driving fun, handling, braking, fuel economy.	Ride, noise, access, vestigial rear seating.
Toyota Avalon Limited (V6)	Ride, quietness, fuel economy, acceleration, rear seat, standard frontal collision avoidance.	Agility, too easy to turn off daytime running lights.
Toyota Camry Hybrid XLE	Fuel economy, ride, powertrain, interior room, reliability.	Too easy to turn off the daytime running lights.
Toyota Camry LE (4-cyl.)	Ride, powertrain, fuel economy, interior room, reliability.	Too easy to turn off the daytime running lights.
Toyota Camry XLE (V6)	Ride, fuel economy, powertrain, acceleration, interior room, reliability.	Too easy to turn off the daytime running lights.

⚠ **Alert:** This vehicle can be outfitted with a semi-autonomous driving package. Consumer Reports believes automakers should take stronger steps to ensure that vehicles with those systems are designed, deployed, and marketed safely. Please heed all warnings, and keep your hands on the wheel.

Make & Model	Highs	Lows
Toyota C-HR	Have not evaluated yet.	
Toyota Corolla (Scion) iM	Agility, fuel economy, hatchback versatility, standard frontal collision avoidance, well-equipped for price.	Acceleration, engine noise, rear seat, rear visibility, lacks common options.
Toyota Corolla LE Plus	Ride, fuel economy, interior space, large trunk, secure emergency handling, standard frontal collision avoidance, reliability, value.	Lackluster handling, inconsistent interior quality, too easy to turn off daytime running lights.
Toyota Highlander Hybrid Limited	Fuel economy, powertrain, quietness, roomy and versatile interior, access, easy-to-use infotainment system, standard frontal collision avoidance, reliability.	Low rear seat, too easy to turn off daytime running lights.
Toyota Highlander XLE (V6)**	Powertrain, fuel economy, roomy and versatile interior, access, standard frontal collision avoidance, reliability, easy-to-use infotainment system.	Low rear-seat, too easy to turn off daytime running lights.
Toyota Land Cruiser **	Ride, quietness, powertrain, acceleration, fit and finish, front and second row seat comfort, off-road capability, towing capacity.	Fuel economy, agility, tight third-row seat, pricey.
Toyota Prius C Two	Fuel economy, smooth transmission, standard frontal collision avoidance, turning circle, relatively roomy rear seat for two, reliability.	Acceleration, ride, noise, driving position, rear visibility, fit and finish.
Toyota Prius Three	Fuel economy, hatchback versatility, ride, standard frontal collision avoidance, reliability.	Rear visibility, acceleration, seat comfort, insubstantial for price, odd shifter and gauges.
Toyota Prius Prime	Have not evaluated redesign.	
Toyota Prius V Three	Fuel economy, transmission, rear seat, access, cargo room, ride, reliability.	Acceleration, agility, engine noise, complicated radio.

Make & Model	Highs	Lows
Toyota RAV4 Hybrid XLE	Fuel economy, access, transmission, roominess, standard frontal collision avoidance, reliability.	Driver's seat lumbar support, too easy to turn off daytime running lights.
Toyota RAV4 XLE	Fuel economy, access, transmission, roominess, standard frontal collision avoidance, reliability.	Driver's seat lumbar support, too easy to turn off daytime running lights.
Toyota Sequoia Limited (5.7)	Powertrain, towing and off-road capability, accommodations, storage, power-retractable rear window, reliability.	Agility, braking, unsettled ride, high step-in, long reach to some controls.
Toyota Sienna XLE (AWD)**	Ride, transmission, interior space and flexibility, rear seat, AWD, reliability.	Agility, road noise, fit and finish.
Toyota Sienna XLE (FWD)**	Ride, transmission, interior space and flexibility, rear seat, fuel economy, reliability.	Agility, road noise, fit and finish.
Toyota Tacoma SR5 (V6)	Fuel economy, resale value, reliability, off-road ability.	Ride, handling, braking, noise, driving position, seat comfort, reliability.
Toyota Tundra SR5 (5.7L V8)	Powertrain, towing, low-effort tailgate, reliability.	Ride, visibility, braking, long reach to some controls, no full-time 4WD.
Toyota Yaris (Scion) iA	Fuel economy, agility, standard front-collision mitigation.	Noise levels, infotainment learning curve, tight rear seat, wet braking.
Toyota Yaris LE	Fuel economy, roomy rear seat, turning circle, standard frontal collision avoidance.	Noise, ride, driving position, front-seat comfort, fit and finish, radio controls, rear visibility.
Volkswagen Beetle 1.8T (AT)	Controls.	Reliability, wind noise, on-limit handling, rear seat, no curtain air bags.
Volkswagen CC Sport (2.0T)	Agility, ride, fit and finish.	Visibility, access, tight rear seat.
Volkswagen Golf SE (1.8T)	Ride, handling, quietness, braking, easy infotainment system, versatility.	Reliability, noisy rear view camera, a bit pricey.
Volkswagen GTI Autobahn	Agility, fuel economy, seat comfort, quiet cabin, hatchback versatility.	Limited rear-view camera availability, reliability, gets pricey.

Make & Model	Highs	Lows
Volkswagen Jetta GLI SE (MT)	Handling, powertrain, rear seat, large trunk.	Long clutch travel, reliability.
Volkswagen Jetta Hybrid SEL Premium	Fuel economy, quietness, ride, transmission, rear seat.	Touchy brake pedal, small trunk, can roll back on hills, premium fuel, reliability.
Volkswagen Jetta SE (1.4T)	Agility, acceleration, refined engine, fuel economy, rear seat, large trunk, visibility.	Ride, reliability, lackluster interior finish.
Volkswagen Jetta Sport (1.8T)	Agility, acceleration, refined engine, fuel economy, rear seat, large trunk, controls, visibility.	Ride, reliability, lackluster interior finish.
Volkswagen Passat SE (1.8T)	Interior room, rear seat, trunk, access, agility, braking, standard frontal collision avoidance, fuel economy.	Transmission refinement at low speeds, reliability.
Volkswagen Passat SEL Premium (V6)	Ride, handling, interior room, acceleration, rear seat, standard frontal collision avoidance access.	Fuel economy, premium fuel, slow touch-screen controls, reliability.
Volkswagen Tiguan SEL	Agility, transmission, access, fit and finish, rear seat.	Ride, noise, touch-screen controls.
Volvo S60 T5**	Transmission, braking, fuel economy, standard frontal collision avoidance, front-seat comfort.	Ride, rear seat, rear visibility.
Volso S90 ⚠	Have not evaluated redesign.	
Volvo V60 Cross Country**	Transmission, braking, plush cabin, standard frontal collision avoidance, front-seat comfort, safety features.	Ride, rear visibility, tight rear seat and cargo area, headlights, no standard rear camera, value.
Volvo XC60 T6**	Transmission, fit and finish, safety features, standard frontal collision avoidance.	Ride, fuel economy, rear visibility.
Volvo XC90 T6 Momentum ⚠	Quietness, seat comfort, fit and finish, visibility, braking, standard frontal collision avoidance, high-beam headlights.	Stiff ride, unintuitive controls, fuel economy, reliability.

⚠ **Alert:** This vehicle can be outfitted with a semi-autonomous driving package. Consumer Reports believes automakers should take stronger steps to ensure that vehicles with those systems are designed, deployed, and marketed safely. Please heed all warnings, and keep your hands on the wheel.

Rating the 2017 Models

INCLUDED HERE ARE RATINGS on 256 vehicles that Consumer Reports has recently tested. Within each category, they are ranked by their overall score.

To earn our Recommendation (✔), vehicles must perform well in our testing; have average or better reliability; and perform adequately if included in a government or industry safety test. Models with subpar crash-test results are identified by a (!).

Price as tested is the sticker price at the time of purchase of our test vehicle, including an automatic transmission (unless noted) and typical equipment.

Overall score accounts for a vehicle's performance in our road tests, results from our reliability and owner satisfaction surveys, the availability of a frontal crash-prevention system, and, if applicable, safety tests by government and insurance-industry.

Survey results include predicted reliability, our forecast of how well a new car will hold up based on its recent history from our 2016 Annual Auto Survey. Owner satisfaction is based on the percentage of subscribers who say they would definitely buy or lease their vehicle again. Reliability and owner satisfaction predictions for new or redesigned models are based on other models from the manufacturer and the history of the previous generation.

A model that is based on limited data is identified with an asterisk (*). Overall MPG is the overall miles per gallon a vehicle achieved based on results from fuel-economy tests, a mix of city and highway driving. A model with a double asterisk (**) indicates the powertrain has changed since our last test. Road-test score is based on results from more than 50 tests and evaluations.

Standout Models by Category

CARS

Subcompacts & Compacts: $14,000-$30,000

Best Overall: Subcompacts
Toyota Yaris iA, Honda Fit, Chevrolet Sonic

Best Overall: Compacts
Chevrolet Cruze
Kia Forte, Mazda3

Fuel-efficient: Sedans
Mazda3, Toyota Corolla ›
Hyundai Elantra

Fuel-efficient: Hatchbacks
Toyota Prius, Ford C-Max

Standout Models by Category

Midsized: $22,000-$33,000

Best Overall
Kia Optima
Honda Accord
Toyota Camry
Subaru Legacy

Best Fuel Economy
Toyota Camry Hybrid
Ford Fusion Hybrid >
Hyundai Sonata Hybrid
Mazda6
Honda Accord (4-cyl.)

Large: $35,000-$42,000

Best Overall
Chevrolet Impala >
Toyota Avalon
Hyundai Azera

Luxury Compact: $35,000-$45,000

Great Value
Buick Regal >

Sporty
Audi A4
BMW 328i

Luxury Midsized: $40,000-$65,000

Best Overall
Audi A6 (3.0T)
Infiniti Q70 (V6) >
Lexus GS 350
Cadillac CT6

Great Value
Lexus ES 350
Lincoln MKZ 2.0 EcoBoost

Luxury Midsized: $40,000-$65,000
Fuel-efficient
BMW 328d xDrive
Lexus ES 300h
Lincoln MKZ Hybrid >

Luxury Large: $70,000-$95,000
Best Overall
BMW 750i xDrive ⚠ >
Lexus LS 460L

Sports: $30,000-$51,000
Best Overall: Sporty
BMW M235i
Chevrolet Corvette >

Rewarding Roadsters
Porsche Boxster

Fun Hatchbacks
Toyota 86
Subaru BRZ

Muscle Car
Chevrolet Camaro SS

SUVs

Small: $25,000-$35,000
Best Overall
Subaru Forester >
Toyota RAV4
Kia Sportage
Hyundai Tucson
Nissan Rogue
Mazda CX-5
Honda CR-V

⚠ **Alert:** This vehicle can be outfitted with a semi-autonomous driving package. Consumer Reports believes automakers should take stronger steps to ensure that vehicles with those systems are designed, deployed, and marketed safely. Please heed all warnings, and keep your hands on the wheel.

Standout Models by Category

SUVs Continued

Midsized $30,000-$40,000

Best Overall: Three Row
Toyota Highlander
Kia Sorento ›
Hyundai Santa Fe

Best Overall: Two rows
Ford Edge
Nissan Murano
Hyundai Santa Fe Sport

Fuel-Efficient
Toyota Highlander Hybrid

Large $40,000-$60,000

Family-Friendly
Chevrolet Traverse
Ford Flex ›

To Tow and Haul
Toyota Sequoia

Luxury Compact $38,000-$50,000

Best Overall
Mercedes-Benz GLC300 ⚠
BMW X3
Audi Q3 ›
Audi Q5 2.0T
Acura RDX

Luxury Midsized $45,000-$60,000

Best Overall
Lexus RX 350
Mercedes-Benz GLE350 ⚠
Acura MDX ›

Sporty
Porsche Cayenne

Fuel-Efficient
Lexus RX450h

⚠ **Alert:** This vehicle can be outfitted with a semi-autonomous driving package. Consumer Reports believes automakers should take stronger steps to ensure that vehicles with those systems are designed, deployed, and marketed safely. Please heed all warnings, and keep your hands on the wheel.

Luxury Midsized/Large $50,000-$80,000
Best Overall
Audi Q7 >
BMW X5
Buick Enclave

 WAGONS

$25,000-$40,000
All-wheel Drive
Subaru Outback >
Audi Allroad

MINIVANS

$35,000-$40,000
Best Overall
Honda Odyssey >
Toyota Sienna

PICKUP TRUCKS

Best Overall
Honda Ridgeline >

Rec.	Make & Model	Price As tested	Overall Score	Predicted Reliability	Owner Satisfaction	Road Test Score	Overall MPG
	ELECTRIC CARS/PLUG-IN HYBRIDS						
✓	**Tesla Model S** P85D** ⚠	$127,820	88	◑	⌃⌃	100	87[1]
✓	**BMW i3** Giga	$50,450	75	◑	◑	79	139[1]
✓	**Ford C-Max** Energi	$34,940	73	◑	⌃	77	94[1]/37[2]
!	**Nissan Leaf** S	$29,860	67	⌃	◑	71	106[1]
	Chevrolet Volt LT	$35,890	54	⌄⌄	⌃⌃	70	105[1]/38[2]
	Ford Focus Electric	$40,990	50	⌄⌄	⌄	72	107[1]
	Mitsubishi i-MiEV SE	$33,630	44	◑*	⌄*	35	111[1]
	CARS: SUBCOMPACT						
✓	**Toyota Yaris** iA	$17,570	67	⌃⌃*	◑*	60	35
✓	**Honda Fit** EX	$19,025	66	◑	⌃	67	33
✓	**Chevrolet Sonic** LT (1.8L)	$17,290	64	◑	⌄	66	28
	Nissan Versa Note SV	$17,495	62	⌃	⌄	61	31
!	**Hyundai Accent** SE	$16,050	61	⌃	⌄	65	31
	Toyota Prius C Two	$20,850	63	⌃	◑	55	43
	Kia Rio EX	$17,275	60	◑*	⌄*	64	30
	Toyota Yaris LE	$17,290	57	⌃⌃*	◑*	47	32
	Nissan Versa SV (sedan)	$15,490	56	◑*	⌄	56	32
	Chevrolet Spark 1LT	$16,660	50	◑*	◑*	47	33
	Ford Fiesta SE (hatchback, 4-cyl. MT)	$17,795	48	⌄⌄	⌄	66	32
	Ford Fiesta SE (3-cyl., MT)	$18,720	47	⌄⌄	⌄	66	35
	Ford Fiesta SE (sedan, 4-cyl.)	$16,595	46	⌄⌄	⌄	64	33
	Smart ForTwo Passion	$18,730	41	⌄*	⌃*	41	36
	Mitsubishi Mirage ES	$16,050	37	◑*	⌄*	29	37
	CARS: SMALL 2-DOOR						
✓	**Hyundai Veloster** (base, MT)	$20,340	63	◑*	◑*	67	31
	Mini Cooper (base, AT)	$27,400	58	⌄	⌃	68	31
	Volkswagen Beetle 1.8T (AT)	$22,485	46	⌄⌄	⌄	59	27
	Fiat 500C Pop (MT)	$21,000	44	⌄⌄	⌄	52	34
!	**Fiat 500** Sport (MT)	$18,600	40	⌄⌄	⌄	54	33

⚠ **Alert:** This vehicle can be outfitted with a semi-autonomous driving package. Consumer Reports believes automakers should take stronger steps to ensure that vehicles with those systems are designed, deployed, and marketed safely. Please heed all warnings, and keep your hands on the wheel.

Rec.	Make & Model	Price	Overall Score	Survey Results		Test Results	
		As tested		Predicted Reliability	Owner Satisfaction	Road Test Score	Overall MPG
CARS: COMPACT							
✓	**Toyota Prius** Three	$27,323	81	⌃⌃	⌃⌃	75	52
✓	**Chevrolet Cruze** LT	$23,145	78	⌃⌃	◐	77	30
✓	**Toyota Prius** V Three	$28,217	76	⌃⌃	⌃	73	41
✓	**Toyota Corolla** LE	$20,652	75	⌃⌃	⌃	71	32
✓	**Ford C-Max** Hybrid SE	$26,685	73	◐	⌃	77	37
✓	**Kia Forte** LX**	$19,570	72	⌃	⌄	78	28
✓	**Mazda3** Grand Touring (hatchback, 2.0L, MT)	$24,040	72	⌃	⌃	73	32
✓	**Mazda3** Touring (2.0L)	$21,740	72	⌃	⌃	72	33
✓	**Kia Soul** Plus	$24,115	71	◐	⌃	74	26
✓	**Toyota Corolla** iM	$19,995	70	⌃⌃*	◐*	64	31
✓	**Hyundai Elantra** SE	$20,090	69	⌃*	⌃⌃	66	33
	Volkswagen Golf SE (1.8T)	$25,315	64	⌄	⌃	82	28
	Mitsubishi Lancer ES	$17,515	61	◐*	⌄*	62	25
	Nissan Sentra SV	$20,125	61	◐	⌄⌄	62	31
	Volkswagen Jetta SE (1.4T)	$21,235	59	⌄⌄	⌄	79	32
	Honda Civic LX	$20,275	58	⌄⌄	⌃	76	32
	Mini Clubman Base (1.5T)	$31,550	57	⌄	⌃	67	28
	Honda Civic EX-T	$23,035	57	⌄⌄	⌃	75	31
	Dodge Dart SXT (2.4L)	$22,025	56	⌄*	⌄⌄*	68	27
	Ford Focus SE (2.0L)	$20,485	47	⌄⌄	⌄	67	29
	Ford Focus SE (1.0T)	$21,455	45	⌄⌄	⌄	62	29
!	**Fiat 500L** **	$24,595	35	⌄⌄	⌄⌄	50	27
CARS: MIDSIZED							
✓	**Kia Optima** EX (2.4L)	$25,860	85	⌃⌃	⌃⌃	86	28
✓	**Toyota Camry** Hybrid XLE	$29,052	85	⌃⌃	⌃	87	38
✓	**Toyota Camry** XLE (V6)	$32,603	84	⌃⌃	⌃	86	26
✓	**Toyota Camry** LE (4-cyl.)	$24,089	83	⌃⌃	⌃	84	28
✓	**Honda Accord** LX (4-cyl.)	$23,270	82	⌃	⌃	85	30

¹Miles-per-gallon equivalent (MPGe). ²Miles per gallon while running on gas engine.

Rec.	Make & Model	Price As tested	Overall Score	Predicted Reliability	Owner Satisfaction	Road Test Score	Overall MPG
	CARS: MIDSIZED (Continued)						
✓	**Honda Accord** EX-L (V6)	$30,860	81	⌃	⌃	84	26
✓	**Subaru Legacy** 2.5i Premium	$24,837	79	◐	⌃	89	26
✓	**Ford Fusion** SE (1.5T)	$27,720	77	⌃	◐	81	24
✓	**Mazda6** Sport	$23,590	77	⌃	⌃	79	32
✓	**Ford Fusion** SE Hybrid	$28,290	76	⌃	◐	80	39
✓	**Chevrolet Malibu** 1LT (1.5T)	$26,790	76	◐	⌃	80	29
✓	**Ford Fusion** Titanium (2.0T)	$33,180	75	⌃	◐	78	22
✓	**Hyundai Sonata** Hybrid SE	$26,950	74	◐	⌃	80	39
✓	**Hyundai Sonata** SE (2.4L)	$23,315	73	◐	⌃	78	28
	Nissan Altima 3.5 SL	$31,610	72	◐	⌄	80	24
	Nissan Altima 2.5 SV	$26,890	67	◐	⌄	71	29
	Volkswagen Passat SE (1.8T)	$27,485	65	⌄	⌄	82	28
	Volkswagen Passat SEL Premium (V6)	$33,720	64	⌄	⌄	79	23
	Chrysler 200 C (V6)	$33,620	49	⌄⌄	⌄	66	25
	Chrysler 200 Limited (4-cyl.)	$25,790	47	⌄⌄	⌄	63	30
	CARS: LARGE						
✓	**Chevrolet Impala** 2LTZ (3.6)	$39,110	84	◐	⌃	91	22
✓	**Toyota Avalon** Limited (V6)	$42,010	83	⌃⌃	⌃	80	24
✓	**Hyundai Azera**	$37,185	80	⌃⌃	⌃	80	23
✓	**Nissan Maxima** Platinum	$41,995	72	◐	⌃	81	25
✓	**Chrysler 300** C (V8)	$45,650	71	◐	⌃	84	20
✓	**Chrysler 300** Limited (V6)	$38,335	71	◐	⌃	83	22
	Ford Taurus Limited (3.5, V6)	$37,885	65	◐	◐	72	21
	Dodge Charger R/T Plus (V8)	$40,375	61	⌄⌄	⌃	85	20
	Dodge Charger SXT (V6)	$34,510	60	⌄⌄	⌃	82	22
	CARS: LUXURY ENTRY-LEVEL						
✓	**Buick Verano** Leather (2.4)	$27,750	76	⌃⌃	◐	73	24
✓	**Lexus CT** 200h Premium	$32,012	71	⌃⌃	⌄	65	40
✓	**Volkswagen CC** Sport (2.0T)	$32,800	70	◐*	⌄*	78	26
	Audi A3 Premium**	$31,495	69	⌄	⌃	77	27

Rec.	Make & Model	Price (As tested)	Overall Score	Predicted Reliability	Owner Satisfaction	Road Test Score	Overall MPG
	CARS: LUXURY ENTRY-LEVEL (Continued)						
	Acura ILX Premium	$30,820	64	↑	↓↓	61	28
	Volkswagen Jetta GLI SE (MT)	$27,740	57	↓↓	↓	74	27
	Mercedes-Benz CLA250	$36,500	56	↓*	↓↓	64	28
	CARS: LUXURY COMPACT						
✓	**Audi A4** Premium Plus	$48,890	85	↑*	↑	88	27
✓	**Buick Regal** Premium I	$34,485	81	↑↑	↑	83	24
✓	**BMW 328d** xDrive	$50,475	78	●	●	86	35
✓	**BMW 328i****	$43,195	76	●	●	84	28
✓	**Volvo S60****	$39,925	74	●	●	80	25
	Mercedes-Benz C300 (4MATIC) ⚠	$47,560	71	↓	●	85	26
	Infiniti Q50 3.0t Premium (AWD)	$44,855	71	↓	↓↓	85	22
	Lexus IS300 (AWD)	$48,149	66	↑↑	↓	56	20
	Cadillac ATS Luxury (turbo)**	$43,295	60	↓↓	↓	79	23
	Acura TLX 2.4L	$35,920	58	↓↓	●	79	27
	Acura TLX SH-AWD	$42,345	55	↓↓	●	75	25
	CARS: LUXURY MIDSIZED						
✓	**Infiniti Q70** (V6)	$53,825	88	↑↑	↑	90	21
✓	**Lexus GS** 350**	$58,858	85	↑↑	↑	83	21
✓	**Audi A6** 3.0 Premium Plus Quattro	$56,295	84	↑	↑	90	22
✓	**Infiniti Q70** Hybrid	$58,655	83	↑↑	↑	83	25
✓	**Lexus ES** 350	$43,702	82	↑↑	↑	78	25
✓	**Lincoln MKZ** 2.0 EcoBoost**	$41,990	82	●	↑	88	23
✓	**Lincoln MKZ** Hybrid	$41,990	82	●	↑	88	34
✓	**Lexus ES** 300h	$44,017	81	↑↑	↑	77	36
✓	**Cadillac CT6** Luxury (3.6, AWD)	$64,485	81	●*	↑*	95	22
✓	**Genesis G80** 3.8 (AWD)	$52,450	80	●	↑↑	89	20
✓	**Cadillac XTS** Premium	$57,200	77	↑	↓	82	22

⚠ **Alert:** This vehicle can be outfitted with a semi-autonomous driving package. Consumer Reports believes automakers should take stronger steps to ensure that vehicles with those systems are designed, deployed, and marketed safely. Please heed all warnings, and keep your hands on the wheel.

Rec.	Make & Model	Price (As tested)	Overall Score	Predicted Reliability	Owner Satisfaction	Road Test Score	Overall MPG
	CARS: LUXURY MIDSIZED (Continued)						
	Acura RLX Tech	$55,345	75	⌃	⌄	75	23
	Chevrolet SS	$47,170	74	⌄*	⌃*	87	17
	BMW 535i	$58,375	73	●	⌃	81	23
	Cadillac CTS Luxury (V6, AWD)	$58,780	71	●	●	83	22
	Jaguar XF Prestige (V6)	$66,586	66	⌄*	⌃*	83	21
	Maserati Ghibli S Q4	$89,010	51	⌄⌄*	⌄*	71	19
	CARS: ULTRA LUXURY						
✓	**BMW 750i** xDrive ⚠	$110,645	89	●*	⌃	99	21
✓	**Tesla Model** S P85D** ⚠	$127,820	88	●	⌃⌃	100	87¹
✓	**Lexus LS** 460L	$82,504	87	⌃⌃	⌃⌃	89	21
✓	**Audi A8** L**	$91,275	86	⌃*	⌃	91	21
	Mercedes-Benz S550 (4MATIC) ⚠	$114,475	73	⌄	⌃	96	18
	Jaguar XJL Portfolio**	$81,575	66	⌄*	⌃*	82	19
	SPORTS/SPORTY CARS OVER $40,000 Equipped with manual transmission						
✓	**BMW M235i**	$50,400	92	⌃⌃	⌃	98	25
✓	**Chevrolet Corvette** Stingray 3LT	$73,260	83	●	⌃⌃	92	20
✓	**Porsche 911** Carrera S**	$110,630	82	●*	⌃⌃	95	23
✓	**Audi TT** 2.0T (AT)	$50,600	81	⌃*	⌃*	84	26
✓	**Chevrolet Camaro** 2SS (V8)	$47,020	76	●*	⌃⌃	85	20
	BMW Z4 sDrive28i	$55,225	71	●*	⌃*	74	28
	Ford Mustang GT Premium (V8)	$43,295	62	⌄⌄	⌃⌃	84	19
	Dodge Challenger R/T Plus (V8)	$40,860	53	⌄⌄	⌃⌃	70	20
	SPORTS/SPORTY CARS UNDER $40,000 Equipped with manual transmission						
✓	**Mazda MX-5 Miata** Club	$29,905	79	⌃	⌃⌃	80	34
✓	**Nissan 370Z** Touring (coupe)	$38,565	75	●*	●*	81	23
✓	**Subaru BRZ** Premium	$27,117	73	●*	●*	79	30

⚠ **Alert:** This vehicle can be outfitted with a semi-autonomous driving package. Consumer Reports believes automakers should take stronger steps to ensure that vehicles with those systems are designed, deployed, and marketed safely. Please heed all warnings, and keep your hands on the wheel.

Rec.	Make & Model	Price (As tested)	Overall Score	Predicted Reliability	Owner Satisfaction	Road Test Score	Overall MPG
	SPORTS/SPORTY CARS UNDER $40,000 Equipped with manual transmission (Continued)						
✓	**Toyota 86**	$25,025	73	❶*	❶*	78	30
	Volkswagen GTI Autobahn	$31,730	71	⌄	⌃	82	29
	Mini Cooper S	$29,945	66	⌄	⌃	81	30
	Buick Cascada Premium	$37,385	60	⌃*	⌃*	53	22
	Subaru WRX Premium	$29,742	59	⌄	⌃	75	26
	Ford Mustang Premium (4-cyl., AT)	$33,080	58	⌄⌄	⌃⌃	76	25
	Fiat 500 Abarth	$26,050	52	⌄⌄	⌄	66	28
	Ford Fiesta ST	$24,985	52	⌄⌄	⌄	74	29
	Ford Focus ST	$28,270	51	⌄⌄	⌄	74	26
	WAGONS (All-wheel Drive)						
✓	**Subaru Outback** 3.6R Limited	$36,835	75	❶	⌃⌃	85	22
✓	**Subaru Outback** 2.5 Premium	$28,852	73	❶	⌃⌃	82	24
	Volvo V60 Cross Country	$46,475	69	❶	❶	73	21
	MINIVANS						
✓	**Toyota Sienna** XLE (FWD)**	$35,810	80	⌃⌃	⌃⌃	80	20
✓	**Honda Odyssey** EX-L	$38,055	79	❶	⌃	84	21
✓	**Toyota Sienna** XLE (AWD)**	$38,201	78	⌃⌃	⌃⌃	78	19
	Ford Transit Connect XLT (2.5L)	$28,015	68	❶*	⌄*	76	21
	Kia Sedona EX	$34,795	67	❶*	⌃	70	20
	Chrysler Pacifica Touring L	$38,245	67	⌄*	⌃⌃*	85	21
!	**Nissan Quest** SL	$39,040	67	❶*	❶*	79	19
!	**Dodge Grand Caravan** R/T	$37,295	62	❶	❶	72	17
	SUVs: SUBCOMPACTS						
✓	**Subaru Crosstrek** Premium	$24,215	76	⌃⌃	⌃	74	26
✓	**Subaru Crosstrek** Hybrid	$27,132	75	⌃⌃	⌃	74	28
✓	**Honda HR-V** LX	$22,045	69	⌃	❶	66	29
✓	**Mazda CX-3** Touring	$25,800	64	❶	❶	64	28

'Miles-per-gallon equivalent (MPGe).

RATINGS KEY

⌄⌄ ⌄ ❶ ⌃ ⌃⌃   ✓
WORSE————BETTER   **RECOMMENDED** These are high-performing models that stand out.

Rec.	Make & Model	Price (As tested)	Overall Score	Predicted Reliability	Owner Satisfaction	Road Test Score	Overall MPG
	SUVs: SUBCOMPACTS (Continued)						
	Chevrolet Trax LT	$25,560	62	⊗	⊙	55	25
	Fiat 500X Easy	$26,600	42	⊗*	⊙*	50	23
	Jeep Renegade Latitude	$27,525	42	⊗	◑	56	24
	SUVs: COMPACT						
✓	**Subaru Forester** 2.5i Premium	$27,145	83	◉	◉	85	26
✓	**Toyota RAV4** XLE	$29,014	79	⊗	◑	75	24
✓	**Toyota RAV4** Hybrid XLE	$29,753	78	⊗	◑	74	31
✓	**Kia Sportage** LX (2.4L)	$26,720	76	◉*	◉*	78	23
✓	**Hyundai Tucson** Sport (1.6T)	$28,670	75	◑	◉	79	26
✓	**Ford Escape** Titanium (2.0T)	$36,600	74	◑	◑	79	22
✓	**Mazda CX-5** Touring (2.5L)	$28,090	74	◉	◉	74	25
✓	**Hyundai Tucson** SE (2.0L)	$25,920	73	◑	◉	76	24
✓	**Honda CR-V** EX	$27,500	72	◉	◉	73	24
✓	**Volkswagen Tiguan** SEL	$37,020	72	◉	◑	74	21
✓	**Ford Escape** SE (1.6T)**	$28,040	71	◑	◑	75	22
✓	**Nissan Rogue** SV	$29,920	71	◉	⊙	74	24
	Mitsubishi Outlander SEL (4-cyl.)	$28,405	60	◑*	⊙*	59	24
	Jeep Cherokee Limited (V6)	$37,525	55	⊙	⊙	71	21
!	**Jeep Patriot** Latitude**	$25,790	53	◉	◉	56	21
	Jeep Cherokee Latitude (4-cyl.)	$27,490	47	⊙	⊙	58	22
	Jeep Compass Latitude**	$26,190	47	⊙*	⊗	52	22
	SUVs: MIDSIZED						
✓	**Toyota Highlander** Hybrid Limited	$50,875	86	◉	◉	85	25
✓	**Toyota Highlander** XLE (V6)**	$38,941	85	◉	◉	84	20
✓	**Kia Sorento** EX (V6)	$37,915	82	◉	◉	84	21
✓	**Hyundai Santa Fe** SE (V6)	$36,290	78	◉	◑	81	20
✓	**Hyundai Santa Fe** Sport (4-cyl.)	$28,370	75	⊗	◉	73	23
✓	**Honda Pilot** EX-L	$39,585	75	◑	◉	80	20
✓	**Mazda CX-9** Touring	$40,470	74	◑*	◉*	80	22
✓	**Ford Edge** SEL (2.0 EcoBoost)	$39,755	73	◑	◉	84	21

Rec.	Make & Model	Price	Overall Score	Survey Results		Test Results	
		As tested		Predicted Reliability	Owner Satisfaction	Road Test Score	Overall MPG
	SUVs: MIDSIZED (Continued)						
✓	**Nissan Murano** SL	$42,065	73	⊙	⌃	77	21
	Chevrolet Equinox LTZ (V6)	$36,925	71	⌃	⊙	69	18
	GMC Terrain SLT2 (V6)	$36,675	71	⌃	⊙	69	18
	Chevrolet Equinox 1LT (4-cyl.)	$26,350	70	⌃	⊙	68	21
	GMC Terrain SLE1 (4-cyl.)	$26,745	70	⌃	⊙	68	21
	Toyota 4Runner SR5 (V6)	$37,425	62	⌃⌃	⌃	55	18
	Jeep Grand Cherokee Limited (diesel)	$49,780	61	⌄⌄	⌃	84	24
	Ford Explorer XLT (V6)	$39,275	59	⌄	⌃	67	18
	Jeep Grand Cherokee Limited (V6)	$41,375	58	⌄⌄	⌃	80	18
	Nissan Pathfinder SL	$40,470	56	⌄	⌄⌄	72	18
!	**Dodge Journey** Limited (V6)	$36,975	49	⌄	⌄⌄	64	16
	Jeep Wrangler Unlimited Sahara	$36,340	26	⌄	⌃	20	17
	SUVs: LARGE						
✓	**Chevrolet Traverse** LT	$39,920	76	⌃	⊙	77	16
✓	**Ford Flex** SEL	$42,155	74	⌃	⌃⌃	73	18
✓	**Ford Expedition** EL Limited	$63,080	67	⌃⌃	⌃⌃	61	14
✓	**Toyota Sequoia** Limited	$54,005	65	⌃*	⌃	60	15
	Dodge Durango GT (V6)	$43,525	63	⌄	⌃⌃	83	18
	Chevrolet Suburban LTZ	$69,790	54	⌄⌄	⌃	74	16
	Chevrolet Tahoe LT	$60,100	51	⌄⌄	⌃	67	16
	GMC Yukon SLT	$62,125	51	⌄⌄	⌃	67	16
	GMC Yukon XL SLT	$67,370	50	⌄⌄	⌃	67	16
	SUVs: LUXURY ENTRY-LEVEL						
✓	**Audi Q3** Premium Plus	$40,125	80	⌃⌃	⌃	77	22
	BMW X1 xDrive28i	$44,745	72	⌃	⌃	74	26
	Buick Encore Leather	$30,555	71	⌃	⊙	69	23
	Mercedes-Benz GLA250	$42,210	70	⊙	⊙	70	26
	Mini Cooper Countryman S	$32,500	68	⌃	⊙	68	26

Rec.	Make & Model	Price	Overall Score	Survey Results		Test Results	
		As tested		Predicted Reliability	Owner Satisfaction	Road Test Score	Overall MPG
SUVs: LUXURY COMPACT							
✓	Mercedes-Benz GLC 300 ▲	$49,105	84	⌃⌃	⌃	81	22
✓	Lexus NX 200t	$43,284	76	⌃⌃	●	74	24
✓	BMW X3 xDrive28i (2.0T)	$44,595	76	●	●	82	23
✓	Audi Q5 Premium Plus (2.0T)	$43,675	75	⌃	⌃	78	21
✓	Lexus NX 300h	$51,224	74	⌃⌃	●	71	29
✓	Porsche Macan S	$63,290	74	●	⌃⌃	85	19
✓	Acura RDX	$38,990	72	⌃	●	75	22
✓	Volvo XC60 T6**	$42,245	70	●	●	71	17
	Cadillac XT5 Luxury	$51,025	68	●*	⌃*	76	20
	Buick Envision Premium	$45,380	66	●*	⌃*	67	21
	Jaguar F-Pace Prestige	$53,895	60	⌄*	⌃*	72	20
	Lincoln MKC Reserve	$46,485	55	⌄⌄	●	72	19
	Land Rover Discovery Sport HSE	$49,895	47	⌄⌄*	●*	58	21
SUVs: LUXURY MIDSIZED							
✓	Audi Q7 Premium Plus	$68,695	94	⌃⌃	⌃⌃	96	20
✓	Lexus RX 450h	$57,565	81	⌃	⌃⌃	80	29
✓	Lexus RX 350	$51,630	79	⌃	⌃⌃	77	22
✓	BMW X5 xDrive35i	$70,050	75	●	⌃	84	21
✓	Lexus GX 460	$58,428	75	⌃⌃	⌃	70	17
✓	Buick Enclave CXL	$43,260	74	●	⌃	77	15
✓	Acura MDX Tech	$51,410	74	●	●	79	21
✓	Mercedes-Benz GLE350 (ML) ▲	$56,960	73	●	⌃⌃	75	18
✓	Porsche Cayenne (V6)	$63,805	72	●	⌃	78	19
	Lincoln MKX (2.7 EcoBoost)	$54,945	67	⌄	⌃	87	18
	Infiniti QX60 (3.5L)	$51,920	65	⌄	⌄⌄	79	19
	Volvo XC90 T6 Momentum ▲	$56,805	65	⌄⌄	⌃	84	20
	Infiniti QX70**	$51,635	60	⌄*	⌄*	72	18

▲ **Alert:** This vehicle can be outfitted with a semi-autonomous driving package. Consumer Reports believes automakers should take stronger steps to ensure that vehicles with those systems are designed, deployed, and marketed safely. Please heed all warnings, and keep your hands on the wheel.

RATINGS KEY

⊗ ⊘ ● ⌃ ⌃⌃   ✓
WORSE ——— BETTER   RECOMMENDED These are high-performing models that stand out.

Rec.	Make & Model	Price (As tested)	Overall Score	Survey Results — Predicted Reliability	Survey Results — Owner Satisfaction	Test Results — Road Test Score	Test Results — Overall MPG
SUVs: LUXURY MIDSIZED (Continued)							
	Tesla Model X 90D ⚠	$110,700	59	⊘	⊙	77	92¹
	Land Rover Range Rover Sport HSE (3.0L)	$74,040	59	⊘*	⊙*	74	18
SUVs: LUXURY LARGE							
✓	**Toyota Land Cruiser****	$84,820	74	⊙*	⊙*	68	14
	Lincoln Navigator Base	$68,895	69	◑*	⊙*	72	15
	Land Rover Range Rover HSE (3.0L)	$88,545	62	⊘*	⊙*	80	17
	Mercedes-Benz GLS (GL) 350d** ⚠	$73,020	61	⊘	◑	82	20
	Infiniti QX80	$63,395	57	⊙*	⊙	68	15
	Cadillac Escalade Premium	$87,360	44	⊘	⊙	61	16
COMPACT PICKUP TRUCKS							
✓	**Honda Ridgeline** RTL	$36,480	75	◑*	⊙*	80	20
	Chevrolet Colorado LT (V6)**	$34,300	57	⊙	◑	69	18
	GMC Canyon SLE (V6)**	$35,835	57	⊙	◑	69	18
	Chevrolet Colorado LT (diesel)	$39,295	56	⊙	◑	67	24
	GMC Canyon SLE (diesel)	$40,895	56	⊙	◑	67	24
	Toyota Tacoma SR5 (V6)	$34,364	41	⊘	◑	46	19
FULL-SIZED PICKUP TRUCKS							
✓	**Toyota Tundra** SR5 (5.7L V8)	$38,715	67	⊙	⊙	63	15
	Ford F-150 XLT (3.5 V6 EcoBoost)**	$46,755	65	⊙	⊙	80	16
	Chevrolet Silverado 1500 LT (5.3L V8)	$42,070	65	⊙	◑	80	16
	GMC Sierra 1500 SLT (5.3L V8)	$43,200	65	⊙	◑	80	16
	Ford F-150 XLT (2.7 V6 EcoBoost)	$45,750	64	⊙	⊙	78	17
	Ram 1500 Big Horn (V6, diesel)	$49,155	58	⊘	⊙	82	20
	Ram 1500 Big Horn (5.7L V8)	$42,810	58	⊘	⊙	81	15
	Nissan Titan XD SV (diesel)	$51,075	50	⊙*	⊙*	55	15

C! = Caution, subpar crash-test results. * Based on limited data.
**Powertrain has changed since last test.

Used Cars
The Most Reliable Models and The Ones to Avoid

BEST OF THE BEST

These models are the top used sedans, wagons, hatchbacks, and SUVs available in four price ranges. Each performed well in our testing when they were new and have been consistently reliable over time. All of the models listed here had electronic stability control (ESC) either as an optional or standard feature during the model years listed.

LESS THAN $10,000

Small Cars
Ford Focus 2009-10
Pontiac Vibe 2006-09
Scion xB 2008-09
The Focus delivers a steady ride, an interior that feels upscale for the price, and sporty handling. The Vibe is a reliable and spacious hatchback similar to the Toyota Matrix. The Scion xB is a cargo box on wheels, ready to haul almost anything you can throw in or at it.

Sedans
Acura TL 2006
Acura TSX 2006
Hyundai Sonata 2007-09
Mazda6 2009
You can stick to your budget and still get a reliable premium car if you choose the slick-handling TL. The smaller TSX is a sportier alternative. The Sonata is an accommodating alternative in a plain package. The sporty Mazda6 has a supple ride.

SUVs and Minivans
Honda CR-V 2006
Honda Pilot 2006
Toyota Sienna 2006
Standard ESC and curtain airbags, combined with acres of space, make the reliable CR-V a can't-miss prospect. For even more room, check out the eight-seat Pilot with its smooth V6 acceleration and car-like handling. Opt for the Sienna if you need the bountiful accommodations and flexibility of a minivan.

$10,000-$15,000

Small Cars
Honda Fit 2011-13
Kia Soul 2011-13
Mazda3 2011-12
The Fit is a bit noisy, but excellent fuel economy and a flexible interior make it a standout among subcompacts. The boxy yet stylish Soul has tons of features for a small car and expansive cargo space, making it a smart choice for recent grads. The Mazda3 has everything most shoppers want in a small car: reliability, fuel efficiency, a fun-to-drive attitude, an interior that feels upscale for the price, and seats that won't leave your back and tailbone screaming.

Sedans
Infiniti G 2006-08
Lincoln MKZ 2009-10
The G35 blends sporty handling with interior refinement. For less of a race-car feel, the MKZ has available AWD and a supple ride. Look for a 2010 model, with its quieter, luxurious interior.

SUVs
Acura MDX 2006
Toyota Highlander 2006-7
The MDX's quiet interior and responsive handling put an enjoyable spin on family-friendly vehicles, showing why it's the standard for three-row crossover SUVs. The rock-solid, reliable Highlander is slightly smaller, but for

some, it's a handier size. It's available with a third-row seat, and the hybrid version delivers the fuel economy of a small SUV.

$15,000-$20,000

Small Cars
Toyota Prius 2012-13
Hyundai Elantra 2014-15
Honda Civic 2013-14
The Prius has always proved that you don't have to give up space or ride comfort to get stellar gas mileage. And its standard ESC is an added bonus. Lots of features for the money, a roomy backseat, and responsive handling make the Elantra a great deal. Go for a 2013 or newer Civic to get its much-needed upgrades in braking, suspension, and the interior.

Sedans
Honda Accord 2011-12
Toyota Camry 2012-13
Lexus ES 2009-10
A cavernous backseat, responsive suspension and 25 mpg overall from the four-cylinder engine make the Accord a perennial winner. The Camry is also a no-brainer thanks to stellar reliability and ample space for five adults. The ES takes the Camry platform and adds luxury appointments, front seats worthy of a road trip, and a hushed cabin.

SUVs
Mazda CX-5 2013

Toyota RAV4 2010-11
Mazda's CX-5 has very good fuel economy, crisp handling, and a generous rear seat. The RAV4 is available with four- and six-cylinder engines, both of which are quite fuel-efficient. Nimble, secure handling is a plus.

$20,000-$25,000

Sedans
Ford Fusion 2014-15
Subaru Legacy 2014-15
Toyota Avalon 2012
The Fusion has sporty handling, a composed ride, and a roomy interior. The spacious and refined Legacy offers a wide variety of advanced safety features. Choose the Avalon if you want a commodious, luxurious sedan without the upscale price.

SUVs
Nissan Murano 2012-13
Subaru Forester 2012-13
Toyota Sequoia 2008
The Murano has long been one of our favorite SUVs, with secure handling and a rich interior. The Forester has standard AWD, plentiful rear-seat accommodations, and a comfortable ride. The Sequoia is a reliable SUV with seating for eight and strong towing capability.

Luxury SUVs
Mercedes-Benz E-Class 2009

Acura RDX 2011
Lexus RX 2010
The smooth-riding E-Class wraps its occupants in a first-class cabin. The RDX blends sporty handling and upscale accoutrements in a small SUV package. The RX upscale SUV has bulletproof reliability, plush seats, and a luxury ride. The hybrid gets an impressive 26 mpg overall.

WORST OF THE WORST
These have had multiple years of much worse than average reliability, listed alphabetically.

BMW 5 Series
Chevrolet Cruze
Chevrolet Traverse
Chrysler PT Cruiser
Dodge Challenger
Dodge Journey
Fiat 500
Ford Fiesta
Ford Focus
GMC Acadia
Jeep Grand Cherokee
Mercedes-Benz GL-Class
Mini Cooper
Mini Countryman
Nissan Pathfinder
Pontiac Torrent
Saturn Outlook
Tesla Model S
Volkswagen GTI
Volkswagen Tiguan

Reliable Used Cars For Every Budget

AS OWNERS HOLD ON TO their vehicles longer, fewer late-model used cars are available for sale. The result: higher prices and a limited supply of reliable vehicles that have low miles. But there are still a large number of good buys to be found. These lists show vehicles in four price categories. Each one of the vehicles featured tested well when new and has had above-average reliability. Try to buy the newest vehicle that your budget allows, so that you can get the most up-to-date safety features. To help, we show the first year that each model offered electronic stability control (ESC), a proven lifesaver, as a standard or optional feature.

Make & Model	Under $10,000	$10,000-$15,000	$15,000-$20,000	$20,000-$25,000	ESC ('06-15) Opt. From	ESC ('06-15) Std. From
CARS: SUBCOMPACT AND COMPACT						
Ford Focus	'08-10	-	-	-	'09	'10
Honda Civic	'06-09	'10-12	'13-14	'15	'09	'12
Honda Fit	'07-09	'10-13	-	-	'09	'11
Hyundai Accent	-	'12-14	-	-	-	'12
Hyundai Elantra	'06-09	-	'14-15	-	'08	'11
Kia Forte	'10-11	-	-	-	-	All
Kia Soul	'10	'11-13	'14	-	-	All
Mazda3	-	'09-12	'13-15	-	'07	'11
Nissan Leaf	-	'12	'14	-	-	All
Pontiac Vibe	'06-09	'10	-	-	'06	'09
Scion xB	'06, '08-09	'10, '12	-	-	-	All
Scion xD	'08	-	-	-	'08	'10
Subaru Impreza	-	-	'11	'13	'08	'09
Toyota Corolla	'06-09	'10-13	'14-15	-	'06	'10
Toyota Matrix	'06-08	'10	-	-	'06	'10
Toyota Prius	'06-08	'09-11	'12-13	'14-15	'06	'10
Toyota Prius C	-	'12	'13-14	-	-	All
Toyota Yaris	'07-10	-	-	-	-	'10

Make & Model	Under $10,000	$10,000-$15,000	$15,000-$20,000	$20,000-$25,000	ESC ('06-15)	
					Opt. From	Std. From
CARS: MIDSIZED AND LARGE						
Ford Fusion	'06-09	-	'12	'14-15	'09	'10
Honda Accord	'06-07	'08-10	'11-12	'13-15	'06	'08
Hyundai Azera	'07	-	-	'12-13	-	All
Hyundai Sonata	'07-09	-	'13-15	-	-	'06
Kia Optima	-	-	'13	'14	-	'06
Mazda6	'09	'10, '12	'14	-	'06	'09
Mercury Milan	'06-09	-	-	-	'09	'10
Nissan Altima	'07	'08-11	'12	-	'07	'10
Nissan Maxima	-	'08	'10-12	'13-14	'06	'09
Subaru Legacy	-	'10	'11-13	'14-15	'07	'09
Toyota Avalon	'06	'07-09	'10-11	'12	'06	'09
Toyota Camry	'06-07	'08-11	'12-13	'14-15	'06	'10
CARS: LUXURY						
Acura ILX	-	-	-	'13-14	-	All
Acura TL	'06	'07-08	'09-10	'11-12	-	All
Acura TSX	'06	'07-09	'10-11	-	-	All
Buick Regal	-	-	'12	'14	-	All
Infiniti G	-	'06-08	'09-10	'11-12	-	All
Infiniti M	-	'06-08	-	'11	-	All
Lexus CT 200h	-	-	'11	'12-13	-	All
Lexus ES	-	'06-08	'09-10	'11-12	'06	'07
Lexus GS	-	-	'07-08	-	-	All
Lexus HS Hybrid	-	-	'10	'12	-	All
Lexus IS	-	-	-	'10-11	-	'06
Lexus LS	-	-	'06	'07-08	-	All
Lincoln MKZ	'07-08	'09-10	'11-12	-	-	'09
Mercedes-Benz C-Class	'06	-	'08-09	'11	-	All
Mercedes-Benz E-Class	-	'06	'07	'09	-	All

Make & Model	Under $10,000	$10,000-$15,000	$15,000-$20,000	$20,000-$25,000	ESC ('06-15)	
					Opt. From	Std. From
SPORTS CARS/CONVERTIBLES						
Chevrolet Camaro	-	-	'10-11	-	-	'10
Ford Mustang	'06	-	'08	'10	-	'10
Mazda MX-5 Miata	'06	'07-10	'11-12	'13	'06	'12
WAGONS AND MINIVANS						
Honda Accord Crosstour	-	-	'10	'12-13	-	All
Mazda5	-	'12	'13-14	-	-	All
Subaru Outback	-	-	'10-11	'12-13	'06	'09
Toyota Prius V	-	-	'12-13	'14	-	All
Toyota Sienna	'06	-	'09	'11-12	'06	'08
Toyota Venza	-	-	'09-11	'12-13	-	All
Volvo V70/XC70	-	'07, '09	'10	-	'06	'07
SUVs: SMALL						
Buick Encore	-	-	-	'13-14	-	All
Chevrolet Equinox	-	-	'12-13	'14	-	'07
GMC Terrain	-	-	'12	'13	-	All
Honda CR-V	'06	'07-09	'10-11	'12-14	-	All
Hyundai Tucson	'07	'10	'13	'14-15	-	All
Mazda CX-5	-	-	'13	'14-15	-	All
Nissan Rogue	-	'10	'11	'15	-	All
Subaru Forester	-	-	-	'12-13	'07	'09
Subaru XV Crosstrek	-	-	-	'11	-	All
Toyota RAV4	-	'09	'10-11	'12-13	-	All

Make & Model	Under $10,000	$10,000-$15,000	$15,000-$20,000	$20,000-$25,000	ESC ('06-15)	
					Opt. From	Std. From
SUVs: MIDSIZED AND LARGE						
Acura MDX	-	'06	-	'09	-	All
Acura RDX	-	'07	'08, '10	'11	-	All
Ford Edge	-	'09	'10	'11	-	All
Honda Pilot	'06	'07-08	'09	'11	-	'06
Lexus GX	-	-	'06-07	'08	-	All
Lexus RX	-	'06-07	'08-09	'10	-	All
Mazda CX-9	-	'08	-	'13	-	All
Mercedes-Benz GLK-Class	-	-	-	'11	-	All
Nissan Murano	-	-	'10-11	'12-13	'06	'09
Toyota 4Runner	-	'06-07	'08	-	-	All
Toyota Highlander	-	'06-07	'08-09	'10-11	-	All
Toyota Sequoia	-	'06	'07	'08	-	All
Volvo XC90	-	'07-08	-	-	-	All
PICKUP TRUCKS						
Chevrolet Silverado 2500HD	-	-	'07-08	'09	'09	'10
GMC Sierra 2500HD	-	-	'07-08	'09	'09	'10
Honda Ridgeline	-	'06-07	'08-09	'10-11	-	All
Nissan Frontier	-	'08	'09-11	'12	'06	'12
Toyota Tacoma	-	'06-07	'08-10	'11-13	'06	'09
Toyota Tundra	-	'06	'07-08	'10	'06	'09

Used Cars to Avoid

Audi A4

These 2006-15 models
have a record of below-
average overall reliability.
They are listed alpha-
betically by make and
model.

ACURA RLX '14; TLX '15

AUDI A4 '06-07, '09-11;
A5 '10-11

BMW 1 Series '12; 3 Series
'06-09, '11; 4 Series '15; 5
Series '06-08, '10-12, '15;
i3 '14; X3 '06-08, '11; X5
'11-14

BUICK Enclave '08-11;
LaCrosse '06-08, '10-11;
Lucerne '07, '09-11; Rainer
'06; Regal '11; Rendezvous
'06; Terraza '06

CADILLAC ATS '13-14; CTS
'06, '08-10;
DTS '06-07; Escalade '15;
SRX '10-13;
XTS '13

CHEVROLET Avalanche
'07-08,'11; Camaro '13;
Cobalt '07; Colorado '08,
'15; Corvette '15; Cruze
'11-13; Equinox '06-11;
HHR '06, '10; Impala '06-
08, '13; Malibu '06-08;
Silverado 1500 '08-09,
'14-15; Sonic '13; Suburban
'08-09, '15; Tahoe '15;
TrailBlazer '06; Traverse
'09-11; Uplander '06

CHRYSLER 200 '12-13, '15;
300 '13-14; Pacifica '07; PT
Cruiser '06-08; Sebring
'06; Town & Country '06-13

DODGE Caliber '07;
Caravan '06-07;
Challenger '13-14; Charger
'13; Dakota '06; Dart '13-14;
Durango '11-12, '14; Grand
Caravan '06-13; Journey '09,
'12-14; Ram 1500 '09-10; Ram
2500 '06; Stratus '06

FIAT 500 '12-13, '15; 500L
'14

FORD C-Max '13; Edge '12;
Escape '06-08, '10, '13;
Expedition '12; Explorer
'06, '10-12; F-150 '11-12;
F-250 '06, '08, '11, '13;
F-350 '06, '08; Fiesta '11-
14; Focus '12-14; Freestyle
'06; Fusion '13; Mustang
'12-13, '15; Taurus '10-11

GMC Acadia '07-14;
Canyon '08, '15; Envoy '06;
Sierra 1500 '08-09, '14-15;

Nissan Juke

Terrain '10-11; Yukon '15; Yukon XL '08-09, '15

HONDA Pilot '10, '15

HYUNDAI Elantra '10-11; Genesis '10, '12; Genesis Coupe '13; Santa Fe '10, '15; Sonata '12; Veracruz '08, '11

INFINITI Q50 '14; JX '13; QX60 '14

JEEP Cherokee '14-15; Grand Cherokee '07, '10-14; Liberty '06; Patriot '08, '14; Wrangler '06-09, '12-13

KIA Forte '12; Rio '13; Rondo '08; Sedona '06; Sorento '11

LINCOLN MKC '15; MKZ '13

MAZDA Mazda5 '06-08; Mazda6 '07; CX-7 '10; Tribute '06-08, '10

MERCEDES-BENZ C-Class '12, '15; CLA '14; CLK '08; GL-Class '13-15; M-Class '07-10, '12; S-Class '14
MERCURY Mariner '06-08, '10; Mountaineer '06, '10

MINI COOPER '06-12, '14; Countryman '11-12

NISSAN Altima '13-14; Frontier '06, '15; Juke '11-12; Leaf '13; Maxima '06-07; Pathfinder '13-14; Quest '12; Rogue '14; Sentra '13; Xterra '06

PONTIAC G5 '06, '08-09; Montana SV6 '06; Torrent '06-09

PORSCHE 911 '12; Cayman '14; Macan '15
RAM 1500 '13-14; 2500 '14

SAAB 9-3 '08

SATURN Aura '09; Ion '07; Outlook '07-09; Vue '08
SMART FORTWO '08-09

SUBARU Forester '06-07; Impreza '07-10; Legacy '06-08; Outback '06-08

TESLA Model S '12-13, '15

VOLKSWAGEN
Beetle '14; CC '10, '12; Eos '08, '12; Golf '15; GTI '10-13; Jetta '06, '15; Passat '06-07, '10, '12; Tiguan '09-12

VOLVO S60 '07; V60 '15; XC60 '14

Detailed Used Car Reliability

THESE CHARTS GIVE YOU a model's complete reliability picture for both its used versions (2010 through 2015) and the predicted reliability for the new one currently on sale. These detailed reliability Ratings are based on our 2015 Annual Car Reliability Survey, for which we received responses on almost 750,000 vehicles.

The Annual Car Reliability Survey is sent to subscribers of Consumer Reports and ConsumerReports.org. Respondents reported on any serious problems they had with their vehicles in any of the trouble spots included in the following charts, during the previous 12 months. These were considered serious because of cost, failure, safety, or downtime. Because high-mileage vehicles tend to have more problems than low-mileage ones, problem rates are standardized to minimize differences related to mileage. The 2015 models were generally less than 6 months old at the time of the survey and had been driven an average of about 3,000 miles. Models with insufficient data are noted with a column of asterisks (*).

HOW TO USE THE CHARTS

Major redesigns
A model year in bold identifies the year the model was introduced or underwent a major redesign.

Trouble spots
To assess a used car in more detail, look at the individual ratings for each of the 17 trouble spots. They will pinpoint a model's strengths and weaknesses. Ratings are based on the percentage of survey respondents who reported problems for that trouble spot, compared with the average of all vehicles for that year.

Models that score a B are not necessarily unreliable, but they have a higher problem rate than the average model. Similarly, models that score a N are not necessarily problem-free, but they had relatively few problems compared with other models.

Because problem rates in some trouble spots are very low, we do not assign a ⊗ or ⊙ unless the model's problem rate exceeds 3 percent. If a problem rate is below 2 percent, it will be assigned a ●; below 1 percent, it will be assigned a ◕.

Used Car Verdicts
To check the overall reliability of a used car, look at the Used-Car Verdict. This Rating shows whether the model had more or fewer problems overall than the average model of that year. The verdict is calculated from the total number of problems reported by subscribers in all trouble spots. Our calculations give extra weight to problems with major engine and transmission systems, the cooling system, and the drive system, because they can be serious and expensive to repair.

What The Trouble Spots Mean
Engine, Major Engine rebuild or replacement, cylinder head, head gasket, turbo or supercharger, timing chain or timing belt. **Engine, Minor** Oil leaks, accessory belts and pulleys, engine mounts, engine knock or ping. **Engine Cooling** Radiator, cooling fan, antifreeze leaks, water pump,

thermostat, overheating.

Transmission, Major
Transmission rebuild or replacement, torque converter, premature clutch replacement.

Transmission, Minor Gear selector or linkage, coolers and lines, rough shifting, slipping transmission, leaks, transmission computer, transmission sensor or solenoid, clutch adjustment, hydraulics (clutch master or slave cylinder).

Drive System Driveshaft or axle, CV joint, differential, transfer case, 4WD/AWD components, driveline vibration, traction control, stability control (ESC), electrical failure.

Fuel System Check engine light, sensors (includes O2 or oxygen sensor), emission control devices (includes EGR), engine computer, fuel cap, fuel gauge/sender, fuel-injection system, fuel pump, fuel leaks, stalling or hesitation.

Electrical Alternator, starter, hybrid battery and related systems, regular battery, battery cables, engine harness, coil, ignition switch, electronic ignition, distributor or rotor failure, spark plugs and wires failure.

Climate System Blower (fan) motor, A/C compressor, condenser, evaporator, heater system, automatic climate control, refrigerant leakage, electrical failure.

Average Problem Rates						
TROUBLE SPOTS	'10	'11	'12	'13	'14	'15
Engine, major	1	1	1	<1	<1	<1
Engine, minor	1	1	1	1	<1	<1
Engine Cooling	1	1	<1	<1	<1	<1
Trans. Major	1	1	1	<1	<1	<1
Trans. Minor	1	1	1	1	1	<1
Drive System	1	1	1	1	1	<1
Fuel System	2	1	1	1	1	<1
Electrical	1	1	<1	<1	<1	<1
Climate System	2	2	1	1	1	<1
Suspension	3	2	1	1	1	<1
Brakes	3	2	2	1	1	<1
Exhaust	1	<1	<1	<1	<1	<1
Paint/Trim	2	1	1	1	1	1
Body Integrity	3	2	3	2	2	1
Body Hardware	1	1	1	1	1	<1
Power Equip.	4	3	2	2	1	1
Audio System	2	2	2	3	2	2

USED CAR VERDICTS

< Sample chart.

Suspension Shocks or struts, ball joints, tie rods, wheel bearings, alignment, steering linkage (includes rack and pinion), power steering, wheel balance, springs or torsion bars, bushings, electronic or air suspension.

Brakes Premature wear, pulsation or vibration, squeaking, master cylinder, calipers, rooters, antilock brake system (ABS), parking brake, brake failure.

Exhaust Muffler, pipes, catalytic converter, exhaust manifold, leaks.

Paint/Trim Paint (fading, chalking, cracking, peeling), loose trim or moldings, rust.

Noises/Leaks Squeaks or rattles, seals and/or weather stripping, air or water leaks, wind noise.

Body Hardware Windows, locks and latches, tailgate, hatch or trunk, doors or sliding doors, mirrors, seat controls, safety belts, sunroof, convertible top, glass defect.

Power Equipment and Accessories Cruise control, clock, warning lights, body control module, keyless entry, wiper motor or washer, tire pressure monitor, interior or exterior light, horn, gauges, 12V power plug, alarm or security system.

In-Car Electronics Audio systems, entertainment systems, navigation system, backup camera/sensors, communication system.

TROUBLE SPOTS

TROUBLE SPOTS	Acura ILX						Acura MDX						Acura RDX						Acura RL, RLX						Acura TL					
	'10	'11	'12	'13	'14	'15	'10	'11	'12	'13	'14	'16	'10	'11	'12	'13	'14	'15	'10	'11	'12	'13	'14	'15	'10	'11	'12	'13	'14	'15
Engine, Major				●	●	*	●	●	●	●	●	●	●	●	●	●	●	●	*	*	*		●	*	●	●	●	●	●	●
Engine, Minor				●	●	*	●	●	●	●	●	●	●	●	●	●	●	●	*	*	*		●	*	●	●	●	●	●	●
Engine Cooling				●	●	*	●	●	●	●	●	●	●	●	●	●	●	●	*	*	*		●	*	●	●	●	●	●	●
Trans., Major				●	●	*	●	●	●	●	●	●	●	●	●	●	●	●	*	*	*		●	*	●	●	●	●	●	●
Trans., Minor				●	●	*	●	●	●	●	●	●	●	●	●	●	●	●	*	*	*		●	*	●	●	●	●	●	●
Drive System				●	●	*	●	●	●	●	●	●	●	●	●	●	●	●	*	*	*		●	*	●	●	●	●	●	●
Fuel System				●	●	*	●	●	●	●	●	●	●	●	●	●	●	●	*	*	*		●	*	●	●	●	●	●	●
Electrical				●	●	*	●	●	●	●	●	●	●	●	●	●	●	●	*	*	*		●	*	●	●	●	●	●	●
Climate System				●	●	*	●	●	●	●	●	●	●	●	●	●	●	●	*	*	*		●	*	●	●	●	●	●	●
Suspension				●	●	*	●	●	●	●	●	●	●	●	●	●	●	●	*	*	*		●	*	●	●	●	●	●	●
Brakes				●	●	*	●	●	●	●	●	●	●	●	●	●	●	●	*	*	*		●	*	●	●	●	●	●	●
Exhaust				●	●	*	●	●	●	●	●	●	●	●	●	●	●	●	*	*	*		●	*	●	●	●	●	●	●
Paint/Trim				●	●	*	●	●	●	●	●	●	●	●	●	●	●	●	*	*	*		●	*	●	●	●	●	●	●
Noises/Leaks				●	●	*	●	●	●	●	●	●	●	●	●	●	●	●	*	*	*		●	*	●	●	●	●	●	●
Body Hardware				●	●	*	●	●	●	●	●	●	●	●	●	●	●	●	*	*	*		●	*	●	●	●	●	●	●
Power Equip.				●	●	*	●	●	●	●	●	●	●	●	●	●	●	●	*	*	*		●	*	●	●	●	●	●	●
In-Car Elec.				●	●	*	●	●	●	●	●	●	●	●	●	●	●	●	*	*	*		●	*	●	●	●	●	●	●
USED-CAR VERDICTS				●	●	*	●	●	●	●	●	●	●	●	●	●	●	●	*	*	*		●	*	●	●	●	●	●	●

TROUBLE SPOTS	Acura TLX						Acura TSX						Audi A3						Audi A4						Audi A5					
	'10	'11	'12	'13	'14	'15	'10	'11	'12	'13	'14	'15	'10	'11	'12	'13	'14	'15	'10	'11	'12	'13	'14	'15	'10	'11	'12	'13	'14	'15
Engine, Major						●	●	●	●	●	*		*	*	*	*		●	●	●	●	●	●	●	●	●	●	●	●	●
Engine, Minor						●	●	●	●	●	*		*	*	*	*		●	●	●	●	●	●	●	●	●	●	●	●	●
Engine Cooling						●	●	●	●	●	*		*	*	*	*		●	●	●	●	●	●	●	●	●	●	●	●	●
Trans., Major						●	●	●	●	●	*		*	*	*	*		●	●	●	●	●	●	●	●	●	●	●	●	●
Trans., Minor						●	●	●	●	●	*		*	*	*	*		●	●	●	●	●	●	●	●	●	●	●	●	●
Drive System						●	●	●	●	●	*		*	*	*	*		●	●	●	●	●	●	●	●	●	●	●	●	●
Fuel System						●	●	●	●	●	*		*	*	*	*		●	●	●	●	●	●	●	●	●	●	●	●	●
Electrical						●	●	●	●	●	*		*	*	*	*		●	●	●	●	●	●	●	●	●	●	●	●	●
Climate System						●	●	●	●	●	*		*	*	*	*		●	●	●	●	●	●	●	●	●	●	●	●	●
Suspension						●	●	●	●	●	*		*	*	*	*		●	●	●	●	●	●	●	●	●	●	●	●	●
Brakes						●	●	●	●	●	*		*	*	*	*		●	●	●	●	●	●	●	●	●	●	●	●	●
Exhaust						●	●	●	●	●	*		*	*	*	*		●	●	●	●	●	●	●	●	●	●	●	●	●
Paint/Trim						●	●	●	●	●	*		*	*	*	*		●	●	●	●	●	●	●	●	●	●	●	●	●
Noises/Leaks						●	●	●	●	●	*		*	*	*	*		●	●	●	●	●	●	●	●	●	●	●	●	●
Body Hardware						●	●	●	●	●	*		*	*	*	*		●	●	●	●	●	●	●	●	●	●	●	●	●
Power Equip.						●	●	●	●	●	*		*	*	*	*		●	●	●	●	●	●	●	●	●	●	●	●	●
In-Car Elec.						●	●	●	●	●	*		*	*	*	*		●	●	●	●	●	●	●	●	●	●	●	●	●
USED-CAR VERDICTS						●	●	●	●	●	*		*	*	*	*		●	●	●	●	●	●	●	●	●	●	●	●	●

TROUBLE SPOTS	Audi A6						Audi A7						Audi Allroad						Audi Q3						Audi Q5					
	'10	'11	'12	'13	'14	'15	'10	'11	'12	'13	'14	'15	'10	'11	'12	'13	'14	'15	'10	'11	'12	'13	'14	'15	'10	'11	'12	'13	'14	'15
Engine, Major																														
Engine, Minor																															
Engine Cooling																															
Trans., Major																															
Trans., Minor																															
Drive System																															
Fuel System																															
Electrical																															
Climate System																															
Suspension																															
Brakes																															
Exhaust																															
Paint/Trim																															
Noises/Leaks																															
Body Hardware																															
Power Equip.																															
In-Car Elec.																															
USED-CAR VERDICTS																															

TROUBLE SPOTS	BMW 1 Series						BMW 2 Series						BMW 3 Series						BMW 4 Series						BMW 5 Series					
	'10	'11	'12	'13	'14	'15	'10	'11	'12	'13	'14	'15	'10	'11	'12	'13	'14	'15	'10	'11	'12	'13	'14	'15	'10	'11	'12	'13	'14	'15
Engine, Major																														
Engine, Minor																															
Engine Cooling																															
Trans., Major																															
Trans., Minor																															
Drive System																															
Fuel System																															
Electrical																															
Climate System																															
Suspension																															
Brakes																															
Exhaust																															
Paint/Trim																															
Noises/Leaks																															
Body Hardware																															
Power Equip.																															
In-Car Elec.																															
USED-CAR VERDICTS																															

TROUBLE SPOTS

TROUBLE SPOTS	BMW X1						BMW X3						BMW X5						BMW i3						Buick Enclave					
	'10	'11	'12	'13	'14	'15	'10	'11	'12	'13	'14	'15	'10	'11	'12	'13	'14	'15	'10	'11	'12	'13	'14	'15	'10	'11	'12	'13	'14	'15
Engine, Major																														
Engine, Minor																														
Engine Cooling																														
Trans., Major																														
Trans., Minor																														
Drive System																														
Fuel System																														
Electrical																														
Climate System																														
Suspension																														
Brakes																														
Exhaust																														
Paint/Trim																														
Noises/Leaks																														
Body Hardware																														
Power Equip.																														
In-Car Elec.																														
USED-CAR VERDICTS																														

TROUBLE SPOTS

TROUBLE SPOTS	Buick Encore						Buick LaCrosse						Buick Regal						Buick Verano						Cadillac ATS					
	'10	'11	'12	'13	'14	'15	'10	'11	'12	'13	'14	'15	'10	'11	'12	'13	'14	'15	'10	'11	'12	'13	'14	'15	'10	'11	'12	'13	'14	'15
Engine, Major																														
Engine, Minor																														
Engine Cooling																														
Trans., Major																														
Trans., Minor																														
Drive System																														
Fuel System																														
Electrical																														
Climate System																														
Suspension																														
Brakes																														
Exhaust																														
Paint/Trim																														
Noises/Leaks																														
Body Hardware																														
Power Equip.																														
In-Car Elec.																														
USED-CAR VERDICTS																														

TROUBLE SPOTS

TROUBLE SPOTS	Cadillac CTS						Cadillac Escalade						Cadillac SRX						Cadillac XTS						Chevrolet Avalanche					
	'10	'11	'12	'13	'14	'15	'10	'11	'12	'13	'14	'15	'10	'11	'12	'13	'14	'15	'10	'11	'12	'13	'14	'15	'10	'11	'12	'13	'14	'15
Engine, Major	●	●	●	●	●	*	*	*	*	*	*	●	●	●	●	●	●	●				●	●	*	*	●	●	*		
Engine, Minor	●	●	●	●	●	*	*	*	*	*	*	●	●	●	●	●	●	●				●	●	*	*	●	●	*		
Engine Cooling	●	●	●	●	●	*	*	*	*	*	*	●	●	●	●	●	●	●				●	●	*	*	●	●	*		
Trans., Major	●	●	●	●	●	*	*	*	*	*	*	●	●	●	●	●	●	●				●	●	*	*	●	●	*		
Trans., Minor	●	●	●	●	●	*	*	*	*	*	*	●	●	●	●	●	●	●				●	●	*	*	●	●	*		
Drive System	●	●	●	●	●	*	*	*	*	*	*	●	●	●	●	●	●	●				●	●	*	*	●	●	*		
Fuel System	●	●	●	●	●	*	*	*	*	*	*	●	●	●	●	●	●	●				●	●	*	*	●	●	*		
Electrical	●	●	●	●	●	*	*	*	*	*	*	●	●	●	●	●	●	●				●	●	*	*	●	●	*		
Climate System	●	●	●	●	●	*	*	*	*	*	*	●	●	●	●	●	●	●				●	●	*	*	●	●	*		
Suspension	●	●	●	●	●	*	*	*	*	*	*	●	●	●	●	●	●	●				●	●	*	*	●	●	*		
Brakes	●	●	●	●	●	*	*	*	*	*	*	●	●	●	●	●	●	●				●	●	*	*	●	●	*		
Exhaust	●	●	●	●	●	*	*	*	*	*	*	●	●	●	●	●	●	●				●	●	*	*	●	●	*		
Paint/Trim	●	●	●	●	●	*	*	*	*	*	*	●	●	●	●	●	●	●				●	●	*	*	●	●	*		
Noises/Leaks	●	●	●	●	●	*	*	*	*	*	*	●	●	●	●	●	●	●				●	●	*	*	●	●	*		
Body Hardware	●	●	●	●	●	*	*	*	*	*	*	●	●	●	●	●	●	●				●	●	*	*	●	●	*		
Power Equip.	●	●	●	●	●	*	*	*	*	*	*	●	●	●	●	●	●	●				●	●	*	*	●	●	*		
In-Car Elec.	●	●	●	●	●	*	*	*	*	*	*	●	●	●	●	●	●	●				●	●	*	*	●	●	*		
USED-CAR VERDICTS	●	●	●	●	●	*	*	*	*	*	*	●	●	●	●	●	●	●				●	●	*	*	●	●	*		

TROUBLE SPOTS

TROUBLE SPOTS	Chevrolet Camaro						Chevrolet Colorado						Chevrolet Corvette						Chevrolet Cruze						Chevrolet Equinox					
	'10	'11	'12	'13	'14	'15	'10	'11	'12	'13	'14	'15	'10	'11	'12	'13	'14	'15	'10	'11	'12	'13	'14	'15	'10	'11	'12	'13	'14	'15
Engine, Major	●	●	●	●	●	*	*	*	●			●	*	●	●	●	●	●		●	●	●	●	*	●	●	●	●	●	●
Engine, Minor	●	●	●	●	●	*	*	*	●			●	*	●	●	●	●	●	●	●	●	●	●	*	●	●	●	●	●	●
Engine Cooling	●	●	●	●	●	*	*	*	●			●	*	●	●	●	●	●	●	●	●	●	●	*	●	●	●	●	●	●
Trans., Major	●	●	●	●	●	*	*	*	●			●	*	●	●	●	●	●		●	●	●	●	*	●	●	●	●	●	●
Trans., Minor	●	●	●	●	●	*	*	*	●			●	*	●	●	●	●	●	●	●	●	●	●	*	●	●	●	●	●	●
Drive System	●	●	●	●	●	*	*	*	●			●	*	●	●	●	●	●	●	●	●	●	●	*	●	●	●	●	●	●
Fuel System	●	●	●	●	●	*	*	*	●			●	*	●	●	●	●	●	●	●	●	●	●	*	●	●	●	●	●	●
Electrical	●	●	●	●	●	*	*	*	●			●	*	●	●	●	●	●	●	●	●	●	●	*	●	●	●	●	●	●
Climate System	●	●	●	●	●	*	*	*	●			●	*	●	●	●	●	●	●	●	●	●	●	*	●	●	●	●	●	●
Suspension	●	●	●	●	●	*	*	*	●			●	*	●	●	●	●	●	●	●	●	●	●	*	●	●	●	●	●	●
Brakes	●	●	●	●	●	*	*	*	●			●	*	●	●	●	●	●	●	●	●	●	●	*	●	●	●	●	●	●
Exhaust	●	●	●	●	●	*	*	*	●			●	*	●	●	●	●	●	●	●	●	●	●	*	●	●	●	●	●	●
Paint/Trim	●	●	●	●	●	*	*	*	●			●	*	●	●	●	●	●	●	●	●	●	●	*	●	●	●	●	●	●
Noises/Leaks	●	●	●	●	●	*	*	*	●			●	*	●	●	●	●	●	●	●	●	●	●	*	●	●	●	●	●	●
Body Hardware	●	●	●	●	●	*	*	*	●			●	*	●	●	●	●	●	●	●	●	●	●	*	●	●	●	●	●	●
Power Equip.	●	●	●	●	●	*	*	*	●			●	*	●	●	●	●	●	●	●	●	●	●	*	●	●	●	●	●	●
In-Car Elec.	●	●	●	●	●	*	*	*	●			●	*	●	●	●	●	●	●	●	●	●	●	*	●	●	●	●	●	●
USED-CAR VERDICTS	●	●	●	●	●	*	*	*	●			●	*	●	●	●	●	●		●	●	●	●	*	●	●	●	●	●	●

TROUBLE SPOTS

TROUBLE SPOTS	Chevrolet HHR						Chevrolet Impala						Chevrolet Malibu						Chevrolet Silverado 1500						Chevrolet Sonic					
	'10	'11	'12	'13	'14	'15	'10	'11	'12	'13	'14	'15	'10	'11	'12	'13	'14	'15	'10	'11	'12	'13	'14	'15	'10	'11	'12	'13	'14	'15
Engine, Major																														
Engine, Minor																														
Engine Cooling																														
Trans., Major																														
Trans., Minor																														
Drive System																														
Fuel System																														
Electrical																														
Climate System																														
Suspension																														
Brakes																														
Exhaust																														
Paint/Trim																														
Noises/Leaks																														
Body Hardware																														
Power Equip.																														
In-Car Elec.																														
USED-CAR VERDICTS																														

TROUBLE SPOTS	Chevrolet Suburban						Chevrolet Tahoe						Chevrolet Traverse						Chevrolet Volt						Chrysler 300					
	'10	'11	'12	'13	'14	'15	'10	'11	'12	'13	'14	'15	'10	'11	'12	'13	'14	'15	'10	'11	'12	'13	'14	'15	'10	'11	'12	'13	'14	'15
Engine, Major																														
Engine, Minor																														
Engine Cooling																														
Trans., Major																														
Trans., Minor																														
Drive System																														
Fuel System																														
Electrical																														
Climate System																														
Suspension																														
Brakes																														
Exhaust																														
Paint/Trim																														
Noises/Leaks																														
Body Hardware																														
Power Equip.																														
In-Car Elec.																														
USED-CAR VERDICTS																														

First Table

TROUBLE SPOTS	Chrysler Sebring, 200						Chrysler Town & Country						Dodge Challenger						Dodge Charger						Dodge Dart					
	'10	'11	'12	'13	'14	'15	'10	'11	'12	'13	'14	'15	'10	'11	'12	'13	'14	'15	'10	'11	'12	'13	'14	'15	'10	'11	'12	'13	'14	'15
Engine, Major	★				★								★	★	★				★	★				★						★
Engine, Minor	★				★								★	★	★				★	★				★						★
Engine Cooling	★				★								★	★	★				★	★				★						★
Trans., Major	★				★								★	★	★				★	★				★						★
Trans., Minor	★				★								★	★	★				★	★				★						★
Drive System	★				★								★	★	★				★	★				★						★
Fuel System	★				★								★	★	★				★	★				★						★
Electrical	★				★								★	★	★				★	★				★						★
Climate System	★				★								★	★	★				★	★				★						★
Suspension	★				★								★	★	★				★	★				★						★
Brakes	★				★								★	★	★				★	★				★						★
Exhaust	★				★								★	★	★				★	★				★						★
Paint/Trim	★				★								★	★	★				★	★				★						★
Noises/Leaks	★				★								★	★	★				★	★				★						★
Body Hardware	★				★								★	★	★				★	★				★						★
Power Equip.	★				★								★	★	★				★	★				★						★
In-Car Elec.	★				★								★	★	★				★	★				★						★
USED-CAR VERDICTS	★				★								★	★	★				★	★				★						★

Second Table

TROUBLE SPOTS	Dodge Durango						Dodge Grand Caravan						Dodge Journey						Fiat 500						Fiat 500L					
	'10	'11	'12	'13	'14	'15	'10	'11	'12	'13	'14	'15	'10	'11	'12	'13	'14	'15	'10	'11	'12	'13	'14	'15	'10	'11	'12	'13	'14	'15
Engine, Major													★	★				★												★
Engine, Minor													★	★				★												★
Engine Cooling													★	★				★												★
Trans., Major													★	★				★												★
Trans., Minor													★	★				★												★
Drive System													★	★				★												★
Fuel System													★	★				★												★
Electrical													★	★				★												★
Climate System													★	★				★												★
Suspension													★	★				★												★
Brakes													★	★				★												★
Exhaust													★	★				★												★
Paint/Trim													★	★				★												★
Noises/Leaks													★	★				★												★
Body Hardware													★	★				★												★
Power Equip.													★	★				★												★
In-Car Elec.													★	★				★												★
USED-CAR VERDICTS													★	★				★												★

TROUBLE SPOTS

Ford C-Max | Ford Edge | Ford Escape | Ford Expedition | Ford Explorer

	\'10	\'11	\'12	\'13	\'14	\'15	\'10	\'11	\'12	\'13	\'14	\'15	\'10	\'11	\'12	\'13	\'14	\'15	\'10	\'11	\'12	\'13	\'14	\'15	\'10	\'11	\'12	\'13	\'14	\'15
Engine, Major																														
Engine, Minor																														
Engine Cooling																														
Trans., Major																														
Trans., Minor																														
Drive System																														
Fuel System																														
Electrical																														
Climate System																														
Suspension																														
Brakes																														
Exhaust																														
Paint/Trim																														
Noises/Leaks																														
Body Hardware																														
Power Equip.																														
In-Car Elec.																														
USED-CAR VERDICTS																														

Ford F-150 | Ford Fiesta | Ford Flex | Ford Focus | Ford Fusion

	\'10	\'11	\'12	\'13	\'14	\'15	\'10	\'11	\'12	\'13	\'14	\'15	\'10	\'11	\'12	\'13	\'14	\'15	\'10	\'11	\'12	\'13	\'14	\'15	\'10	\'11	\'12	\'13	\'14	\'15
Engine, Major																														
Engine, Minor																														
Engine Cooling																														
Trans., Major																														
Trans., Minor																														
Drive System																														
Fuel System																														
Electrical																														
Climate System																														
Suspension																														
Brakes																														
Exhaust																														
Paint/Trim																														
Noises/Leaks																														
Body Hardware																														
Power Equip.																														
In-Car Elec.																														
USED-CAR VERDICTS																														

TROUBLE SPOTS

TROUBLE SPOTS	Ford Mustang						Ford Taurus						GMC Acadia						GMC Canyon						GMC Sierra 1500					
	'10	'11	'12	'13	'14	'15	'10	'11	'12	'13	'14	'15	'10	'11	'12	'13	'14	'15	'10	'11	'12	'13	'14	'15	'10	'11	'12	'13	'14	'15
Engine, Major																														
Engine, Minor																														
Engine Cooling																														
Trans., Major																														
Trans., Minor																														
Drive System																														
Fuel System																														
Electrical																														
Climate System																														
Suspension																														
Brakes																														
Exhaust																														
Paint/Trim																														
Noises/Leaks																														
Body Hardware																														
Power Equip.																														
In-Car Elec.																														
USED-CAR VERDICTS																														

TROUBLE SPOTS

TROUBLE SPOTS	GMC Terrain						GMC Yukon						GMC Yukon XL						Honda Accord						Honda Accord Crosstour					
	'10	'11	'12	'13	'14	'15	'10	'11	'12	'13	'14	'15	'10	'11	'12	'13	'14	'15	'10	'11	'12	'13	'14	'15	'10	'11	'12	'13	'14	'15
Engine, Major																														
Engine, Minor																														
Engine Cooling																														
Trans., Major																														
Trans., Minor																														
Drive System																														
Fuel System																														
Electrical																														
Climate System																														
Suspension																														
Brakes																														
Exhaust																														
Paint/Trim																														
Noises/Leaks																														
Body Hardware																														
Power Equip.																														
In-Car Elec.																														
USED-CAR VERDICTS																														

TROUBLE SPOTS

Honda Models

TROUBLE SPOTS	Honda CR-V						Honda Civic						Honda Fit						Honda Odyssey						Honda Pilot					
	'10	'11	'12	'13	'14	'15	'10	'11	'12	'13	'14	'15	'10	'11	'12	'13	'14	'15	'10	'11	'12	'13	'14	'15	'10	'11	'12	'13	'14	'15
Engine, Major																														
Engine, Minor																														
Engine Cooling																														
Trans., Major																														
Trans., Minor																														
Drive System																														
Fuel System																														
Electrical																														
Climate System																														
Suspension																														
Brakes																														
Exhaust																														
Paint/Trim																														
Noises/Leaks																														
Body Hardware																														
Power Equip.																														
In-Car Elec.																														
USED-CAR VERDICTS																														

Honda / Hyundai Models

TROUBLE SPOTS	Honda Ridgeline						Hyundai Accent						Hyundai Azera						Hyundai Elantra						Hyundai Equus					
	'10	'11	'12	'13	'14	'15	'10	'11	'12	'13	'14	'15	'10	'11	'12	'13	'14	'15	'10	'11	'12	'13	'14	'15	'10	'11	'12	'13	'14	'15
Engine, Major																														
Engine, Minor																														
Engine Cooling																														
Trans., Major																														
Trans., Minor																														
Drive System																														
Fuel System																														
Electrical																														
Climate System																														
Suspension																														
Brakes																														
Exhaust																														
Paint/Trim																														
Noises/Leaks																														
Body Hardware																														
Power Equip.																														
In-Car Elec.																														
USED-CAR VERDICTS																														

TROUBLE SPOTS	Hyundai Genesis						Hyundai Santa Fe						Hyundai Santa Fe Sport						Hyundai Sonata						Hyundai Tucson					
	'10	'11	'12	'13	'14	'15	'10	'11	'12	'13	'14	'15	'10	'11	'12	'13	'14	'15	'10	'11	'12	'13	'14	'15	'10	'11	'12	'13	'14	'15
Engine, Major																														
Engine, Minor																														
Engine Cooling																														
Trans., Major																														
Trans., Minor																														
Drive System																														
Fuel System																														
Electrical																														
Climate System																														
Suspension																														
Brakes																														
Exhaust																														
Paint/Trim																														
Noises/Leaks																														
Body Hardware																														
Power Equip.																														
In-Car Elec.																														
USED-CAR VERDICTS																														

TROUBLE SPOTS	Hyundai Veloster						Infiniti G						Infiniti JX, QX60						Infiniti M, Q70						Infiniti Q50					
	'10	'11	'12	'13	'14	'15	'10	'11	'12	'13	'14	'15	'10	'11	'12	'13	'14	'15	'10	'11	'12	'13	'14	'15	'10	'11	'12	'13	'14	'15
Engine, Major																														
Engine, Minor																														
Engine Cooling																														
Trans., Major																														
Trans., Minor																														
Drive System																														
Fuel System																														
Electrical																														
Climate System																														
Suspension																														
Brakes																														
Exhaust																														
Paint/Trim																														
Noises/Leaks																														
Body Hardware																														
Power Equip.																														
In-Car Elec.																														
USED-CAR VERDICTS																														

Top table

TROUBLE SPOTS	Jeep Cherokee						Jeep Grand Cherokee						Jeep Wrangler						Kia Cadenza						Kia Optima					
	'10	'11	'12	'13	'14	'15	'10	'11	'12	'13	'14	'15	'10	'11	'12	'13	'14	'15	'10	'11	'12	'13	'14	'15	'10	'11	'12	'13	'14	'15
Engine, Major																														
Engine, Minor																														
Engine Cooling																														
Trans., Major																														
Trans., Minor																														
Drive System																														
Fuel System																														
Electrical																														
Climate System																														
Suspension																														
Brakes																														
Exhaust																														
Paint/Trim																														
Noises/Leaks																														
Body Hardware																														
Power Equip.																														
In-Car Elec.																														
USED-CAR VERDICTS																														

Bottom table

TROUBLE SPOTS	Kia Rio						Kia Sorento						Kia Soul						Kia Forte						Kia Sportage					
	'10	'11	'12	'13	'14	'15	'11	'12	'13	'14	'15	'16	'10	'11	'12	'13	'14	'15	'10	'11	'12	'13	'14	'15	'10	'11	'12	'13	'14	'15
Engine, Major																														
Engine, Minor																														
Engine Cooling																														
Trans., Major																														
Trans., Minor																														
Drive System																														
Fuel System																														
Electrical																														
Climate System																														
Suspension																														
Brakes																														
Exhaust																														
Paint/Trim																														
Noises/Leaks																														
Body Hardware																														
Power Equip.																														
In-Car Elec.																														
USED-CAR VERDICTS																														

TROUBLE SPOTS

TROUBLE SPOTS	Lexus CT 200h						Lexus ES						Lexus GS						Lexus GX						Lexus HS Hybrid					
	'10	'11	'12	'13	'14	'15	'10	'11	'12	'13	'14	'15	'10	'11	'12	'13	'14	'15	'10	'11	'12	'13	'14	'15	'10	'11	'12	'13	'14	'15
Engine, Major	⊝	⊝	⊝	⊝	★		⊝	⊝	⊝	⊝	⊝	⊝	★	★		⊝	⊝	⊝	★	★	★	⊝	⊝	⊝	⊝	★	⊝			
Engine, Minor	⊝	⦿	⊝	⊝	★		⊝	⊝	⊝	⊝	⊝	⊝	★	★		⊝	⊝	⊝	★	★	★	⊝	⊝	⊝	⊝	★	⊝			
Engine Cooling	⊝	⊝	⊝	⊝	★		⊝	⊝	⊝	⊝	⊝	⊝	★	★		⊝	⊝	⊝	★	★	★	⊝	⊝	⊝	⊝	★	⊝			
Trans., Major	⊝	⊝	⊝	⊝	★		⊝	⊝	⊝	⊝	⊝	⊝	★	★		⊝	⊝	⊝	★	★	★	⊝	⊝	⊝	⊝	★	⊝			
Trans., Minor	⊝	⊝	⊝	⊝	★		⊝	⊝	⊝	⊝	⊝	⊝	★	★		⊝	⊝	⊝	★	★	★	⊝	⊝	⊝	⊝	★	⊝			
Drive System	⊝	⊝	⊝	⊝	★		⊝	⊝	⊝	⊝	⊝	⊝	★	★		⊝	⊝	⊝	★	★	★	⊝	⊝	⊝	⊝	★	⊝			
Fuel System	⊝	⊝	⊝	⊝	★		⊝	⊝	⊝	⊝	⊝	⊝	★	★		⊝	⊝	⊝	★	★	★	⊝	⊝	⊝	⊝	★	⊝			
Electrical	⊝	⊝	⊝	⊝	★		⊝	⊝	⊝	⊝	⊝	⊝	★	★		⊝	⊝	⊝	★	★	★	⊝	⊝	⊝	⊝	★	⊝			
Climate System	⊝	⊝	⊝	⊝	★		⊝	⊝	⊝	⊝	⊝	⊝	★	★		⊝	⊝	⊝	★	★	★	⊝	⊝	⊝	⊝	★	⊝			
Suspension	⊝	⊝	⊝	⊝	★		⊝	⊝	⊝	⊝	⊝	⊝	★	★		⊝	⊝	⊝	★	★	★	⊝	⊝	⊝	⊝	★	⊝			
Brakes	⊝	⊝	⊝	⊝	★		⊝	⊝	⊝	⊝	⊝	⊝	★	★		⊝	⊝	⊝	★	★	★	⦵	⊝	⊝	⊝	★	⊝			
Exhaust	⊝	⊝	⊝	⊝	★		⊝	⊝	⊝	⊝	⊝	⊝	★	★		⊝	⊝	⊝	★	★	★	⊝	⊝	⊝	⊙	★	⊝			
Paint/Trim	⊝	⊝	⊝	⦵	★		⊝	⊝	⊝	⊝	⊝	⊝	★	★		⊝	⊝	⊝	★	★	★	⊝	⊝	⊝	⊙	★	⊝			
Noises/Leaks	⊝	⦿	⦿	⊝	★		⊝	⊝	⊝	⊝	⊝	⊝	★	★		⊝	⊝	⊝	★	★	★	⊝	⊝	⊝	⊝	★	⊝			
Body Hardware	⊝	⊝	⊝	⊝	★		⊝	⊝	⊝	⊝	⊝	⊝	★	★		⊝	⊝	⊝	★	★	★	⊝	⊝	⊝	⊝	★	⊝			
Power Equip.	⊝	⊝	⊝	⊝	★		⊝	⊝	⊝	⊝	⊝	⊝	★	★		⊝	⊝	⊝	★	★	★	⊝	⊝	⊝	⊝	★	⊝			
In-Car Elec.	⊝	⊝	⊝	⊝	★		⊝	⊝	⊝	⊝	⊝	⊝	★	★		⊝	⊝	⊝	★	★	★	⊝	⦿	⦵	⊝	★	⊝			
USED-CAR VERDICTS	⊝	⊝	⊝	⊝	★		⊝	⊝	⊝	⊝	⊝	⊝	★	★		⊝	⊝	⊝	★	★	★	⊝	⊝	⊝	⊝	★	⊝			

TROUBLE SPOTS	Lexus IS						Lexus LS						Lexus NX						Lexus RX						Lincoln MKC					
	'10	'11	'12	'13	'14	'15	'10	'11	'12	'13	'14	'15	'10	'11	'12	'13	'14	'15	'10	'11	'12	'13	'14	'15	'10	'11	'12	'13	'14	'15
Engine, Major	⊝	⊝	⊝	★	⊝	⊝	⊝	⊝	⊝	⊝	⊝	★						⊝	⊝	⊝	⊝	⊝	⊝	⊝						⊝
Engine, Minor	⦿	⊝	⊝	★	⊝	⊝	⊝	⊝	⊝	⊝	⊝	★						⊝	⊝	⊝	⊝	⊝	⊝	⊝						⊝
Engine Cooling	⊝	⊝	⊝	★	⊝	⊝	⊝	⊝	⊝	⊝	⊝	★						⊝	⊝	⊝	⊝	⊝	⊝	⊝						⊝
Trans., Major	⊝	⊝	⊝	★	⊝	⊝	⊝	⊝	⊝	⊝	⊝	★						⊝	⊝	⊝	⊝	⊝	⊝	⊝						⊝
Trans., Minor	⊝	⊝	⊝	★	⊝	⊝	⊝	⊝	⊝	⊝	⊝	★						⊝	⊝	⊝	⊝	⊝	⊝	⊝						⊝
Drive System	⊝	⊝	⊝	★	⊝	⊝	⊝	⊝	⊝	⊝	⊝	★						⊝	⊝	⊝	⊝	⊝	⊝	⊝						⊝
Fuel System	⊝	⊝	⊝	★	⊝	⊝	⊝	⊝	⊝	⊝	⊝	★						⊝	⊝	⊝	⊝	⊝	⊝	⊝						⊝
Electrical	⊝	⊝	⊝	★	⊝	⊝	⊝	⊝	⊝	⊝	⊝	★						⊝	⊝	⊝	⊝	⊝	⊝	⊝						⊝
Climate System	⊝	⊝	⊝	★	⊝	⊝	⊝	⊝	⊝	⊝	⊝	★						⊝	⊝	⊝	⊝	⊝	⊝	⊝						⊝
Suspension	⊝	⊝	⊝	★	⊝	⊝	⊙	⊝	⊝	⊝	⊝	★						⊝	⊝	⦿	⊝	⊝	⊝	⊝						⊝
Brakes	⊝	⊝	⊝	★	⊝	⊝	⊝	⊝	⊝	⊝	⊝	★						⊝	⊝	⊝	⊝	⊝	⊝	⊝						⊝
Exhaust	⊝	⊝	⊝	★	⊝	⊝	⊝	⊝	⊝	⊝	⊝	★						⊝	⊝	⊝	⊝	⊝	⊝	⊝						⊝
Paint/Trim	⊝	⊝	⊝	★	⊝	⊝	⊝	⊝	⊝	⊝	⊝	★						⊝	⊝	⊝	⊝	⊝	⊝	⊝						⊝
Noises/Leaks	⊙	⊝	⊝	★	⊝	⊝	⊝	⊝	⊝	⊝	⦿	★						⊝	⊝	⊝	⊝	⊝	⊝	⊝						⊝
Body Hardware	⊝	⊝	⊝	★	⊝	⊝	⊝	⊝	⊝	⊝	⊝	★						⊝	⊝	⊝	⊝	⊝	⊝	⊝						⊝
Power Equip.	⊝	⊝	⊝	★	⊝	⊝	⊝	⊝	⊝	⊝	⊝	★						⊝	⊝	⊝	⊝	⊝	⊝	⊝						⊝
In-Car Elec.	⊝	⦿	⊝	★	⊙	⊝	⊝	⊝	⊝	⊝	⦿	★						⊝	⊝	⊝	⊝	⊝	⊝	⊝						⊙
USED-CAR VERDICTS	⊝	⊝	⊝	★	⊝	⊝	⊝	⊝	⊝	⊝	⊝	★						⊝	⊝	⊝	⊝	⊝	⊝	⊝						⊙

TROUBLE SPOTS

TROUBLE SPOTS	Lincoln MKS						Lincoln MKX						Lincoln MKZ						Mazda 3						Mazda 5					
	'10	'11	'12	'13	'14	'15	'10	'11	'12	'13	'14	'15	'10	'11	'12	'13	'14	'15	'10	'11	'12	'13	'14	'15	'10	'11	'12	'13	'14	'15
Engine, Major	*	*	*	●	*	*	●	●	●	●	●	*	●	●	●	●	●	●	●	●	●	●	●	●	●		●	●	●	*
Engine, Minor	*	*	*	●	*	*	●	●	●	●	●	*	●	●	●	●	●	●	●	●	●	●	●	●	●		●	●	●	*
Engine Cooling	*	*	*	●	*	*	●	●	●	●	●	*	●	●	●	●	●	●	●	●	●	●	●	●	●		●	●	●	*
Trans., Major	*	*	*	●	*	*	●	●	●	●	●	*	●	●	●	●	●	●	●	●	●	●	●	●	●		●	●	●	*
Trans., Minor	*	*	*	●	*	*	●	●	●	●	●	*	●	●	●	●	●	●	●	●	●	●	●	●	●		●	●	●	*
Drive System	*	*	*	●	*	*	●	●	●	●	●	*	●	●	●	●	●	●	●	●	●	●	●	●	●		●	●	●	*
Fuel System	*	*	*	●	*	*	●	●	●	●	●	*	●	●	●	●	●	●	●	●	●	●	●	●	●		●	●	●	*
Electrical	*	*	*	●	*	*	●	●	●	●	●	*	●	●	●	●	●	●	●	●	●	●	●	●	●		●	●	●	*
Climate System	*	*	*	●	*	*	●	●	●	●	●	*	●	●	●	●	●	●	●	●	●	●	●	●	●		●	●	●	*
Suspension	*	*	*	●	*	*	●	●	●	●	●	*	●	●	●	●	●	●	●	●	●	●	●	●	●		●	●	●	*
Brakes	*	*	*	●	*	*	●	●	●	●	●	*	●	●	●	●	●	●	●	●	●	●	●	●	●		●	●	●	*
Exhaust	*	*	*	●	*	*	●	●	●	●	●	*	●	●	●	●	●	●	●	●	●	●	●	●	●		●	●	●	*
Paint/Trim	*	*	*	●	*	*	●	●	●	●	●	*	●	●	●	●	●	●	●	●	●	●	●	●	●		●	●	●	*
Noises/Leaks	*	*	*	●	*	*	●	●	●	●	●	*	●	●	●	●	●	●	●	●	●	●	●	●	●		●	●	●	*
Body Hardware	*	*	*	●	*	*	●	●	●	●	●	*	●	●	●	●	●	●	●	●	●	●	●	●	●		●	●	●	*
Power Equip.	*	*	*	●	*	*	●	●	●	●	●	*	●	●	●	●	●	●	●	●	●	●	●	●	●		●	●	●	*
In-Car Elec.	*	*	*	●	*	*	●	●	●	●	●	*	●	●	●	●	●	●	●	●	●	●	●	●	●		●	●	●	*
USED-CAR VERDICTS	*	*	*	●	*	*	●	●	●	●	●	*	●	●	●	●	●	●	●	●	●	●	●	●	●		●	●	●	*

TROUBLE SPOTS	Mazda 6						Mazda CX-5						Mazda CX-9						Mazda MX-5 Miata						Mercedes-Benz C-Class					
	'10	'11	'12	'13	'14	'15	'11	'12	'13	'14	'15	'16	'10	'11	'12	'13	'14	'15	'10	'11	'12	'13	'14	'15	'10	'11	'12	'13	'14	'15
Engine, Major	●	*	●	*	●	●		●	●	●	●		●	●	●	●	●	*	●	●	●	●	*	*	●	●	●	●	●	●
Engine, Minor	●	*	●	*	●	●		●	●	●	●		●	●	●	●	●	*	●	●	●	●	*	*	●	●	●	●	●	●
Engine Cooling	●	*	●	*	●	●		●	●	●	●		●	●	●	●	●	*	●	●	●	●	*	*	●	●	●	●	●	●
Trans., Major	●	*	●	*	●	●		●	●	●	●		●	●	●	●	●	*	●	●	●	●	*	*	●	●	●	●	●	●
Trans., Minor	●	*	●	*	●	●		●	●	●	●		●	●	●	●	●	*	●	●	●	●	*	*	●	●	●	●	●	●
Drive System	●	*	●	*	●	●		●	●	●	●		●	●	●	●	●	*	●	●	●	●	*	*	●	●	●	●	●	●
Fuel System	●	*	●	*	●	●		●	●	●	●		●	●	●	●	●	*	●	●	●	●	*	*	●	●	●	●	●	●
Electrical	●	*	●	*	●	●		●	●	●	●		●	●	●	●	●	*	●	●	●	●	*	*	●	●	●	●	●	●
Climate System	●	*	●	*	●	●		●	●	●	●		●	●	●	●	●	*	●	●	●	●	*	*	●	●	●	●	●	●
Suspension	●	*	●	*	●	●		●	●	●	●		●	●	●	●	●	*	●	●	●	●	*	*	●	●	●	●	●	●
Brakes	●	*	●	*	●	●		●	●	●	●		●	●	●	●	●	*	●	●	●	●	*	*	●	●	●	●	●	●
Exhaust	●	*	●	*	●	●		●	●	●	●		●	●	●	●	●	*	●	●	●	●	*	*	●	●	●	●	●	●
Paint/Trim	●	*	●	*	●	●		●	●	●	●		●	●	●	●	●	*	●	●	●	●	*	*	●	●	●	●	●	●
Noises/Leaks	●	*	●	*	●	●		●	●	●	●		●	●	●	●	●	*	●	●	●	●	*	*	●	●	●	●	●	●
Body Hardware	●	*	●	*	●	●		●	●	●	●		●	●	●	●	●	*	●	●	●	●	*	*	●	●	●	●	●	●
Power Equip.	●	*	●	*	●	●		●	●	●	●		●	●	●	●	●	*	●	●	●	●	*	*	●	●	●	●	●	●
In-Car Elec.	●	*	●	*	●	●		●	●	●	●		●	●	●	●	●	*	●	●	●	●	*	*	●	●	●	●	●	●
USED-CAR VERDICTS	●	*	●	*	●	●		●	●	●	●		●	●	●	●	●	*	●	●	●	●	*	*	●	●	●	●	●	●

TROUBLE SPOTS

TROUBLE SPOTS	Mercedes-Benz CLA						Mercedes-Benz E-Class						Mercedes-Benz GL-Class						Mercedes-Benz GLK-Class						Mercedes-Benz M-Class					
	'10	'11	'12	'13	'14	'15	'10	'11	'12	'13	'14	'15	'10	'11	'12	'13	'14	'15	'10	'11	'12	'13	'14	'15	'10	'11	'12	'13	'14	'15
Engine, Major					⌃	★	⌃	⌃	⌃	⌃	⌃	⌃	★	★	★	⌃	⌃	⌃	⌃	⌃	⌃	⌃	⌃	⌃	⌃	⌃	⌃	⌃	⌃	⌃
Engine, Minor					⌃	★	⌃	⌃	⌵	❶	⌃	⌃	★	★	★	⌃	⌃	⌃	⌃	⌃	⌃	⌃	⌃	⌃	⌵	⌵	❶	⌵	⌃	⌃
Engine Cooling					⌃	★	⌃	⌃	⌃	⌃	⌃	⌃	★	★	★	⌃	⌃	⌃	⌃	⌃	⌃	⌃	⌃	⌃	⌃	⌃	⌃	⌃	⌃	⌃
Trans., Major					⌃	★	⌃	⌃	⌃	⌃	⌃	⌃	★	★	★	⌃	⌃	⌃	⌃	⌃	⌃	⌃	⌃	⌃	⌃	⌃	⌃	⌃	⌃	⌃
Trans., Minor					❶	★	⌃	⌃	⌃	⌃	⌃	⌃	★	★	★	⌃	⌃	⌃	⌃	⌃	⌃	⌃	⌃	⌃	⌃	⌃	⌃	⌃	⌃	⌃
Drive System					❶	★	⌃	⌃	⌃	⌃	⌃	⌃	★	★	★	⌃	⌵	⌃	❶	⌃	⌃	⌃	⌃	⌃	⌃	⌃	⌃	⌃	⌃	⌃
Fuel System					⌃	★	⌃	❶	❶	⌃	⌃	⌃	★	★	★	⌃	⌃	⌃	⌃	⌃	⌃	⌃	⌃	⌃	⌵	⌵	❶	⌵	⌃	⌃
Electrical					⌃	★	⌃	⌃	⌃	⌃	⌃	⌃	★	★	★	⌃	⌃	⌃	⌃	⌃	⌃	⌃	⌃	⌃	⌵	⌃	⌃	⌃	⌃	⌃
Climate System					⌃	★	⌃	⌃	⌃	⌃	⌃	⌃	★	★	★	⌃	⌃	⌃	⌃	⌃	⌃	⌃	⌃	⌃	⌵	⌃	⌃	⌃	⌃	⌃
Suspension					⌃	★	⌃	⌃	⌃	⌃	⌃	⌃	★	★	★	⌵	⌵	⌃	⌃	⌃	⌃	⌃	⌃	⌃	⌃	❶	⌵	⌃	⌃	⌃
Brakes					⌵	★	⌃	⌃	⌃	⌃	⌃	⌃	★	★	★	⌵	⌵	⌃	⌃	⌃	⌃	⌃	⌃	⌃	⌵	❶	⌵	⌃	⌃	⌃
Exhaust					⌃	★	⌃	⌃	⌃	⌃	⌃	⌃	★	★	★	⌃	⌃	⌃	⌃	⌃	⌃	⌃	⌃	⌃	⌃	⌃	⌃	⌃	⌃	⌃
Paint/Trim					⌃	★	⌃	⌃	⌃	⌃	⌃	⌃	★	★	★	❶	❶	⌃	⌃	⌃	⌃	⌃	⌃	⌃	⌃	⌃	⌃	⌃	⌃	⌃
Noises/Leaks					⌵	★	❶	⌃	⌃	⌃	⌃	⌃	★	★	★	⌵	❶	⌃	⌃	❶	⌵	❶	⌃	⌃	❶	⌃	⌃	❶	⌃	⌃
Body Hardware					⌃	★	⌃	⌃	⌃	⌃	⌃	⌃	★	★	★	⌃	❶	⌵	⌃	⌃	⌃	⌃	⌃	⌃	⌃	⌃	⌃	❶	⌃	⌃
Power Equip.					⌃	★	⌵	❶	❶	❶	⌃	⌃	★	★	★	❶	⌵	⌵	⌵	⌃	⌃	⌃	⌃	❶	⌵	⌵	⌵	⌃	⌃	⌃
In-Car Elec.					⌃	★	❶	⌵	❶	❶	⌃	⌃	★	★	★	⌵	❶	❶	⌵	⌃	⌃	❶	⌃	⌃	⌵	⌵	❶	⌵	⌃	⌃
USED-CAR VERDICTS					⌵	★	⌃	❶	❶	❶	❶	❶	★	★	★	⌵	⌵	⌵	❶	⌃	⌃	⌃	⌃	❶	⌵	❶	⌵	❶	❶	⌃

TROUBLE SPOTS

TROUBLE SPOTS	Mercedes-Benz S-Class						Mini Cooper						Mini Cooper Countryman						Nissan Altima						Nissan Frontier					
	'10	'11	'12	'13	'14	'15	'10	'11	'12	'13	'14	'15	'10	'11	'12	'13	'14	'15	'10	'11	'12	'13	'14	'15	'10	'11	'12	'13	'14	'15
Engine, Major	★	★	★	★	⌃	⌃	⌵	⌃	⌃	⌃	⌃	⌃	❶	❶	⌃	⌃	★		⌃	⌃	⌃	⌃	⌃	⌃	⌃	⌃	⌃	⌃	⌃	⌃
Engine, Minor	★	★	★	★	⌃	⌃	⌵	⌵	⌵	⌃	⌃	⌃	⌵	❶	⌃	⌃	★		⌃	⌃	⌃	⌃	⌃	⌃	⌃	⌃	⌃	⌃	⌃	⌃
Engine Cooling	★	★	★	★	⌃	⌃	⌵	❶	❶	⌃	⌃	⌃	⌵	❶	⌃	⌃	★		⌃	⌃	⌃	⌃	⌃	⌃	⌃	⌃	⌃	⌃	⌃	⌃
Trans., Major	★	★	★	★	⌃	⌃	⌃	⌃	⌃	⌃	⌃	⌃	⌃	⌵	⌃	⌃	★		⌃	⌃	⌃	⌃	⌃	⌃	⌃	⌃	⌃	⌃	⌃	⌃
Trans., Minor	★	★	★	★	⌃	⌃	⌃	⌃	⌃	⌃	⌃	⌃	⌵	❶	⌃	⌃	★		⌃	⌃	⌃	⌃	⌃	⌃	⌃	⌃	⌃	⌃	⌃	⌃
Drive System	★	★	★	★	⌃	⌃	⌃	⌃	⌃	⌃	⌃	⌃	⌵	⌵	⌃	⌃	★		⌃	⌃	⌃	⌃	⌃	⌃	⌃	⌃	⌃	⌃	⌃	⌃
Fuel System	★	★	★	★	⌃	⌃	⌵	❶	⌃	⌃	⌃	⌃	⌵	⌵	⌃	⌃	★		⌃	❶	⌃	⌃	⌃	⌃	⌃	⌃	⌃	⌃	⌃	⌃
Electrical	★	★	★	★	⌃	⌃	⌵	⌵	⌃	⌃	⌃	⌃	⌵	⌵	⌃	⌃	★		⌃	⌃	⌃	⌃	⌃	⌃	⌃	⌃	⌃	⌃	⌃	⌃
Climate System	★	★	★	★	❶	⌃	⌵	⌃	⌃	⌃	⌃	⌃	⌵	⌃	⌃	★			⌃	⌃	⌃	⌃	⌃	⌃	⌃	⌃	⌃	⌃	⌃	❶
Suspension	★	★	★	★	⌵	⌃	⌃	⌃	⌃	⌃	⌃	⌃	⌃	⌃	⌵	★			⌃	⌃	⌃	⌃	⌃	⌃	⌃	⌃	⌃	⌃	⌃	⌃
Brakes	★	★	★	★	⌵	⌃	⌵	⌃	❶	⌃	⌃	⌃	⌵	⌃	⌃	★			⌵	❶	⌃	⌃	⌃	⌃	⌵	❶	⌃	⌃	⌃	⌃
Exhaust	★	★	★	★	⌃	⌃	⌃	⌃	⌃	⌃	⌃	⌃	⌃	⌃	⌃	★			⌃	⌃	⌃	⌃	⌃	⌃	⌃	⌃	⌃	⌃	⌃	⌃
Paint/Trim	★	★	★	★	⌃	⌃	❶	⌃	⌃	⌃	⌃	⌃	⌃	⌃	⌃	★			⌃	⌃	⌃	⌵	⌃	⌃	⌃	⌃	⌃	⌃	⌃	⌃
Noises/Leaks	★	★	★	★	⌵	⌃	⌵	⌵	❶	⌃	⌃	❶	⌵	⌵	⌃	★			❶	⌃	❶	⌵	⌃	❶	⌃	⌃	⌃	⌃	❶	⌵
Body Hardware	★	★	★	★	⌃	⌃	⌃	⌃	⌃	⌃	⌃	⌃	⌃	⌃	⌃	★			⌃	⌃	⌃	⌃	⌃	⌃	⌃	⌃	⌃	⌃	⌃	❶
Power Equip.	★	★	★	★	⌃	⌃	❶	⌃	⌵	❶	❶	⌃	⌵	⌵	⌃	★			⌃	❶	❶	⌃	⌃	⌃	⌃	⌃	⌃	⌃	⌃	❶
In-Car Elec.	★	★	★	★	⌵	❶	⌃	⌃	⌃	⌃	⌃	⌵	⌵	⌵	⌃	★			⌃	⌃	❶	⌵	⌵	❶	⌃	⌃	⌃	⌃	⌃	⌵
USED-CAR VERDICTS	★	★	★	★	⌵	❶	⌵	⌵	⌵	⌃	⌵	❶	⌵	⌵	❶	⌃	★		⌃	⌃	⌃	⌵	⌃	❶	⌃	⌃	⌃	❶	❶	⌵

TROUBLE SPOTS

Table 1

TROUBLE SPOTS	Nissan Juke '10 '11 '12 '13 '14 '15	Nissan Leaf '10 '11 '12 '13 '14 '15	Nissan Maxima '10 '11 '12 '13 '14 '15	Nissan Murano '10 '11 '12 '13 '14 '15	Nissan Pathfinder '10 '11 '12 '13 '14 '15
Engine, Major					
Engine, Minor					
Engine Cooling					
Trans., Major					
Trans., Minor					
Drive System					
Fuel System					
Electrical					
Climate System					
Suspension					
Brakes					
Exhaust					
Paint/Trim					
Noises/Leaks					
Body Hardware					
Power Equip.					
In-Car Elec.					
USED-CAR VERDICTS					

Table 2

TROUBLE SPOTS	Nissan Rogue '10 '11 '12 '13 '14 '15	Nissan Sentra '10 '11 '12 '13 '14 '15	Nissan Versa Hatchback, Note '10 '11 '12 '13 '14 '15	Porsche 911 '10 '11 '12 '13 '14 '15	Porsche Boxster '10 '11 '12 '13 '14 '15
Engine, Major					
Engine, Minor					
Engine Cooling					
Trans., Major					
Trans., Minor					
Drive System					
Fuel System					
Electrical					
Climate System					
Suspension					
Brakes					
Exhaust					
Paint/Trim					
Noises/Leaks					
Body Hardware					
Power Equip.					
In-Car Elec.					
USED-CAR VERDICTS					

TROUBLE SPOTS

TROUBLE SPOTS	Porsche Cayenne						Porsche Macan						Ram 1500						Scion FR-S						Scion xB					
	'10	'11	'12	'13	'14	'15	'10	'11	'12	'13	'14	'15	'10	'11	'12	'13	'14	'15	'10	'11	'12	'13	'14	'15	'10	'11	'12	'13	'14	'15
Engine, Major																														
Engine, Minor																														

(This page consists of a Consumer Reports reliability symbol grid comparing Porsche Cayenne, Porsche Macan, Ram 1500, Scion FR-S, Scion xB, Subaru BRZ, Subaru Forester, Subaru Impreza, Subaru Impreza WRX/STi, and Subaru Legacy across model years 2010–2015 for trouble spots including Engine Major, Engine Minor, Engine Cooling, Trans. Major, Trans. Minor, Drive System, Fuel System, Electrical, Climate System, Suspension, Brakes, Exhaust, Paint/Trim, Noises/Leaks, Body Hardware, Power Equip., In-Car Elec., and Used-Car Verdicts. The individual rating symbols cannot be reliably transcribed.)

TROUBLE SPOTS	Subaru Outback						Subaru XV Crosstrek						Tesla Model S						Toyota 4Runner						Toyota Avalon					
	'10	'11	'12	'13	'14	'15	'10	'11	'12	'13	'14	'15	'10	'11	'12	'13	'14	'15	'10	'11	'12	'13	'14	'15	'10	'11	'12	'13	'14	'15
Engine, Major																														
Engine, Minor																														
Engine Cooling																														
Trans., Major																														
Trans., Minor																														
Drive System																														
Fuel System																														
Electrical																														
Climate System																														
Suspension																														
Brakes																														
Exhaust																														
Paint/Trim																														
Noises/Leaks																														
Body Hardware																														
Power Equip.																														
In-Car Elec.																														
USED-CAR VERDICTS																														

Bottom table

TROUBLE SPOTS	Toyota Camry						Toyota Corolla						Toyota Highlander						Toyota Prius						Toyota Prius C					
	'10	'11	'12	'13	'14	'15	'10	'11	'12	'13	'14	'15	'10	'11	'12	'13	'14	'15	'10	'11	'12	'13	'14	'15	'10	'11	'12	'13	'14	'15
Engine, Major																														*
Engine, Minor																														*
Engine Cooling																														*
Trans., Major																														*
Trans., Minor																														*
Drive System																														*
Fuel System																														*
Electrical																														*
Climate System																														*
Suspension																														*
Brakes																														*
Exhaust																														*
Paint/Trim																														*
Noises/Leaks																														*
Body Hardware																														*
Power Equip.																														*
In-Car Elec.																														*
USED-CAR VERDICTS																														*

TROUBLE SPOTS

TROUBLE SPOTS	Toyota Prius V '10 '11 '12 '13 '14 '15	Toyota RAV4 '10 '11 '12 '13 '14 '15	Toyota Sequoia '10 '11 '12 '13 '14 '15	Toyota Sienna '10 '11 '12 '13 '14 '15	Toyota Tacoma '10 '11 '12 '13 '14 '15
Engine, Major					
Engine, Minor					
Engine Cooling					
Trans., Major					
Trans., Minor					
Drive System					
Fuel System					
Electrical					
Climate System					
Suspension					
Brakes					
Exhaust					
Paint/Trim					
Noises/Leaks					
Body Hardware					
Power Equip.					
In-Car Elec.					
USED-CAR VERDICTS					

TROUBLE SPOTS	Toyota Tundra '10 '11 '12 '13 '14 '15	Toyota Venza '10 '11 '12 '13 '14 '15	Volkswagen Beetle '10 '11 '12 '13 '14 '15	Volkswagen CC '10 '11 '12 '13 '14 '15	Volkswagen GTI '10 '11 '12 '13 '14 '15
Engine, Major					
Engine, Minor					
Engine Cooling					
Trans., Major					
Trans., Minor					
Drive System					
Fuel System					
Electrical					
Climate System					
Suspension					
Brakes					
Exhaust					
Paint/Trim					
Noises/Leaks					
Body Hardware					
Power Equip.					
In-Car Elec.					
USED-CAR VERDICTS					

TROUBLE SPOTS

TROUBLE SPOTS	Volkswagen Golf						Volkswagen Jetta						Volkswagen Jetta SportWagen						Volkswagen Passat						Volkswagen Tiguan					
	'10	'11	'12	'13	'14	'15	'10	'11	'12	'13	'14	'15	'10	'11	'12	'13	'14	'15	'10	'11	'12	'13	'14	'15	'10	'11	'12	'13	'14	'15
Engine, Major																														★
Engine, Minor																														★
Engine Cooling																														★
Trans., Major																														★
Trans., Minor																														★
Drive System																														★
Fuel System																														★
Electrical																														★
Climate System																														★
Suspension																														★
Brakes																														★
Exhaust																														★
Paint/Trim																														★
Noises/Leaks																														★
Body Hardware																														★
Power Equip.																														★
In-Car Elec.																														★
USED-CAR VERDICTS																														★

TROUBLE SPOTS	Volkswagen Touareg						Volvo S60						Volvo V60						Volvo V70, XC70						Volvo XC60					
	'10	'11	'12	'13	'14	'15	'10	'11	'12	'13	'14	'15	'10	'11	'12	'13	'14	'15	'10	'11	'12	'13	'14	'15	'10	'11	'12	'13	'14	'15
Engine, Major	★	★				★	★	★													★			★						
Engine, Minor	★	★				★	★	★													★			★						
Engine Cooling	★	★				★	★	★													★			★						
Trans., Major	★	★				★	★	★													★			★						
Trans., Minor	★	★				★	★	★													★			★						
Drive System	★	★				★	★	★													★			★						
Fuel System	★	★				★	★	★													★			★						
Electrical	★	★				★	★	★													★			★						
Climate System	★	★				★	★	★													★			★						
Suspension	★	★				★	★	★													★			★						
Brakes	★	★				★	★	★													★			★						
Exhaust	★	★				★	★	★													★			★						
Paint/Trim	★	★				★	★	★													★			★						
Noises/Leaks	★	★				★	★	★													★			★						
Body Hardware	★	★				★	★	★													★			★						
Power Equip.	★	★				★	★	★													★			★						
In-Car Elec.	★	★				★	★	★													★			★						
USED-CAR VERDICTS	★	★				★	★	★													★			★						

QUICK GUIDE
Tires

Tires have a direct impact on your car's handling, braking, ride comfort, and fuel economy. More important, the cornering grip, braking distances, and resistance to hydroplaning affect your safety on the road.

Types and Features
All-season—These are the tires that come standard on many cars, minivans, and SUVs.
■ **Best for:** Year-round traction, long tread life, and a comfortable ride. But they may lack the precise handling and grip of performance tires.
■ **Speed ratings:** Most are S (112 mph) or T (118 mph).
■ **Treadwear warranty:** None or 40,000 to 100,000 miles.
Performance all-season —They come standard on many newer cars.
■ **Best for:** Improved handling and grip over all-season tires on wet roads, but often have shorter treadwear than many all-season tires.
■ **Speed ratings:** H (130 mph) and V (149 mph).
■ **Treadwear warranty:** None or 40,000 to 75,000 miles.
Ultra-high performance all-season—Found on sports cars, sports

sedans, and some lower-priced sporty models.
■ **Best for:** Wet and dry braking and handling. But they trade winter performance for ultimate warm-weather grip.
■ **Speed ratings:** Z (more than 149 mph), W (168 mph), and Y (186 mph).
■ **Treadwear warranty:** None or 40,000 to 60,000 miles.
Ultra-high performance summer—Found mostly on high-performance sports cars and sports sedans.
■ **Best for:** Wet and dry braking and handling. But they're not suited for use in winter conditions.
■ **Speed ratings:** Z (more than 149 mph), W (168 mph), and Y (186 mph).
■ **Treadwear warranty:** Usually none.
Winter/Snow—Specially made for use in freezing temperatures and on snow and ice.
■ **Best for:** Maintaining traction on snow and ice. But fast wear and so-so

wet and dry braking make them suitable only for cold-weather use.
■ **Speed ratings:** Q (99 mph and higher).
■ **Treadwear warranty:** Usually none.
SUV/Pickup—Designed for the rigors of truck use.
■ **Best for:** All-terrain models are designed for on-road and light-duty off-pavement use; all-season models are made primarily for on-road use.
■ **Treadwear warranty:** None or 40,000 to 80,000 miles.
Winter/Snow truck— Designed for the rigors of severe winter conditions.
■ **Speed ratings:** S (112 mph and higher).

BUYING ADVICE
Remember that if you buy tires online, you may have to pay for shipping and for mounting and balancing when the tires arrive.

For more buying advice, go to ConsumerReports.org/tires

QUICK PICKS
All-Season Tires

Best balance of long tread life and mostly good all-weather protection:

Michelin Defender
Pirelli P4 Four Seasons Plus

Within types, in performance order.

Rec.	Brand & Model	Score	Three Season Driving				Winter Driving		Comfort		Other	
			Dry Braking	Wet Braking	Handling	Hydroplaning	Snow Traction	Ice Braking	Ride	Noise	Rolling Resistance	Tread Life, Miles
	ALL-SEASON TIRES											
✓	**Michelin** Defender	70	⌃	●	⌃	⌃	⌃	●	●	⋀	⌃	90,000
	Continental TrueContact	68	⌃	●	⌃	⌃	⌃	⌄	⌃	⌃	⋀	60,000
	General Altimax RT43	66	⌃	●	⌃	⌃	⋀	●	⌃	⌃	⌃	65,000
✓	**Pirelli** P4 Four Seasons Plus	66	⌃	●	●	⌃	⌃	●	⌃	⌃	⋀	100,000
	Nexen Aria AH7	64	⌃	●	●	●	⌃	●	⌃	⋀	⌃	75,000
	Goodyear Assurance TripleTred All-Season	62	⌃	●	⌃	⌃	●	⊗	●	⌃	●	80,000
	Kumho Solus TA11	62	⌃	⌄	●	⌃	⌃	●	●	⌃	⋀	55,000
	Cooper CS5 Grand Touring	62	⌃	●	●	⌃	●	⊗	⌃	⌃	⌃	70,000
	Yokohama Avid Ascend	60	⌃	⌄	●	⌃	●	⌄	⌃	⌃	⌃	90,000
	BFGoodrich Advantage T/A	58	⌃	⌄	●	⌃	●	●	⌃	●	⌄	75,000
	Uniroyal Tiger Paw Touring	56	⌃	⌄	●	⌃	●	⌄	⌃	●	●	65,000
	Sumitomo HTR Enhance L/X	56	⌃	⌄	●	●	●	⌄	⌃	⌃	●	70,000
	Toyo Extensa A/S	54	⌃	⌄	●	●	●	⌄	●	⌃	●	60,000
	Firestone Precision Touring	54	⌃	●	●	●	⌄	⌄	⌃	●	⌃	55,000
	Firestone FR710	52	⌃	●	●	●	⊗	⌄	●	●	⌃	55,000
	GT Radial Champiro VP1	50	⌃	●	●	⌃	⊗	⌄	⌃	⌃	⌃	45,000

RATINGS KEY

⊗　⌄　●　⌃　⋀　　✓
WORSE ⟵――――⟶ BETTER　　RECOMMENDED These are high-performing models that stand out.

QUICK PICKS
Performance
All-season
H-Speed rated

Best balance of long tread life and mostly good all-weather protection:

Pirelli Cinturato P7 All Season Plus

Michelin Premier A/S

Within types, in performance order.

Rec.	Brand & Model	Score	Three Season Driving				Winter Driving		Comfort		Other	
			Dry Braking	Wet Braking	Handling	Hydroplaning	Snow Traction	Ice Braking	Ride	Noise	Rolling Resistance	Tread Life, Miles
	PERFORMANCE ALL-SEASON, H-SPEED RATED											
	Continental PureContact	70	˄	˄	˄	˄	˄	˅	˄	˄	˄	55,000
✓	**Pirelli** Cinturato P7 All Season Plus	70	˄	◑	◑	˄	˄	◑	˄	˄	˄˄	70,000
✓	**Michelin** Premier A/S	70	˄	˄	◑	˄	˄	◑	˄	˄	˄	85,000
	Goodyear Assurance Fuel Max	68	˄	˄	˄	˄	◑	◑	◑	˄	˄˄	60,000
	General Altimax RT43	68	˄	◑	˄	˄	◑	◑	˄	˄	˄	65,000
	Nokian Entyre 2.0	68	˄	˄	˄	˄˄	◑	˅	˄	˄	˄	35,000
	Nexen N5000 Plus	66	˄	˅	˄	˄	˄	◑	˄	˄	˄˄	75,000
	Cooper CS5 Ultra Touring	64	˄	◑	˄	˄	◑	˅˅	˄	˄	◑	60,000
	Dunlop SP Sport 7000 A/S	64	˄	◑	◑	◑	◑	◑	◑	˄	◑	65,000
	Kumho Solus TA31	64	˄	◑	˄	◑	◑	˅	◑	◑	˄˄	55,000
	Toyo Versado Noir	60	˄	◑	◑	◑	˄	˅	˄	◑	˄	65,000
	Uniroyal Tiger Paw Touring	60	˄	◑	◑	˄	◑	˅	˄	◑	˄	60,000
	BFGoodrich Advantage T/A	58	˄	˅	◑	◑	◑	˅	˄	◑	◑	65,000
	Sumitomo HTR Enhance L/X	58	˄	˅	◑	◑	◑	˅	˄	˄	◑	55,000
	Falken Ziex ZE950 A/S	56	˄	◑	◑	◑	˄	˅	◑	◑	˅	55,000
	GT Radial Champiro VP1	52	˄	◑	◑	˄	˅˅	˅˅	◑	◑	˄	50,000

Best balance of long tread life and mostly good all-weather protection:

Michelin Premier A/S

Pirelli Cinturato P7 All Season Plus

Within types, in performance order.

Rec.	Brand & Model	Score	Three Season Driving				Winter Driving		Comfort		Other	
			Dry Braking	Wet Braking	Handling	Hydroplaning	Snow Traction	Ice Braking	Ride	Noise	Rolling Resistance	Tread Life, Miles
PERFORMANCE ALL-SEASON, V-SPEED RATED												
	Continental PureContact	70	▲	▲	▲	▲	▲	⊙	▲	▲	▲	55,000
✓	**Michelin** Premier A/S	70	▲	▲	▲	▲	▲	⊙	▲	▲	●	80,000
✓	**Pirelli** Cinturato P7 All Season Plus	70	▲	●	●	▲	▲	⊙	▲	▲	⊕	65,000
	General Altimax RT43	68	▲	●	▲	▲	●	⊙	▲	▲	▲	55,000
	Goodyear Eagle Sport All-Season	64	▲	▲	▲	▲	●	⊗	●	●	▲	70,000
	Goodyear Assurance ComforTred Touring	62	▲	⊙	●	▲	▲	⊙	▲	▲	▲	75,000
	Yokohama Avid Ascend	62	▲	⊙	●	▲	●	●	▲	▲	●	85,000
	Cooper CS5 Ultra Touring	60	▲	●	●	▲	●	⊗	▲	▲	⊙	50,000
	Kumho Solus TA71	60	▲	●	▲	⊕	●	⊙	▲	▲	⊙	40,000
	Bridgestone DriveGuard	60	▲	▲	●	▲	●	⊗	●	▲	●	50,000
	Bridgestone Turanza Serenity Plus	60	▲	●	●	▲	⊙	⊙	▲	▲	●	60,000
	Goodyear Assurance TripleTred All-Season	58	▲	●	●	▲	●	⊗	●	●	●	85,000
	BFGoodrich Advantage T/A	56	▲	⊙	●	▲	●	⊙	▲	●	●	60,000
	Falken Ziex ZE950 A/S	56	▲	●	●	●	▲	⊙	●	●	●	55,000
	Uniroyal Tiger Paw Touring	56	▲	●	●	●	●	⊙	▲	●	●	60,000
	Sumitomo HTR Enhance L/X	52	▲	⊙	●	▲	▲	⊗	▲	▲	●	55,000

RATINGS KEY

⊗ ⊙ ❶ ▲ ⊕

WORSE — BETTER   ✓ **RECOMMENDED** These are high-performing models that stand out.

QUICK PICKS
UHP All-Season tires

Best for most weather conditions:

Michelin Pilot Sport A/S 3+
Pirelli P Zero All Season Plus

Continental ExtremeContact SWS06
BFGoodrich g-Force COMP-2 A/S

Within types, in performance order.

Rec.	Brand & Model	Score	Three Season Driving					Winter Driving		Comfort		Other	
			Dry Braking	Dry Handling	Wet Braking	Wet Handling	Hydroplaning	Snow	Ice	Ride	Noise	Rolling Resistance	Tread Life
	UHP ALL-SEASON												
✓	**Michelin** Pilot Sport A/S 3+	78	⌃⌃	⌃⌃	⌃	⌃⌃	⌃	—	—	—	⌃	⌄	55,000
✓	**Pirelli** P Zero All Season Plus	76	⌃	⌃⌃	⌃	⌃⌃	⌃	—	—	—	⌃⌃	⌄	50,000
✓	**Continental** ExtremeContact DWS06	76	⌃⌃	⌃	⌃	⌃⌃	⌃	⌄	—	—	⌃	⌄	45,000
✓	**BFGoodrich** g-Force COMP-2 A/S	74	⌃	⌃	⌃	⌃	⌃	⌄	⌄	⌄⌄	⌃	⌄	60,000
	Goodyear Eagle Sport All-Season	72	⌃	⌃	⌃	—	—	⌃	—	—	⌃	—	70,000
	Yokohama ADVAN Sport A/S	72	⌃	⌃	⌃	⌃	⌃	⌄	—	⌃	⌃	—	60,000
	Goodyear Eagle F1 Asymmetric All-Season	72	⌃⌃	⌃	⌃	⌃	⌃	⌄	—	⌄	⌄	⌄	50,000
	Hankook Ventus S1 noble 2	72	⌃⌃	⌃	—	⌃	⌃	⌄	—	⌃	⌃	⌄	45,000
	Dunlop Signature HP	72	⌃⌃	⌃⌃	⌃	⌃	⌃	⌄	—	⌃	—	—	40,000
	General G-Max AS-03	70	⌃	⌃	⌃	⌃	⌃⌃	—	—	⌄⌄	⌄⌄	⌄	50,000
	Falken Azenis FK450 A/S	68	⌃⌃	⌃	⌃	⌃	⌃⌃	—	⌄	⌄	⌃	—	40,000
	Kumho ECSTA 4X II	68	⌃	⌃⌃	⌃	⌃	⌃	⌄	—	—	—	⌄⌄	40,000
	Cooper Zeon RS3-G1	68	⌃	⌃	⌃	⌃	⌃	⌄	—	⌄	⌃	⌄	35,000
	Bridgestone Potenza RE970 AS Pole Position	68	⌃	⌃	⌃	⌃	⌃	⌄	⌄	—	⌃	⌄	45,000
	Laufenn S Fit AS	68	⌃	⌃	—	⌄	—	⌄	⌄	—	⌃	—	60,000
	Nitto Motivo	66	⌃	⌃	—	⌃	⌃	⌄	—	⌄	⌃	⌄	50,000
	Fuzion UHP Sport A/S	64	⌃	—	⌃	⌃	—	—	⌄	⌄	—	⌄	55,000
	Toyo Proxes 4 Plus	62	⌃	⌃	⌄	—	⌃	—	⌄	—	⌃	⌄	50,000
	Sumitomo HTR A/S PO2	60	⌃	⌃⌃	—	—	—	⌄⌄	⌄	—	⌃	⌄	30,000
	Sumitomo HTR En-hance L/X	60	⌃	—	⌃	⌄	⌃	⌄	⌄	—	⌃	⌄	55,000
	GT Radial Champiro UHP AS	58	⌃	—	⌄	—	⌃	⌄⌄	⌄	—	—	—	40,000

QUICK PICKS
UHP Summer tires

Best-performing tires:

Michelin Pilot Super Sport

Goodyear Eagle F1 Asymmetric 3

Nokian zLine

Yokohama ADVAN Sport V105

Pirelli P Zero

Within types, in performance order.

Rec.	Brand & Model	Score	Dry Braking	Dry Handling	Wet Braking	Wet Handling	Hydroplaning	Ride	Noise	Rolling Resistance	Tread Life
	UHP SUMMER										
✓	**Michelin** Pilot Super Sport	82	⌃⌃	⌃⌃	⌃	⌃⌃	⌃⌃	⌄	⌃	⌄	40,000
✓	**Goodyear** Eagle F1 Asymmetric 3	80	⌃⌃	⌃⌃	⌃	⌃⌃	⌃⌃	●	⌃	●	35,000
✓	**Nokian** zLine	80	⌃⌃	⌃⌃	⌃	⌃⌃	⌃	●	⌃	●	35,000
✓	**Yokohama** ADVAN Sport V105	78	⌃⌃	⌃⌃	⌃	⌃	⌃	⌄	⌃	⌄	35,000
✓	**Pirelli** P Zero	78	⌃⌃	⌃⌃	⌃	⌃⌃	⌃	⌄	⌄	⌄	35,000
	Kumho ECSTA PS91	76	⌃⌃	⌃⌃	⌃	⌃⌃	⌃	⌄	⌃	⌄	25,000
	Bridgestone Potenza S-04 Pole Position	76	⌃⌃	⌃⌃	⌃	⌃	⌃	⌄	●	⌄	30,000
	Vredestein Ultrac Vorti	76	⌃⌃	⌃⌃	⌃	⌃⌃	⌃	⌄	⌃	⌄	40,000
	Hankook Ventus V12 evo2	76	⌃⌃	⌃⌃	⌃	⌃	⌃	⌄	●	●	35,000
	Nexen N Fera SU1	76	⌃⌃	⌃⌃	⌃	⌃	⌃⌃	⌄	⌃	●	35,000
	Toyo Proxes T1 Sport	74	⌃⌃	⌃⌃	⌃	⌃	⌃⌃	⌄	⌃	⌄	25,000
	Firestone Firehawk Indy 500	74	⌃⌃	⌃⌃	⌃	⌃	⌃	●	●	●	40,000
	Bridgestone Potenza RE760 Sport	72	⌃⌃	⌃⌃	●	⌃	⌃⌃	⌄	⌃	⌄	40,000
	Sumitomo HTR ZIII	70	⌃⌃	⌃⌃	●	⌃	⌃	⌄	⌃	⌄	35,000
	BFGoodrich g-Force Sport Comp-2	70	⌃⌃	⌃⌃	⌃	⌃	⌃	⌄	⌄	⌄	35,000
	Nitto iNVO	68	⌃⌃	⌃⌃	●	⌃	⌃	⌄	⌄	⌄	30,000
	Cooper Zeon RS3-S	66	⌃	⌃⌃	●	⌃	⌃⌃	⌄	⌄	⌄	25,000
	Dunlop Direzza DZ102	66	⌃	⌃	●	●	⌃⌃	⌄	●	⌄	40,000

QUICK PICKS
Winter/Snow Tires

Best for severe winter driving conditions:

Yokohama W.drive V905
Michelin Pilot Alpin PA4

Within types, in performance order.

Rec.	Brand & Model	Score	Winter Driving		Three Season Driving					Comfort		Other
			Snow	Ice	Dry Braking	Dry Handling	Wet Braking	Wet Handling	Hydroplaning	Ride	Noise	Rolling Resistance
	PERFORMANCE WINTER/SNOW											
✓	**Yokohama** W.drive V905	70	⊚	⊚	●	●	●	∧	∧	●	⊘	●
✓	**Michelin** Pilot Alpin PA4	66	⊚	⊚	●	●	●	∧	∧	●	●	⊘
	Bridgestone Blizzak LM-32	62	∧	⊚	●	●	●	●	●	∧	⊘	⊘
	Hankook Winter i*cept evo2	62	∧	⊚	●	●	⊘	●	∧	●	∧	●
	Falken Espia EZP II	50	⊚	⊚	⊘	●	⊗	⊗	●	⊘	⊘	⊘

Guide to the Ratings
Score is based on 12 to 14 tests, with braking, handling, and hydroplaning resistance weighed heavily for most tires. Snow traction and ice braking weigh more heavily for winter tires. **Braking** tests on dry and wet pavement are from 60 mph; on ice, from 10 mph. **Handling**, in most cases, combines how well a tire did in wet and dry cornering grip, steering feel, and an emergency handling maneuver. **Wet Handling** for UHP tires is evaluated by driving the car through a wet slalom course, and includes wet cornering grip. **Dry Handling** for UHP tires combines the emergency handling maneuver, dry cornering grip, and steering feel. **Hydroplaning** denotes a tire's ability to resist skimming along the surface of standing water and causing loss of steering ability. **Snow Traction** tests denote how far a vehicle has to travel to accelerate from 5 to 20 mph on flat, moderately packed snow. **Ride Comfort** and **Noise** are evaluated subjectively, on rough and smooth roads. **Rolling Resistance**, as measured by a dynamometer, is a factor in fuel economy. **Tread Life** is an indicator of wear potential from CR's extended mixed-driving test run on the government's treadwear course.

RATINGS KEY
⊗ ⊘ ● ∧ ⊚   ✓
WORSE———BETTER   RECOMMENDED These are high-performing models that stand out.

QUICK PICKS
Winter/Snow Tires

Best for most winter driving conditions:

Michelin Latitude X-Ice Xi2

Continental Extreme WinterContact

Nokian Hakkapeliitta R2 SUV

Within types, in performance order.

Rec.	Brand & Model	Score	Winter Driving — Snow Traction	Winter Driving — Ice Braking	Three Season — Dry Braking	Three Season — Wet Braking	Three Season — Handling	Three Season — Hydroplaning	Comfort — Ride	Comfort — Noise	Other — Rolling Resistance
	WINTER/SNOW TRUCK										
✓	**Michelin** Latitude X-Ice XI2	68	⌃⌃	⌃⌃	●	⌄	●	●	⌃	⌃	⌃⌃
✓	**Continental** ExtremeWinterContact	66	⌃⌃	⌃	⌃	⌄	●	⌃	●	⌃	●
✓	**Nokian** Hakkapeliitta R2 SUV	66	⌃	⌃	⌃	●	●	⌃⌃	●	⌃	●
	Yokohama Ice Guard iG51v	64	⌃	⌃	●	⊗	●	⌃⌃	⌃	⌃	●
	Bridgestone Blizzak DM-V1	64	⌃⌃	⌃⌃	●	⊗	⊗	⌃	●	●	⌄
	Nexen Winguard winSpike	62	⌃	⌃	●	⌄	●	⌃	⌃	⌃	●
	Firestone Winterforce UV	58	⌃⌃	●	●	⌄	⌄	⌃	⌃	⊗	⊗
	Cooper Discoverer M+S	52	⌃	●	●	⌄	●	⌃⌃	⌃	●	⊗

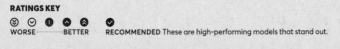

RATINGS KEY

⊗ ⌄ ● ⌃ ⌃⌃   ✓
WORSE ———— BETTER   **RECOMMENDED** These are high-performing models that stand out.

QUICK PICKS
All-Season Truck Tires

Best for all-weather conditions and excellent tread life:
Michelin LTX M/S2
Goodyear Assurance CS TripleTred All-Season

Very good for most weather conditions:
Pirelli Scorpion Verde All Season Plus
Continental CrossContact LX20 EcoPlus
Cooper Discoverer SRX

Within types, in performance order.

Rec.	Brand & Model	Score	Three Season Driving				Winter Driving		Comfort		Other	
			Dry Braking	Wet Braking	Handling	Hydroplaning	Snow Traction	Ice Braking	Ride Comfort	Noise	Rolling Resistance	Tread Life
	ALL-SEASON TRUCK											
✔	**Michelin** LTX M/S2	74	⌃	⌃	⌃	⌃⌃	⌃	–	⌃	⌃⌃	–	⌃⌃
✔	**Goodyear** Assurance CS TripleTred All-Season	70	⌃⌃	⌃	–	⌃⌃	–	–	–	⌃⌃	–	⌃⌃
✔	**Pirelli** Scorpion Verde All Season Plus	68	⌃⌃	⌃	⌃	⌃⌃	–	–	⌃	⌃	⌃	⌃
✔	**Continental** CrossContact LX20 EcoPlus	68	⌃⌃	⌃⌃	–	⌃⌃	–	⌄	⌃	⌃⌃	–	–
✔	**Cooper** Discoverer SRX	68	⌃	⌃	⌃	⌃⌃	⌃	–	–	–	–	⌃
	Nokian WR G3 SUV	66	⌃	⌃	⌃	⌃⌃	⌃	–	–	–	–	⌄
	Uniroyal Laredo Cross Country Tour	66	⌃	⌃	⌃	⌃	–	–	⌃	⌃	⌄	⌃
	Firestone Destination LE 2	66	⌃	⌃	–	⌃⌃	⌃	–	–	–	–	–
	General Grabber HTS	66	⌃⌃	⌃	–	⌃⌃	–	–	⌃⌃	–	⌄	–
	Falken WildPeak H/T 01	64	⌃	–	–	⌃⌃	–	–	–	–	⌄	–
	Hankook Dynapro HT	64	⌃	⌃	⌃	⌃⌃	–	–	–	–	–	–
	GT Radial Savero HT2	64	⌃	–	⌃	⌃⌃	–	⌄	–	⌃	⌃	⌄
	Toyo Open Country H/T	62	⌃⌃	–	⌃	⌃	–	–	⌃	⌃	⌄⌄	⌃
	Kumho Road Venture APT KL51	62	⌃	–	–	⌃⌃	–	–	–	⌃	–	⌄
	Maxxis Bravo HT-770	60	⌃⌃	–	⌃	⌃⌃	⌄	–	⌃	⌃⌃	–	–
	Bridgestone Dueler H/L Alenza Plus	60	⌃	⌃	⌃	⌃⌃	–	⌄	–	–	–	–
	Geostar GS716	58	⌃⌃	–	–	⌃⌃	⌄	⌄	–	–	–	–
	Sunny SN3606	54	⌃⌃	–	–	⌃⌃	⌄⌄	⌄	⌄	⌄	⌄⌄	⌄

QUICK PICKS
All-Terrain Truck Tires

Best for all-weather driving and tread life:

Hankook Dynapro AT-M

Goodyear Wrangler All-Terrain Adventure with Kevlar

Michelin LTX A/T2

Cooper Discoverer A/TW

Very good for most weather conditions:

Falken WildPeak A/TO1

Within types, in performance order.

Rec.	Brand & Model	Score	Three Season Driving				Winter Driving		Comfort		Other	
			Dry Braking	Wet Braking	Handling	Hydroplaning	Snow Traction	Ice Braking	Ride Comfort	Noise	Rolling Resistance	Tread Life
	ALL-TERRAIN TRUCK											
✓	**Hankook** Dynapro AT-M	66	⌃⌃	●	●	⌃	⌃	●	●	●	●	⌃⌃
✓	**Goodyear** Wrangler All-Terrain Adventure with Kevlar	66	⌃⌃	⌃	⌃	⌃	●	●	●	●	⊘	⌃
✓	**Michelin** LTX A/T2	66	⌃	●	●	⌃⌃	⌃	●	⌃	●	⌃	⌃⌃
✓	**Cooper** Discoverer A/TW	64	⌃	●	⌃	⌃⌃	⌃	●	●	●	●	●
✓	**Falken** WildPeak A/TO1	64	⌃⌃	⌃	●	⌃⌃	⌃	⊘	●	●	●	●
	Maxxis Bravo AT-771	62	⌃⌃	●	●	⌃	●	●	●	●	●	●
	BFGoodrich Rugged Terrain T/A	62	⌃⌃	⌃	⌃	⌃	●	●	⊘	⊘	⊘	⌃
	Cooper Discoverer A/T3	60	⌃⌃	●	⌃	⌃⌃	●	⊘	⌃	●	⊘	●
	Nokian Rotiiva AT	60	⌃⌃	●	●	⌃	⌃	⊘	⌃	●	●	●
	Nexen Roadian AT Pro	60	⌃⌃	●	●	⌃	⌃	●	●	●	⊘	●
	Kumho Road Venture AT KL78	58	⌃	●	●	●	⌃	●	●	●	⊘	●
	Dick Cepek Trail Country	58	⌃⌃	●	●	⌃	⌃	●	●	●	⊗	●
	Yokohama Geolandar A/T-S	58	⌃⌃	●	●	⌃⌃	●	⊗	●	●	⊘	⊘
	Bridgestone Dueler A/T Revo 2	58	⌃⌃	⌃	●	⌃⌃	●	●	●	●	⊘	⊘
	Firestone Destination A/T	56	⌃	⊘	●	⌃⌃	●	●	●	●	⊘	●

RATINGS KEY

⊗ ⊘ ● ⌃ ⌃⌃   ✓

WORSE————BETTER   **RECOMMENDED** These are high-performing models that stand out.

Statement of Ownership, Management, and Circulation

(Required by 39 U.S.C. 3685)

1. Publication Title: Consumer Reports. 2. Publication No: 0010-7174. 3. Filing Date: Sept. 20, 2016. 4. Issue Frequency: Monthly, except two issues in December. 5. No. of Issues Published Annually: 13. 6. Annual Subscription Price: $30. 7. Complete Mailing Address of Known Office of Publication: Consumer Reports Inc., 101 Truman Avenue, Yonkers, NY 10703-1057. 8. Complete Mailing Address of Headquarters or General Business Office of Publisher: Consumer Reports Inc., 101 Truman Avenue, Yonkers, NY 10703-1057. 9. Full Names and Complete Mailing Addresses of Publisher, Editor, and Managing Editor. Publisher: Consumer Reports Inc., 101 Truman Avenue, Yonkers, NY 10703-1057. President and CEO: Marta L. Tellado; Editor-in-Chief: Diane Salvatore; Managing Editor, Content: Nancy Crowfoot. 10. Owner: (If the publication is published by a nonprofit organization, its name and address must be stated.) Full Name: Consumer Reports Inc., a nonprofit organization. Complete Mailing Address: 101 Truman Avenue, Yonkers, NY 10703-1057. 11. Known Bondholders, Mortgagees, and Other Security Holders Owning or Holding 1 Percent or More of Total Amount of Bonds, Mortgages, or Other Securities: None. 12. For Completion by Nonprofit Organizations Authorized to Mail at Special Rates: The purpose, function, and nonprofit status of this organization and the exempt status for federal income tax purposes has not changed during preceding 12 months. 13. Publication Title: Consumer Reports. 14. Issue Date for Circulation Data Below: October 2016.

15. Extent and Nature of Circulation: Print Magazine, U.S. and Canada	Average no. copies each issue during past 12 mo.	No. copies of single issue published nearest to filing date
A. Total no. of copies (net press run)	4,293,625	4,218,796
B. Paid circulation		
1. Mailed outside-county paid subscriptions stated on Form 3541	3,851,022	3,830,988
2. Mailed in-county paid subscriptions stated on Form 3541	0	0
3. Sales through dealers, carriers, street vendors, counter sales, and other non-USPS paid distribution	56,985	43,650
4. Other classes mailed through the USPS	0	0
C. Total paid distribution (sum of 15b(1), (2), (3), and (4))	3,908,007	3,874,638
D. 1. Free or Nominal Rate Outside-County Copies included on PS Form 3541	1,580	1,421
2. Free or Nominal Rate In-County included on PS form 3541	0	0
3. Free or Nominal Rate Copies Mailed at Other Classes Through the USPS (e.g. First-Class Mail)	0	0
4. Free or Nominal Rate Distribution Outside the Mail (Carriers or other means)	12,665	9,555
E. Total free distribution (sum of 15d(1) and (4))	14,245	10,976
F. Total distribution (sum of 15c and 15e)	3,922,252	3,885,614
G. Copies not distributed	371,373	333,182
H. TOTAL (sum of 15f and 15g)	4,293,625	4,218,796
I. Percent paid and/or requested circulation	99.64%	99.72%

I certify that the statements made by me above are correct and complete.

Brent Diamond, VP, Magazine and Newsletter Products

CONSUMER REPORTS BUYING GUIDE 2017 VOLUME 81, No. 13

CONSUMER REPORTS magazine (ISSN 0010-7174) is published monthly, except twice in December, by CONSUMER REPORTS, 101 Truman Avenue, Yonkers, NY 10703-1057. Periodicals postage paid at Yonkers, NY, and at other mailing offices. Canadian postage paid at Mississauga, Ontario, Canada. Canadian publications registration no. 2665247-98, agreement number 40015148. CONSUMER REPORTS® is a registered trademark in the United States, Canada and Mexico. Contents of this issue copyright © 2017 by CONSUMER REPORTS. All rights reserved. Reproduction in whole or in part is forbidden without prior written permission (and is never permitted for commercial purposes). CR is a member of Consumers International. **Mailing lists:** CR rents or exchanges its customer postal list so it can be provided to other publications, companies, and nonprofit organizations. If you wish your name deleted from lists and rentals, send your address label with a request for deletion to CONSUMER REPORTS, P.O. Box 2127, Harlan, IA 51593-0316. **U.S. Postmaster:** Send address changes to P.O. Box 2109, Harlan, IA 51593-0298. If the Post Office alerts us that your magazines are undeliverable, we have no further obligation to fulfill your magazines unless we have a corrected address within two years. **Canada Post:** If copies are undeliverable, return to CONSUMER REPORTS, P.O. Box 481, Station Main, Markham, ON L3P 0C4. **Back issues:** Single copies of 12 preceding issues, $7.95 each; Buying Guide, $14.49 each (includes shipping and handling). Write Back Issues, CONSUMER REPORTS, Customer Relations, 101 Truman Ave., Yonkers, N.Y. 10703-1057.